The Kitchen Spoon's Handle

The Kitchen Spoon's Handle

*Transnationalism and
Sri Lanka's Migrant Housemaids*

Michele Ruth Gamburd

CORNELL UNIVERSITY PRESS

ITHACA AND LONDON

First published 2000 by Cornell University Press
First printing, Cornell Paperbacks, 2000

Printed in the United States of America

Library of Congress Cataloging-in-Publication Data

Gamurg, Michele Ruth, 1965-
    The kitchen spoon's handle : transnationalism and Sri Lanka's migrant housemaids / Michele Ruth Gamburd.
        p. cm.
    Includes bibliographical references and index.
    ISBN 0-8014-3738-5 (cloth) — ISBN 0-8014-8644-0 (pbk.)
    1. Ethnology—Sri Lanka—Naeaegama. 2. Sex role—Sri Lanka—Naeaegama. 3. Caste—Sri Lanka—Naeaegama. 4. Women domestics—Employment— Middle East. 5. Women—Sri Lanka—Naeaegama—Economic conditions. 6. Social classes—Sri Lanka—Naeaegama. 7. Naeaegama (Sri Lanka)—Social conditions. 8. Naeaegama (Sri Lanka)—Economic conditions. 9. Naeaegama (Sri Lanka)—Emigration and immigration—Economic aspects. I.Title.
    GN635.S72 G36 2000
    306.'095493—dc21
                                                            00-008931

Cornell University Press strives to use environmentally responsible suppliers and materials to the fullest extent possible in the publishing of its books. Such materials include vegetable-based, low-VOC inks and acid-free papers that are recycled, totally chlorine-free, or partly composed of nonwood fibers. Books that bear the logo of the FSC (Forest Stewardship Council) use paper taken from forests that have been inspected and certified as meeting the highest standards for environmental and social responsibility. For further information visit our website at www.cornellpress.cornell.edu.

Cloth printing   10 9 8 7 6 5 4 3 2 1
Paperback printing   10 9 8 7 6 5 4 3 2 1

The epigraph to the book is reprinted with the permission of Simon and Schuster, Inc., from *The Poems of W. B. Yeats: A New Edition*, edited by Richard J. Finneran. Copyright © 1928 by Macmillan Publishing Company, renewed 1956 by Georgie Yeats.

FSC FSC Trademark © 1996 Forest Stewardship Council A.C.
       SW-COC-098

In memory of my father,
Samuel Gamburd

Labour is blossoming or dancing where
The body is not bruised to pleasure soul,
Nor beauty born out of its own despair,
Nor blear-eyed wisdom out of midnight oil.
O chestnut-tree, great-rooted blossomer,
Are you the leaf, the blossom or the bole?
O body swayed to music, O brightening glance,
How can we know the dancer from the dance?

—W. B. Yeats, "Among School Children"

Contents

Acknowledgments

Many people have contributed their time, energy, passion, knowledge, and humor to the writing of this book. For their sage counsel on its grand scheme down to its particulars, and for their critical comments and insightful suggestions on multiple versions of numerous chapters, special thanks go to Sharon Carstens, Nicole Constable, and Patricia Rainey. Thanks also go to E. Valentine Daniel, Bruce Mannheim, Tom Trautmann, and Crisca Bierwert for their encouragement in the completion of my fieldwork, and to the members of the Feminist Anthropology Reading Group, especially Laura Ahearn, Lessie Jo Frazier, Lisa Gezon, Bridget Hayden, and Katherine Zirbel for their warm support and sound advice during the early phases of this work. I am also grateful to William Cornett, Sara Dickey, Margaret Everett, Caitrin Lynch, Ellen Ostern, Brent Schauer, and Anne Waters for their assistance during the preparation of this manuscript.

My mother, Geraldine Gamburd, has inspired me to follow in her anthropological footsteps, sharing with me her expertise, field site, and wisdom. She has pushed me in new directions, drawn out hidden connections, and provided a sounding board for my ideas. My father, Samuel Gamburd, generously offered his services as photographer and videoproducer and pointed me toward insights not easily put into words.

This research was made possible in part by a National Science Foundation Dissertation Research Award (grant number DBS 9207143), a National Science Foundation Graduate Research Fellowship, an Andrew W. Mellon Dissertation Fellowship, a grant from the Oregon Council for the Humanities, and a Faculty Development Grant from Portland State University. Financial assistance provided by a Foreign Language Area Studies summer grant for language study (Sinhala) at Cornell University and a Rackham Summer Research Grant from the University of Michigan is gratefully acknowledged.

Portions of this book incorporate information from previously published materials. Chapter 5 is based on my article, "Sri Lanka's 'Army of Housemaids': Control of Remittances and Gender Transformations," *Anthropologica* 37:49–88. Chapter 8 is based on my essay, "Nurture for Sale: Sri Lankan Housemaids and the Work of Mothering," in *Home and Hegemony*, edited by Kathleen M. Adams and Sara Dickey (Ann Arbor: University of Michigan Press, 2000), 179–205. Several chapters use arguments first published in "Class Identity and the International Division of Labor: Sri Lanka's Migrant Housemaids," *Anthropology of Work Review* 19, no. 3:4–8. Reprinted by permission of the American Anthropological Association. Not for further reproduction.

Numerous people in Sri Lanka have offered their wisdom, advice, and support, including L. K. Ruhunage, Sarath Mananwatte, and Nilam and Shukri Hameed. Radhika Coomaraswamy, the late Neelan Thiruchelvam, and the staff at the International Center for Ethnic Studies provided generous aid on all fronts during my fieldwork. Thanks are due to the staff at the Sri Lanka Bureau of Foreign Employment (SLBFE), the Centre for Women's Research (CENWOR), the Marga Institute, and the United States Education Foundation (USEF). I have a special place in my heart for the staff at the Rotunda Gardens YWCA guest house, especially Jessie Sivanantham, for making my stays in Colombo so comfortable. For her friendship, generosity, and unflagging kindness, special thanks go to Kusuma Karunaratne of the University of Colombo.

For the serenity and unstinting enthusiasm with which they coached me through my initial butchery of the Sinhala language, I thank W. S. Karunatillake and Rev. K. Gnanadhaja of the University of Kelaniya and James Gair and Milan Rodrigo at Cornell University.

Most of all, I stand indebted to all those in the village of Naeaegama who shared their stories and their lives with me, relating their experiences at home and abroad. For opening their home to me, my love and gratitude go to D. Telsie Mendis Karunaratne, D. Seelawathie de Zoysa, and R. Sujeewa de Zoysa. For sharing their knowledge of village life, I am beholden to R. J. G. de Zoysa, R. M. de Zoysa, and Rev.

Kosgoda Mahinda. For drawing me into the lives of women, for teaching me Sinhala, and for listening, special thanks go to my research associate K. Sita Perera. And finally, this work would never have been possible without the patience, perception, and devotion of my mentor and guide R. B. H. "Siri" de Zoysa, who taught me many of the most worthwhile things I know.

W. S. Karunatillake shared with me a Sanskrit poem:

> One quarter of knowledge comes from the teacher,
> One quarter comes through one's own intelligence,
> One quarter comes from fellow students,
> And the remainder comes in the fullness of time.

Many thanks to all of my teachers, colleagues, and fellow students, who guided me through the reading and the writing while awaiting the insights of time.

MICHELE RUTH GAMBURD

Portland, Oregon

Introduction

"He's good-hearted guy, but what a fool!"[1] Priyanthi exclaimed, laughing, as we sat in her living room three days after her return to Polwatta from two years' work in the Middle East.[2] Referring affectionately to her alcoholic husband, she continued to say that any money he had, he spent right away: "Today he's like a white man, tomorrow like a beggar."[3] Every time she came home from abroad, she found only the four walls of their house remaining; during her last trip he had even sold the kitchen knives. Despite her complaints, Priyanthi radiated an excited, good-humored conviction that she could reform her husband and build a better life for her four sons with the money she had earned abroad.

Like Priyanthi, many Sri Lankan women have found the changes generated by migration neither straightforward nor unambiguously positive.

---

[1] "mooD*a*yaa unat hit*a* ho*n*dayi." Upper case letters and underlining denote pronunciation of consonants particular to Sinhala. Capitalization in Sinhala transliterations will not follow English conventions. Please see appendix A for an orthography of spoken Sinhala.

[2] Throughout this book I use the terms "Middle East," "West Asia," and "Gulf States" interchangeably to designate the six oil-producing nations in the Persian Gulf that form the Gulf Cooperative Council (GCC): Bahrain, Kuwait, Oman, Qatar, Saudi Arabia, and the United Arab Emirates (UAE). By generalizing in this way, I have inevitably lost some nuances and ignored some details about particular countries and populations.

[3] "ad*a* suddhaa, heT*a* paddaa."

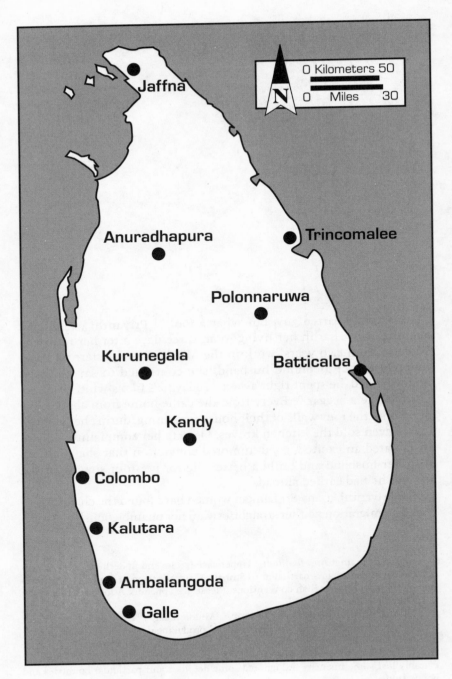

Map 1. The island of Sri Lanka

The money they earn as housemaids does not operate solely for the ends they have envisioned, since many other people and patterns intervene in its use. This book examines how the migration of female labor to the Middle East has spurred changes in gender relations, class status, and caste hierarchies in a coastal village in Sri Lanka. Like dancers challenging the bounds of their choreography, both improvising and following the rules, village women and men constantly transform and re-create their lived systems of values and meanings through their everyday practices, sending older structures of power and authority into flux.

Roughly the size of West Virginia, Sri Lanka, the island nation off the southern tip of India, is home to more than eighteen million people. Colonized sequentially by the Portuguese, Dutch, and British, Ceylon, as it was then called, attained independence in 1948. Rivalries between the Sinhala-speaking Buddhist majority and the Tamil-speaking Hindu and Muslim minorities have disrupted the course of post-colonial government, plunging the country into an armed conflict that has claimed tens of thousands of lives since 1983. In addition to the civil war in the North and East, two insurgencies in the South, the first in 1970–71 and the second in 1988–90, have further torn the fabric of national unity. Despite high literacy rates and relatively high quality of life, unemployment and lack of opportunity fuel ethnic and regional hostilities.

The British colonists once prized this tropical island for its spices, and established tea, rubber, and coconut plantations whose exports still bring in large amounts of foreign exchange. Current entrepreneurs and international travelers have shifted their attention to the beautiful beaches and reefs that ring the island. Ever-growing numbers of sun-worshipping tourists visit ancient ruins and coastal resorts. More recently, a third large source of foreign exchange has joined tea exports and the tourism industry: beginning in 1976, streams of Sri Lankans have migrated for work to the Gulf States in the Middle East. Indeed, the story of migration begins with the worldwide demand for the oil lying beneath the desert in West Asia.

Current discussions of transnationalism study the global movement of people, money, goods, and ideas. The concept of *globalization* suggests that theorists cannot adequately explain the local without reference to international and transnational dynamics; the concept of *global implosion* suggests that the world grows smaller and more interconnected day

Map 2. South and West Asia

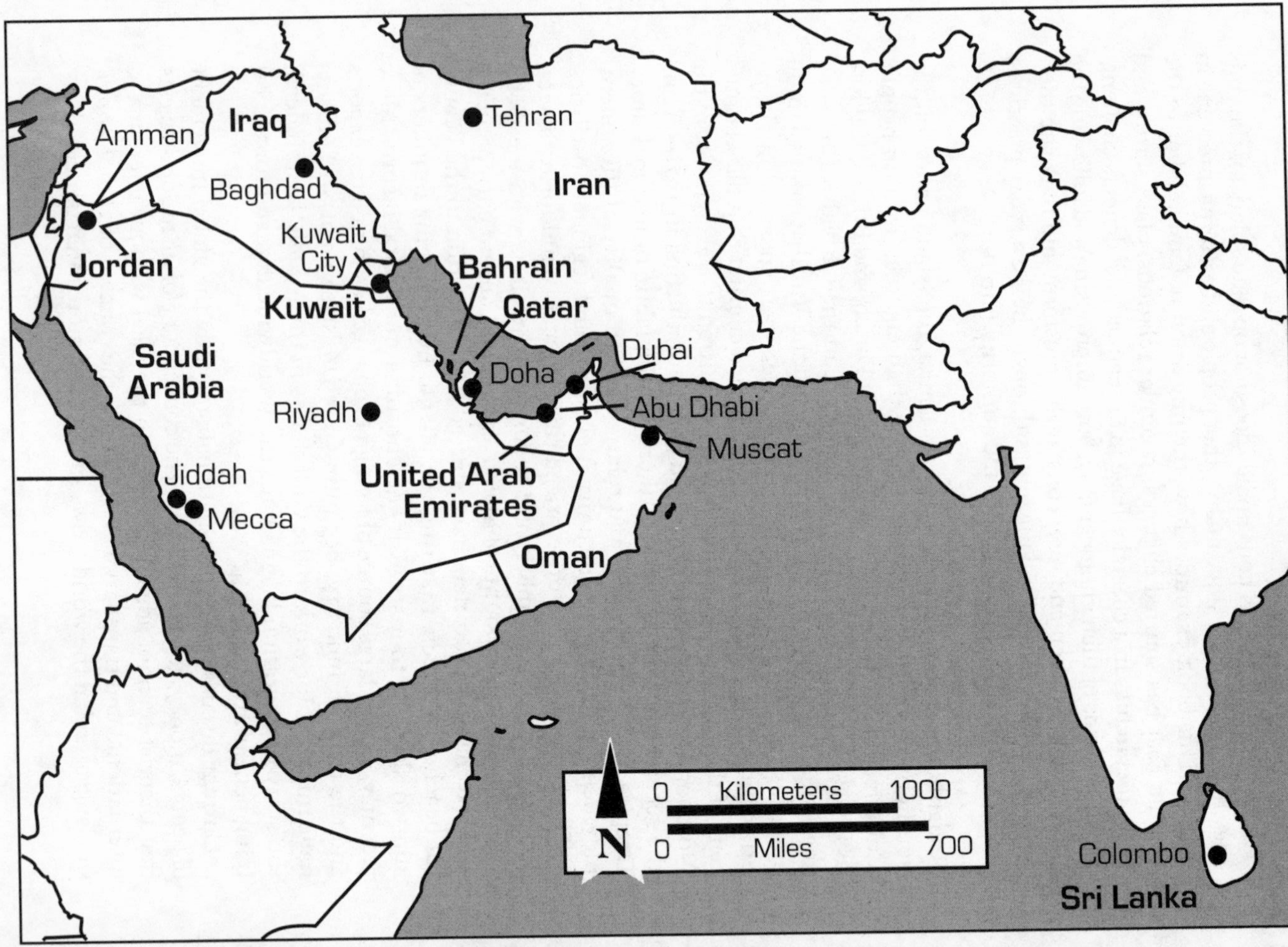

by day. This book discusses women's lives in a rural Sri Lankan village in the context of the global movement of petroleum products, petrodollars, migrant laborers, and Western free-market ideologies.

A common Sinhala proverb denigrating women's domesticity suggests that "a woman's understanding reaches only the length of the kitchen spoon handle."[4] But how long is the kitchen spoon's handle? Since the early 1980s, spurred by urban and rural unemployment and poverty, Sri Lankan women from all over the island have packed their metaphorical spoons and gone to work as housemaids in Saudi Arabia, Kuwait, the United Arab Emirates (UAE), and other oil-producing countries in the Persian Gulf. Women's migration affects the international division of labor, Sri Lanka's national economy, the meaning of women's work, and local social relations such as family structures, caste stratification, class hierarchies, and gender roles. I argue that to understand either the global or the local, one must view each in the context of the other. Focusing on the qualitative experiences of individual migrants, this book explores how new economic opportunities transform local, national, and international power structures.

Previous Anthropological Research Done in Naeaegama[5]

The village that I call Naeaegama, or "The Village of Relatives," lies in the thirty-mile area between the towns of Kalutara and Ambalangoda on the Southwest coast of Sri Lanka, about a mile inland from the main highway, Galle Road (see map 3). I acquired my connection to Naeaegama through my mother, Geraldine E. Gamburd. As a graduate student in anthropology at Columbia University, my mother, accompanied by my father and my self (age two), came to the island of Sri Lanka (then Ceylon) in January 1968. Although she had planned to investigate myth and ritual, my mother found herself drawn into a study of the nine-generation kinship network central to all village interactions and relations (G. Gamburd 1972). My father brought the eye of a fine artist to bear, wielding camera, tape recorder, and movie camera in his role as my mother's audiovisual support team. His gener-

---

[4] "*gaehaeniyagee nuwaṇa haeṇdimiTee durayi.*"

[5] "Naeaegama" should be pronounced like the English word "nag" + ah + mah. The vowel in "nag" should be exaggerated slightly. I have designated the village in question by a pseudonym to protect the privacy of individuals and families whose stories I tell.

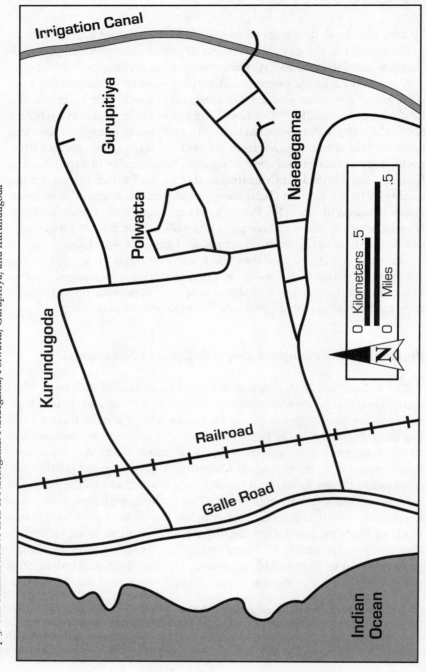

Map 3. The administrative area of Naeaegama: Naeaegama, Polwatta, Gurupitiya, and Kurundugoda

Fig. 1. Three playmates in Naeaegama. My father took this photograph and gave it to the family of the girl in the middle in 1968. She gave it back to me when I was in Sri Lanka in 1994. (Courtesy of Samuel Gamburd.)

osity with cigarettes, his love of storytelling, and his many card games with local men on the back porch solidified a growing network of personal relations in the village.

My parents rented the spacious cement house newly constructed by two school teachers very well respected in the village. Their eldest son, Siri, served as my mother's research associate, my father's firm friend, and as my older brother, protector, and piggyback pony. Sita, the young woman hired to take care of me, proved a much more able researcher than babysitter.[6] Left happily with Siri's mother in "the back house,"

---

[6] While I have kept Siri's and Sita's names unchanged, I have disguised the identity of other individuals to protect their privacy. Villagers usually carry three or more official names; the first indicates their patriline, the second is their personal name, and the third (in the coastal areas often a Portuguese name, like "Mendis" or "de Silva") is an additional honorific passed from father to children and husband to wife. Throughout this book I have referred to individuals by pseudonyms resembling common "house" names or nicknames. I have not, however, included the fictive kin terms (such as *"malli"* [younger brother] or *"akkaa"* [older sister]) that usually accompany the name in conversation.

I quickly acquired, with the effortless ease of the toddler, more fluency in Sinhala and more taste for curry than either of my parents. Memories of my childhood in Naeaegama, the village that was our home for two years, are few and fragmented, bolstered by pictures and the stories told and retold by my parents. The king cobra under the house, the seven-foot iguana on the front lawn ("Daddy, there's a creature in the yard ..."), the howling dogs terrified into silence by the tape of their own howling, the kite-flying contests, the cook and his weekly requests for more pepper, all carry for me a resonance of "once upon a time."

Years later, as an English literature major (insisting that one anthropologist per family should suffice), I eluded my college's social science requirement by taking Latin. Despite my lack of training and initial reluctance, my mother persuaded me to serve as her research assistant during a sabbatical leave. In 1985 I joined my parents for another stint of field research in Sri Lanka, and returned to college determined that the family would have at least two anthropologists. Having embarked on graduate study in anthropology at the University of Michigan, I returned to Naeaegama briefly in 1991, again in 1992 for eighteen months of my own dissertation fieldwork (M. Gamburd 1995a), and again for several months in 1997.

The Journey to Naeaegama

The bus journey down the coastal road to Naeaegama starts two and a half hours away in the teeming chaos of the private bus terminal in Colombo's Pettah market district. Young men eagerly guide foreigners toward vans and buses whose conductors shout out destinations, lazily at first, then with more vigor as the bus slowly fills with passengers. With all seats occupied, the bus begins the forty-odd-mile trip south, picking up standing passengers along the way. Agile and balanced, the conductor lithely makes his way through the packed aisle, issuing tickets for the Rs. 16/ (U.S.$ .32) trip, while the driver, hand to the horn, makes his perilous way through traffic. On busy days, crowded buses canting dangerously to their door-sides charge along Galle Road, their packed human cargo swaying and sweating in the heat. Those lucky few with window views watch as cityscape slowly gives way to slum and suburb.

A jostled hour (and twenty miles) later, the conductor taps a coin on the metal handrail on which he is perched, and small change offerings for safe travel flow from passenger to passenger into his hands. As the white dome of the Kalutara Bodhi (a Buddhist temple with a sacred bo tree) looms into sight, the music blaring from the sound system suddenly goes silent, and the bus pulls to the side of the road amid vehicles of all description. Seated passengers rise in respect as the conductor leaps to the ground, dashes to one of the many red tills on the side of the road, deposits the collected offerings, bows his head in worship, and sprints back to the bus, which is already in motion when his foot hits the running board.

From Kalutara, Galle Road winds its way south through coconut groves interspersed with towns, villages, and tourist resorts bordering the beach. About a mile before my destination I begin the laborious process of working my way through the seemingly solid wall of bodies in the aisle toward the door, murmuring, "*bahinavaa, mehe bahinavaa*" [I'm getting down, I'm getting down here]. As if squeezed from its bowels, I watch the bus pull away in a cloud of black diesel smoke. With ringing ears and a sigh of relief, I open my umbrella against the sun or rain and, having persuaded the tourist touts that I truly do not want to visit the five-star hotel just south of the junction, I begin the twenty-minute walk to Naeaegama.

After two years' residence, I rarely go from the junction to the house without meeting and greeting dozens of friends and acquaintances along the way. Basket-bearing women clad in tight blouses and long cloth skirts look up from their marketing to call greetings; youthful cyclists ring their bells as they pass. Stopping at this shop for my newspaper, at that shop for a cake of laundry soap, and at a third to visit the shopkeeper's new granddaughter, I make my way from the main road to the village. Each quarter of a mile the road narrows; the trees grow taller, the temperature cooler, and the people warmer, until with growing pleasure I find myself lifting the latch on the front gate, leaving bag and shoes on the veranda, calling "*gedara kavuda?*" [who's at home?] as I make my way through the house to the washbasin on the back porch.

During my time in the village, I stay with Siri's family in the large house my parents had rented in 1968–69. One of the nicest in the village, this cement house has had a sporadic supply of electricity since it was built in 1967 but still depends on a nearby well for drinking and bathing water. Siri's mother and father, now retired, live in the back house, a smaller brick structure in the same one-acre compound. In addition to coconut trees and cinnamon bushes, Siri has filled his garden with numerous edible, medicinal, and flowering plants. The family provides me with a bedroom and an office; from the office window, through the branches of a mango tree, I can see the dome of the *cheetya*[7] at the Buddhist temple across the road.

Although my memories of the village, like my casual childhood fluency in Sinhala, have faded over the years, many older people remember my family, while others have heard stories of our presence. During my first few months in the village, hardly a day passes without a new acquaintance relating a story or two about my parents, usually starting with the tale of "the accident." In June 1968, while my parents were filming an all-night ceremony in Ambalangoda, a nearby town, the balcony on which they were standing came loose from the building and fell to the ground, killing several people underneath and injuring many more. My mother's chipped teeth and broken jaw, my father's back injury, and Siri's broken arm have entered not only our family history but also the collective memory of the village. Our shared past legitimizes my presence in the village and eases most suspicions about what I am doing and why. My role as a daughter following in her mother's footsteps and living with long-standing friends of the family satisfies most people's sense of propriety, if not their curiosity.

Methodology

Sita, my former nanny and my mother's skilled research associate, had fallen in love with and married the young man next door in 1969. In 1992 she still lived with her husband and two grown children two hundred yards down the road, and she gladly agreed to work with me, tutoring me in my still-elementary Sinhala and interpreting when necessary during interviews.

If Sita was tutor, companion, and guide, Siri was all that and even more. Siri (recently retired as storekeeper at a tourist hotel), his wife Telsie, and their son Sujeewa welcomed me into their household. The day of my arrival, Siri remarked that "of course" I would need kinship charts and sent his son to the shop for a dozen large sheets of white paper, upon which he proceeded to sketch out four, five, and some-

---

7 The *cheetya* or *stupa* is a whitewashed dome-shaped structure containing relics, around which the faithful circumambulate in worship.

Fig. 2. The research team: Sita Perera, Michele Gamburd, and Siri de Zoysa. (Courtesy of Margaret Thomas.)

times even six generations' genealogy for all the major families in the village area. Trained in kinship diagrams many years before by my mother, he often worked late into the night wearing the reading glasses I purchased for him. Siri also drew a map of the village, on which we numbered the houses, thereafter coding information by household. With the help of an election list, we completed a census of the village, gradually filling in a survey of housing styles, furniture, appliances, garden land use, and transportation. When the government began a poverty alleviation program in the village, Siri kept elaborate records of attendance at meetings and work done on projects. His intricate grapevine of information kept us abreast not only of upcoming rituals, ceremonies, and meetings but also (to Telsie's laughing embarrassment) of all the latest village gossip. Siri's fine eye for detail, his meticulous patience, his unflagging enthusiasm, and his artistic talents were all invaluable resources for my work.

Sita, Siri, and I attended numerous weddings, funerals, coming-of-age ceremonies, healing rituals, temple festivals, political rallies, village meetings, holiday parties, and other gatherings during my stay in the village. These activities brought me into contact with many villagers and familiarized me with formal and informal aspects of village life. In the late afternoons, easily distracted from entering field notes into my computer, I often joined the group of family members and passersby who gathered to chat on the front steps or the back porch. These free-flowing conversations helped me practice my Sinhala and gave me some firsthand experience with *oopaaduupa* [gossip] and stories about village life.

Interviews made up the bulk of my research in Naeaegama. Siri often set our appointments ahead of time, scheduling meetings for mid-morning and mid-afternoon to avoid conflicting with our interviewees' household chores. Usually either he or Sita accompanied me to the house of the person I was to interview; on other occasions we asked interviewees to come and sit on Siri's porch to talk. When I interviewed migrant women, I often asked Sita to interpret, thinking that they might be more frank in an all-female context. By the end of my fieldwork, interviews took place nearly exclusively in Sinhala, with the occasional English clarification provided by my research associates. Returning to Siri's porch after an interview, two or sometimes all three of us would discuss the case, with Siri and Sita contributing relevant elements of village history and current gossip that brought me insight and understanding far beyond any I could have reached on my own. Siri's and Sita's intuitive grasp of ethnography and their years of fieldwork experience with my mother were priceless assets.

Caste, Class, and Gender in the Village of Naeaegama

Several hundred yards past our gate, the main paved road, a patchy twelve-foot-wide strip of potholed asphalt, gave way entirely to a red dirt path. A network of gravel roads and less formal footpaths running through backyards connected important locations. Naeaegama proper, and the neighboring three villages of Polwatta [Coconut Garden], Gurupitiya [Teacher's Place], and Kurundugoda [Plentiful Cinnamon], made up the *Graama Seevaka* division (a local-level administrative district) of Naeaegama and covered a little over one square mile, with housing plots interspersed between paddy fields, cinnamon gardens, and coconut groves (see Map 3). Wealthier villagers in Naeaegama lived in large cement or brick houses with tile roofs, whereas poorer families made do with single-room clay houses topped with tin sheets, tar sheets, or woven coconut-frond mats.[8] The majority of villagers could not afford toilets, using neighboring cinnamon gardens instead. Wells with good drinking water supported many besides their owners. Fulfilling a 1994 election promise, the government extended electricity lines into the interior of the village.[9] The availability of electricity clearly divided the community between those who could and those who could not afford wiring and service connection fees.

Caste Relations

Many complex layers of kinship and caste relations characterize village life in South Asia. Castes are ranked status groups often associated with a profession. Individuals inherit their caste status from their parents, and members, in theory (and often in practice), marry only within their caste. Numerous special behaviors and taboos associated with ideas of ritual purity and impurity mark caste identity. Despite efforts by colonial and post-colonial governments in India and Sri Lanka to downplay and eradicate this aspect of social stratification, caste considerations continue to shape many local patterns of association and play an important role in village social organization.

The Sinhala-speaking Buddhists and the Tamil-speaking Hindus in Sri Lanka have separate caste hierarchies. The Sinhala caste hierarchy consists of twenty-odd castes whose relative rankings differ in areas around the country. Although the Halaagama caste makes up only a small fraction of the total Sinhala population, it dominates local politics and economics in the coastal district around Naeaegama where most of its members reside, and ranks third in the local caste hierarchy.[10] Four sub-grades within the caste represent further distinctions of status and prestige. The caste occupation has centered on the production of cinnamon since the Portuguese colonized the coastal areas

---

[8] "Clay" houses were constructed of wattle (a wood and twig framework) covered with daub (a special mixture of mud, lime, and straw).

[9] To provide space for poles, workers felled many trees, including a large jak tree nicknamed "The Fib Tree," in the shade of which Polwatta-area residents used to gather and socialize.

[10] "Halaagama" and "Salagama" are interchangeable names for this caste. While most educated Sri Lankans preferred to use the prestigious up-country (inland) "s," those in the low-country (coastal) community in which I lived called themselves Halaagama, with an "h" and an "aa," and I follow their usage here. For more on caste in Sri Lanka, see Chapter 6 and Ryan, 1953.

in the sixteenth century. Cinnamon peelers tend cinnamon gardens, carefully pruning the bushes and stripping the rich, red inner bark from six- to ten-foot shoots harvested every four to six months. Garden owners sell their harvest to dealers, paying peelers between a third and a half of the profit. While most people involved with cinnamon are of the Halaagama caste, only about a fifth of the Naeaegama-area Halaagama work in the caste occupation. In Naeaegama, a small number of Halaagama families had monopolized positions of village authority for at least the past fifty years, controlling the temple and the *Graama Seevaka* [village administrator] position, and owning the bulk of the land.

In 1994 the Halaagama made up approximately 78 percent of the one thousand residents in the Naeaegama *Graama Seevaka* division. Members of the Berava caste made up a significant minority of 15 percent. The Berava, a caste group distributed throughout the Sinhala areas of Sri Lanka, falls in the lower ranks of the local caste hierarchy, well below the Halaagama. About a quarter of the Naeaegama-area Berava engaged in the caste profession, specializing in ceremonial drumming, astrology, and ritual healing practices. Members of other castes, all ranked lower than the Halaagama, resided in neighboring *Graama Seevaka* divisions.

Caste has played an important role in residence patterns. In 1968–69 the Halaagama lived mostly in Naeaegama and Kurundugoda, while the two neighboring villages of Polwatta and Gurupitiya housed families from the Berava caste. Government land reform in Polwatta undertaken in 1980, and subsequent land disputes, worked to the disadvantage of many Berava families, whose Halaagama neighbors usurped much of the land the Berava used to occupy. Neither as economically nor as politically influential as the village Halaagama, many of the lower-ranked Berava moved to several nearby Berava enclaves and to the capital city of Colombo to escape discrimination and intimidation.

Employment: Gender and Class

In the late 1960s villagers in southern Sri Lanka were already integrated into larger regional, national, and international economic networks through the manufacture and trade of cinnamon, rubber, and coconut fiber (coir) products grown and processed in the area. Halaagama men, often accompanied by their entire families, migrated to work in the cinnamon estates throughout the southern coastal region;

processed and packaged, the cinnamon they prepared found its way around the world. Families of both the Halaagama and the Berava castes employed in the coconut fiber business manufactured rope, brooms, mats, mattresses, and other coir products, which they sold to local and international dealers. Villagers from neighboring areas tended and tapped rubber trees on nearby plantations. The labor migration that started in the late 1970s sustained these international links in a different form.

Patterns of gender, caste, and class have shaped village employment. Between 1969 and 1994, many well-off members of both castes left the village and moved permanently to the capital city, Colombo; in 1994 many spoke English fluently, educated their children in nationally acclaimed schools, and returned to Naeaegama only occasionally for large village functions. Several of the best-educated Halaagama secured employment and citizenship in England and the United States, and they could no longer be considered part of the local community except insofar as they sent financial assistance to their poorer relatives. Villagers who worked in the larger cities of Galle, Kalutara, and Colombo as clerks, bank tellers, tailors, or masons commuted daily by train, rising before dawn and returning after dark. While some villagers extolled the benefits of country living, most said that they would eagerly take the chance to move to the city. Siri once said, "We are all frogs in a well, jumping and jumping, hoping that one day the water level will rise enough so that we, too, can escape."

The area population nearly doubled from roughly five hundred in 1969 (G. Gamburd 1972, 68) to roughly one thousand in 1994, creating chronic under- and unemployment in the village area that reflected a similar countrywide situation.[11] On a limited scale, job opportunities in the armed forces provided an outlet for about a dozen village men stationed in conflict areas in the North and East. The tourist trade employed a half-dozen men directly and others indirectly. Opportunities for women created by the United National Party (UNP) government of the late President Ranasinghe Premadasa included jobs in newly constructed local garment factories for those whose family in-

[11] The national population has grown dramatically over this period; the census of 1963 put the figure at 10,625,000 (Yalman 1967, 13), while the 1981 census counted 14,848,364 people (Rand McNally 1987, 253). Subsequent censuses have not been held due to civil unrest, but estimates put the 1995 population around 18.1 million people (Sri Lanka National Department of Census and Statistics 1996).

come fell below the official poverty level. Some fifteen to twenty women and several men found work in these export-oriented activities. Most significantly, female migration to the Middle East financed the daily subsistence of a large and growing number of village families. Finding that they could no longer earn enough locally to make ends meet, let alone purchase land, build a house, or start a business, many village families opted to send women to work in the Middle East.

Over the thirty years from 1968 to 1997, women's work changed significantly. In the late 1960s, with the exception of several teachers from better-off Halaagama families, most women worked with cinnamon or coconut fiber. The migration of labor changed these patterns. In 1994 I found that in the Naeaegama *Graama Seevaka* division, over a quarter of the households (48 out of 161) had or had had a member working abroad; approximately an eighth of the people over 18 (61 out of 462) were or had been abroad. By 1997 the number of women abroad had increased still further. Contrary to many other migrant flows, the vast majority (90 percent) of village migrants were women, and in 1994 about a quarter of the women over 18 in the village (55 out of approximately 225) had current or former overseas experience.[12] Clearly this migration represented the largest single change in village economic orientation in the recent past.

Tables 1 and 2 list the main occupations of women and men in the Naeaegama *Graama Seevaka* division. As table 1 indicates, in 1994 40 percent of the village women occupied their time with household duties such as tending the household garden, fetching water, gathering firewood, doing the marketing, cooking food, washing laundry, and caring for children. Women's jobs reflected age and marriage patterns within the female population: all the teachers came from the richest, most respected Halaagama families; poor, older women did odd jobs and servant work for patron families; unmarried women worked in factories; married women went abroad. Housemaids, about a sixth of the village women at any particular point in time, earned substantial salaries (twice as much as male day-laborers earned) for performing in the Middle East many of the same tasks they did "for free" at home. The resulting commodification of housework created an accompanying revaluation of gendered roles among village men and women.

---

12 For more information on the composition of the Sri Lankan workforce abroad, see chapter 1.

Table 1. Non-exhaustive list of jobs done by women in the Naeaegama area, 1994

Women's occupations	Number of people
Domestic worker for own family	90
Middle East migrant	38
Former Middle East migrant[a]	17
Broom and rope maker	17
Factory worker	14
Teacher	14
Moneylender/rope merchant	11
Odd jobs worker and servant	8
Cinnamon peeling assistant	6
City jobs and government service worker	5
Escort for school children	4
Insurance provider	3
Food vendor	3
Bakery worker	2
Prostitute[b]	2
Crafts and mask maker	2
University student	1
Dairy worker	1
Research associate	1
Shopkeeper	1
Beggar	1
Small trader	1
Total	225

[a] Former Middle East migrants were counted again elsewhere in the table but not included twice in the total.
[b] The individuals in question never confirmed this occupation, but their neighbors referred to it frequently.

Although table 1 captures the general categories of women's work in 1994, it does not indicate the diversity of jobs individuals undertook. Many of the poorer women whom I have categorized as doing domestic work for their own families occasionally offered their services as servants for rich neighbors. Women and children also frequently labored part-time in family industries. For example, family members often helped cinnamon peelers by scraping the outer bark from the cinnamon branches, and children often helped their parents make brooms after school. In the late afternoon and evening, or when their hands were not otherwise engaged, women, especially older ones, often made skeins of coir rope to pass the time and earn some extra cash.

Table 2.   Non-exhaustive list of jobs done by men in the Naeaegama
area, 1994

Men's occupations	Number of people
Unemployed/odd jobs worker	42
Cinnamon peeler	31
Army/navy/police officer	20
Broom maker and/or peddler	18
Day laborer	13
Government servant	11
Tourism worker	10
Baker	8
Security guard	8
Drummer	6
Carpenter	5
Mason	5
Sawmill worker and timber cutter	5
Shop clerk	4
Driver	4
Monk	4
Teacher	4
Businessman	4
Landed proprietor	4
Coconut plucker	3
Ritual specialist and astrologer	3
Middle East migrant	3
Former Middle East migrant[a]	3
Construction worker/contractor	3
Illicit liquor producer	3
Barber	2
Bicycle repairman	2
Welder	2
Hospital worker	2
Middle East job agent	2
Lawyer	2
Farmer	2
Fisherman	1
Bus conductor	1
Painter	1
Tailor	1
Umbrella and shoe repairman	1
Veterinary surgeon	1
University student	1
Factory worker	1
Research associate	1
Rail gate watcher	1
Mask maker	1
Total	246

[a] Former Middle East migrants were counted again elsewhere in the
table but not included twice in the total.

Like women, men also held multiple positions simultaneously. For instance, men who made brooms might also take odd jobs, and men who plucked coconuts might also work occasionally for illicit liquor producers. Most of the Berava caste men who drummed also did masonry, carpentry, or other manual labor. A retired army sergeant worked as a security guard at a garment factory. In both tables I count as "Middle East migrants" those who were abroad at any point between October 1992 and April 1994; in other contexts I have counted both returnees and current migrants as Middle East migrants. Siri and I counted each woman and man only once, under what seemed to us the individual's most significant current occupation.

Preview of Chapters

The migration of labor from Sri Lanka forms part of a complex transnational movement of populations, commodities, currencies, and ideologies. As oil flows out of wells, money flows into countries in the Persian Gulf, creating jobs filled by men and women from around the world. The flow of guest workers in turn generates a multitude of government and private institutions at the local, regional, national, and international levels that extend credit, secure job contracts, and seek to control and regulate migration. In an increasingly interconnected world, events at the local level often reflect close links with global systems. Similarly, large-scale international dynamics often reflect the particular economic, political, and cultural practices of small communities. In Naeaegama, the international migration of labor has spurred changes in family structures, gender ideology, caste hierarchies, and class relations. These village-level dynamics reciprocally influence men's and women's participation in the international labor market. Ordinary individuals and families, through their everyday actions, adapt to changing circumstances. In the process they both recreate and transform the cultural practices and social structures that surround them. By tacking back and forth between different levels of analysis, I hope to show the interconnections between international, national, and local phenomena.

To set the international context for Sri Lankan labor migration, in chapter 1 I discuss the transnational movement of goods (oil), people (labor), money (petrodollars), and ideas (development ideology). Oil production, largely controlled by the Organization of Petroleum Ex-

porting Countries (OPEC), generates wealth and jobs in the Persian
Gulf. Using the available statistical data, I sketch out the characteristics of the workforce in the Middle East, discussing the changing proportion of Arabs and Asians among guest workers and noting the increasing numbers of migrant women from Sri Lanka, the Philippines,
Indonesia, Thailand, and India. Although trade and migration have distinguished human societies for centuries, the speed and volume of current exchanges exceed historical precedents.

At the national and regional levels, a number of interdependent public and private institutions operate to control migration. In chapter 2
I focus on how rules and regulations channel power and authority. The
Sri Lanka Bureau of Foreign Employment (SLBFE), a government body,
supervises both migrants and job agents. The SLBFE trains, registers,
and medically examines migrants; it sets fee structures and enforces
licensing requirements for job agents; and it negotiates labor agreements with foreign countries. Manpower recruiting agencies in Sri
Lanka and in the Middle East control how sponsors find employees
and how employees get jobs. Study of these systems shows that although bureaucratic structures do to a large extent shape how people
behave, those systems rarely work exactly as planned. Put slightly differently, individuals learn not only the official rules but also the rules
for breaking the official rules. Inconsistencies within and between organizations create opportunities for fraud, corruption, and individual
initiatives for people at all points in the system.

Government bureaucracy, private job agencies, and local moneylenders play significant roles in migration. Having discussed bureaucracy and job agencies in chapter 2, in chapter 3 I discuss the power
dynamics and money flows surrounding moneylending in Naeaegama.
Moneylenders facilitate poor women's migration by providing ready
cash to cover agency fees while simultaneously draining the bulk of
migrants' profits by charging high rates of interest. Moneylenders,
many of them female, also play a central part in patron-client relations
and complex local economic networks. With the decline in the coconut fiber industry, Naeaegama moneylenders have adapted their operations to cater to migrant women. Through two case studies, I explore not only the practical aspects of lending money, but also the
diversity of local attitudes toward female entrepreneurship and the
proper use of money, concluding that caste status, family structure,
personal experiences, and age affect these powerful women's concepts
of class and gender identity.

In chapter 4 I discuss women's work experiences abroad, focusing on the structures and rules that control women's behavior, and on the avenues for individual initiative open to women. Complex power relations and intricate behavioral norms keep domestic servants at once marginal insiders and intimate outsiders in the houses of their employers. Within the bounds of existing standards, sponsors and housemaids negotiate work duties and wages. Through emotional ties and the exchange of gifts they also negotiate more subtle matters such as diligence, loyalty, and respect. Presenting a series of case studies, I investigate work situations from the mundane to the extraordinary, concluding the chapter with a housemaid's narrative of her escape from Kuwait during the Gulf War.

When the migration of women originally burgeoned in the early 1980s, many Sri Lankan social scientists predicted a shift in household roles and an upheaval of family structure, with a concomitant increase in power and decision-making for wage-earning women. In chapter 5 I look at the complex relations between female migrants and the people responsible for spending and saving the money those migrants remit to the village. An individual migrant's prosperity depends more on family choices than on his or her own hard work. While in chapter 1 I present several scholarly systems for assessing the "success" and "failure" of migrations, in chapter 5 I compare these Western perspectives with the local standards by which villagers judged whether migrants and their families had prospered or "improved" through their migration. Although at many points village criteria overlapped with the scholars' economic rationale, motives other than finances also prompted migration. Wage labor for domestic service certainly raised the status of women's work, but women negotiated their new gender roles against a background of preexisting norms and values that limited their power and authority.

Migration sent ripples of change through a variety of village social structures and forms of identity. Having presented a brief history of caste relations in Sri Lanka, in chapter 6 I look at how individuals use money earned through migration to improve their social standing, either through symbolic and religious strategies in the local caste hierarchy or through business ventures in the emerging class hierarchy. The example of a local land reform project reveals the roles of political allegiance, sexual assault, and Middle East money in facilitating the displacement of Berava by Halaagama in the formerly Berava village of Polwatta. The case studies in this chapter illustrate how caste identity interacts with financial prosperity, religious practice, political affiliation, and gender ideology at the village level.

The migration of female labor to the Middle East has created many challenges to local gender ideologies. Defining gender as cultural knowledge about sexual difference, I focus on gender roles as learned behaviors based on a culturally constructed view of how the world should work. Although relatively arbitrary and inherently flexible, gender categories are also intensely meaningful, deeply ingrained, central to an individual's sense of self, and painful to change. In Naeaegama, changes in women's work have affected issues of manhood and masculinity. In chapter 7, through a series of case studies, I examine how local men have dealt with identity issues emerging from the migration of a female family member. Although men with wage-earning jobs maintained their prestige and self-respect when a woman went abroad, under- and unemployed husbands regularly confronted images of their financial and sexual impotence. Men who had lost the culturally valued role of breadwinner often reasserted their masculinity through all-male drinking groups. The values of the drinking community stood in implicit opposition to those channeling family resources toward "improving," the dominant village idiom of successful migration. Despite the stigma attached to performing women's work in the domestic sphere, several local men I encountered pragmatically accepted their emerging place in the gendered division of labor.

Migration has also brought about changes in women's roles as mothers. Setting themselves in direct opposition to older images of the ideal South Asian woman, over half of the female migrants I interviewed left children at home to work abroad. Fragmented by migration, the bundle of duties and dispositions thought of as "mothering" was suddenly redistributed to a number of different people, forcing a reevaluation of the nature of mother-love. Migrant women came to "mother" two sets of children in two different ways: they nurtured their Arabic charges (for money) while providing material benefits to their biological offspring (for love). Sri Lankan mothers became breadwinners to secure a good life for their sons and daughters; but faced charges of greed and heartlessness for "abandoning" their children to search for money. By building on the themes of the commodification of labor and changes in gender roles, in chapter 8 I explore the effects of migration on the children left behind, the role conflicts experienced by migrant mothers, and the growing awareness of the value of women's work.

Migration raises issues about morality and identity that reverberate at the local, national, and international levels. Many Naeaegama villagers preferred to relate secondhand tales of dramatic disasters rather than their own firsthand stories of more mundane and benign experiences of migration. In chapter 9 I discuss the wide circulation of a genre of "horror stories" about migration, stories peopled by caricatures of immoral or victimized migrant women and their abusive employers, with plots full of exploitation, abuse, rape, prostitution, theft, death, and a menagerie of other misfortunes. Themes such as national pride, female chastity, respectability, promiscuity, hard work, and harsh punishments recurred regularly in stories told by men, women, Sri Lankans, Arabs, villagers, employers, bureaucrats, media reporters, and anthropologists. In my analysis, leaving aside for the moment the important issues of actual instances of violence and abuse, I focus on the politics of representation and the motivations behind particular narratives. The horror story images affect decisions and opinions on all levels, from the formation of Sri Lankan national policy down to the strategic maneuvering of individual village storytellers. Highlighting the space between fact and fiction, I examine the political forces creating and manipulating the dense, contradictory images surrounding the migrant housemaid.

Many of the points that I make about agency, power, identity, resistance, and social change are illustrated through stories. As I discuss in chapter 9, no storyteller relates just the facts. In response, every critical mind should question information, asking, "Why did you tell me this, and why did you tell it like that?" Pierre Bourdieu suggests that "The construction of reality ... is a major dimension of political power" (1977, 165). Like any spinner of stories, I too engage in the politics of representation.

Some authors criticize feminist anthropologists for condescending to the women whose lives they study. Chandra Mohanty (1988) notes that much of Western feminist literature portrays the "Third World Woman" as sexually constrained, ignorant, poor, tradition-bound, domestic, family-oriented, victimized, and passive. By contrast, her foil, the Western feminist, is educated, modern, in control of her body and her sexuality, and free. Hazel Carby (1982) cautions white female scholars not to place Western-style feminism, capitalism, and the nuclear family at the pinnacle of liberation, goals to be achieved by all women. In order to avoid this superior stance, Carby advises immersion in the specificity of women's lives, with analysis focusing on local values and experiences.

In the case studies in this book, I have tried to show how women in the Naeaegama area contest power relations with their families, job agents, moneylenders, and employers. I have inevitably edited out some of the immense complexity of daily existence. Have I represented general patterns, or merely focused on idiosyncratic occasions? Have I shown too much conflict, or not enough? "Readers should not ... regard the stories themselves as unmediated and disinterested accounts of 'real' experience" (Steedly 1993, 37). In picking and choosing which stories to relate, and in giving voice to particular people and perspectives, I craft a narrative that represents my own situated view of continuity and change, concord and discord in the village. I hope in the process that I have given adequate, accurate, and respectful voice to the individuals in my stories.

1 Labor Migration: National and International Contexts

The concept of globalization suggests that in the modern age one can no longer fully understand the local except with reference to the global. The staggering advances in communication and transportation of the past half-century lead to a sense of implosion, the feeling that the world grows smaller every day. Money, goods, people, and ideas move around the planet, detached from their points of origin. Current discussions of subjects as diverse as ecology, commerce, demography, and the mass media illustrate the blurring of conceptual boundaries between different places and cultures, demonstrating the multiple interconnections among local, national, and international phenomena. Intricate financial, political, and social relations that have evolved with the transnational sale of petroleum provide the global context for the national and local particulars of labor migration from Sri Lanka.

The first section of this chapter discusses the international movement of commodities. Energy, oil in particular, has commanded a large portion of global trade for many years: "Petroleum accounts for half the tonnage, two-thirds of the ton miles, and one-fourth of the value of all commodities exchanged in international markets; it is by far the most important internationally traded commodity, as measured by volume and monetary value" (Danielsen 1982, 1). Persian Gulf countries control nearly two-thirds of the world's proven oil reserves and produce over a quarter of the world's oil (Energy Information Administration

1999c, 1; 1997, 15). Five Persian Gulf nations—Saudi Arabia, Kuwait, Qatar, UAE, and Iraq—control and produce over half of the oil sold by the Organization of Petroleum Exporting Countries (OPEC), a powerful cartel that plays a large role in regulating the global price of petroleum products. OPEC control of this vital resource makes the Persian Gulf area a dominant player in international commerce and finance.[1]

The second section of this chapter discusses the international movement of labor. Money and jobs generated in the Middle East through the export of oil draw Sri Lankan migrants abroad. The six Gulf Cooperative Council (GCC) countries—Bahrain, Kuwait, Oman, Qatar, Saudi Arabia, and UAE—hosted 5.14 million "temporary migrant workers" from all over the world in 1990 (Shah 1994, 3). This figure represents 5 percent of the total worldwide stock of international migrant laborers, estimated at about a hundred million in 1992 (Shah 1994, 3). Current migration between West Asia and South and Southeast Asia takes place within a complex framework of long-standing regional power relations.

The concept of transnationalism focuses not only on the movement of populations, capital, and commodities but also on the circulation of ideas. The last section of this chapter notes the prominence of Western discourses of development in evaluations of women's work and the "success" and "failure" of migration experiences. Official calculations of economic activity often ignore the work done by women in the privacy of the home. Since Western modes of thinking dominate analysis of social and economic reality in "underdeveloped" countries, the goals of "industrial civilization" come to seem natural, normal, and transparently obvious to all, erasing local categories and priorities (Escobar 1988). Case studies from Naeaegama provide a critical perspective on Western views of economic rationality and the domestic economy.

OPEC and the International Oil Market

According to the Energy Information Administration," the price of oil is of critical importance to today's world economy, given that oil is the

---

[1] The eleven members of OPEC, and the dates they joined the organization, are as follows: Algeria, 1969; Indonesia, 1962; Iran, 1960; Iraq, 1960; Kuwait, 1960; Libya, 1962; Nigeria, 1971; Qatar, 1961; Saudi Arabia, 1960; United Arab Emirates, 1967; and Venezuela, 1960 (Energy Information Administration 1999d, 1).

largest internationally traded good, both in volume and value terms (creating what analysts have called a 'hydrocarbon economy')" (1999b, 11). Formed in 1960, OPEC produces about 40 percent of the world's oil; controls 77 percent of the world's proved reserves of crude oil (Energy Information Administration 1999d, 1); and strongly influences world petroleum prices. With oil production costs at an average of U.S.$4–$5 per barrel, and as low as U.S.$1 per barrel in the Persian Gulf OPEC nations, high market prices reflect neither production costs nor immediate shortages but rather the successful efforts of the eleven cartel members to fix prices above market values (al-Chalabi 1991, 3; Energy Information Administration 1997, 9).

In the past thirty years, oil prices have jumped several times, rising in response to perceived threats to supply from political crises and wars. From a stable price of $3 per barrel in 1969, in the wake of the fourth Arab-Israeli war (the Yom Kippur War) and the subsequent Arab oil embargo, oil prices rose in 1973 to $11–$12 per barrel. In 1979, following the overthrow of the Shah of Iran in the Iranian Revolution, prices jumped to $17 a barrel, followed by a further rise to $34 in 1981 due to the beginning of the eight-year Iran-Iraq War in 1980 (see Danielsen 1982, 160, 191; al-Chalabi 1991, 5; Kohl 1991, xvii). Sharp increases in oil prices "have been identified as a major cause in seven out of the 8 post–World War II recessions in the United States" (Energy Information Administration 1999b, 11). These same price increases mean prosperity for citizens in the Gulf countries, especially those countries with small populations and large reserves, such as UAE, Kuwait, Qatar, and Saudi Arabia, where oil revenues provide health care, education, and jobs. This prosperity also draws millions of foreign guest workers to the region from other Arab countries and from Asia.

Oil prices have also fallen several times over the past twenty-five years. In December 1985 the price of oil dropped precipitously from U.S.$28 a barrel down to U.S.$6–$9 (al-Chalabi 1991, 1; Kohl 1991, xiii). By keeping prices high, OPEC inadvertently encouraged development of other sources of oil, many of which had been brought "on stream" by 1985. Although OPEC holds the largest, cheapest, and most easily accessible oil, its high prices, coupled with American and European anxieties about dependence on foreign oil, made development of other oil sources feasible. OPEC became a "residual supplier," making up whatever world oil needs other sources could not meet. Within OPEC, Saudi Arabia operated as a "price defender," producing less or more oil as required to keep OPEC as a whole within its quotas (thus keeping oil supplies at a level to support the high prices). OPEC's share of the market, 66 percent in 1973, fell to only 40 percent in 1985 (al-Chalabi 1991, 12). Saudi Arabia suffered the most, with its "swing production" dropping to absorb declines in demand for expensive OPEC oil. When Saudi Arabia began producing more oil in 1985, oil prices fell worldwide (al-Chalabi 1991, 16). Realizing that it could not maintain both the price of oil and its share of the oil market, OPEC adopted a set price system, and in 1986 oil prices leveled out at a value of U.S.$18 per barrel.

A quarrel between cartel members precipitated the Gulf War. During the summer of 1990, with oil selling below the official set price, Iraq accused Kuwait and UAE of driving oil prices down by producing beyond their quotas. While some countries could increase production to offset lower prices, Iraq, already producing near capacity, found its financial well-being challenged. Declaring Kuwait's overproduction an act of aggression against Iraq, and further accusing Kuwait of taking more than its fair share of oil out of an oil field on the border between the two countries, on 2 August 1990 Iraq turned its impressive military might (honed by eight years of war with Iran) against Kuwait.

Iraq's attack temporarily altered control over world supplies of oil. Iraq controls 5 percent of the world's reserves of crude oil, Kuwait controls 9 percent, and Saudi Arabia controls 26 percent. Iraq's military offensive gave it direct control over its own and Kuwait's reserves of crude oil, and posed an implicit military threat against Saudi Arabia and the rest of the Gulf area (Danielsen 1982, 290; Energy Information Administration 1998a, 1; 1999a, 1, 2). Anxiety about access to oil caused prices to soar briefly to $40 per barrel (al-Chalabi 1991, 215) and directed international attention to the region. Under harsh punitive sanctions by the United Nations, Iraq retained its hold over its small oil-producing neighbor until March 1991, when, after severe aerial bombardment by United Nations forces led by the United States, Iraq withdrew. UN sanctions against Iraq greatly reduced the sale of Iraqi oil, leaving Iraq's portion of the market open for other oil-producing countries until 1996, when sanctions began to ease.

Between 1991 and 1997, oil prices averaged between $15 and $20 a barrel, until surplus production in 1998 led to "the lowest real (i.e., inflation-adjusted) oil export revenues since 1972" (Energy Information Administration 1999b, 1). Hurt by declining revenues, cartel members and other oil-producing nations agreed to cut production in

March 1999, and prices rebounded to what OPEC termed "acceptable levels" (OPEC Press Release 1999, 2). As illustrated above, fluctuations in oil prices affect commercial and financial exchanges around the globe, and reflect and influence political relationships between countries. In an energy-dependent society, control over production and pricing of this vital resource will doubtless continue to concern individuals, nation-states, and international institutions for years to come.

The South Asian Diaspora

Transnationalism focuses on the worldwide movement of populations, commodities, and ideas. In light of current human mobility, many people mistakenly assume that "traditional" cultures are easily bounded and identified, their inhabitants static and intrinsically attached to a native territory. Archaeological and historical data show instead that people have moved from place to place around the planet for millennia. Nor should we imagine that the current global movement of goods is a uniquely modern phenomenon: trade among the Arabian peninsula, India, Sri Lanka, and Southeast Asia flourished as early as the seventh century A.D. (McGilvray 1998); medieval merchants transported dyes and fabrics across Europe and Asia (Schneider 1978); and explorers brought plants and animals to and from the New World shortly after its discovery (Crosby 1972). The significance of changes during the colonial and post-colonial era lies not in the facts of global travel and trade, which have existed for centuries, but rather in the dramatic increase in the speed and magnitude of the connections, in the conscious awareness individuals have of global relationships, and in the relatively new concepts of citizenship and national boundaries, which have radically altered ideas of identity and the interpretation of travel (Anderson 1991; Gupta and Ferguson 1992; Ong 1999; van der Veer 1995).

The age of colonialism accelerated the processes of global integration and cultural contact. For nearly five centuries, from the discovery of the New World in 1492 until the end of World War II in 1945, European powers conquered territories in the Americas, Africa, and Asia, imposing their religious and political views, and expropriating natural resources and human labor for their own profit. Despite the formal independence of former colonies, the commercial, ideological, and political relationships that characterized colonization continue into the present. Masao Miyoshi cautions that the "post" in post-colonialism does not mean that relations of international dominance and subordination have ended (1993, 728). Unequal trade arrangements between nations, international financial organizations managing foreign aid and third-world debt, and transnational corporations that re-create world domination all operate to reproduce relations of power and dependency similar to those found during the colonial era.

The recent migration of Sri Lankans to the Middle East takes place against a historical background of colonization and forced labor. Conquered sequentially by the Portuguese, Dutch, and British, Sri Lanka has participated in colonial and post-colonial trade networks since the early sixteenth century. European administrative powers drew on labor pools from India, China, and smaller colonies to work plantations and mines in other countries. For example, the British left an indelible mark on ethnic stratification in Sri Lanka by importing Tamil-speaking laborers from South India to work on the tea plantations in the predominantly Sinhala hill country. Spread over the world at the whims of colonial powers, South Asian communities now populate areas as widespread as Fiji, the Caribbean, Guyana, and Malaysia. In 1995 approximately eight million people of South Asian descent lived outside South Asia, some brought by colonial powers, some drawn abroad more recently (van der Veer 1995, 1). South Asian labor has served the world elite for centuries.

Although labor migration to the Middle East currently motivates a major portion of Sri Lanka's travelers, Sri Lanka has sent émigrés from diverse social groups abroad since its independence in 1948. Economic and social pressures in the 1950s, 60s, and 70s drove educated and wealthy Sri Lankans to Europe, Australia, Canada, and the United States. Ethnic violence, which surged into civil war in 1983, spurred an out-migration of Tamil-speaking Sri Lankans from the Northeast and augmented the return of Tamil plantation workers to South India from Sri Lanka's central highlands (Gunatilleke 1995, 684; Shah 1995, 559). As refugees, emigrants, and laborers, many different portions of the Sri Lankan community have traveled abroad, with a wide range of motivations.

The mass migration of labor from Sri Lanka to the Middle East started in 1976, corresponding to the first major jump in oil prices. In the early 1980s demand for male construction workers tapered off, but growing numbers of women began working abroad as domestic servants. Sensitized to their dependence on migrant labor, since the Gulf War many GCC countries have instituted policies to replace guest workers with their own citizens but with only partial success (Energy Information Administration 1999a, 2; Looney 1992; Energy Information Administration 1998b, 1; *Migration News* 1996c, 1997, 1996b). Given continued financial prosperity, it seems relatively unlikely that citizens of GCC countries will wish to take over the menial jobs done by housemaids and other unskilled migrant laborers. With the increased efficiency of global transportation, relations of domestic servitude that used to take place in colonial times between the visiting colonial and the native servant are now reproduced in the Middle East, with the servant now the visitor and the master now the native.

Statistical Information on Migration

Statistical information on transnational labor migration presupposes a cognitive framework that holds citizenship in a nation-state as a straightforward, obvious, salient identity. Calling nations "imagined communities" created by a collective act of belief, Benedict Anderson argues that a close examination of the concept of "the nation" reveals both its political power and its conceptual incoherence (1991, 5). Indoctrinated as patriotic subjects through "symbols such as flags, maps, statuary" (Anderson 1994, 319), educated in the history and language of the motherland, and raised in a world with no unadministered populations or places, many people find it difficult to recognize the nation as a cultural construct, let alone to conceptualize conflicting or contradicting modes of classifying political allegiance.

The transnational movement of people, money, goods, and ideas challenges the transparency of the nation as a straightforward category of identity. Recent scholarship questions commonsense assumptions of clearly bounded spaces and sedentary populations, proposing instead a theory of identity based on hybrid loyalties, overlapping cultures, and regular travel (Gupta 1992; Malkki 1992). Temporary and permanent migrants, naturalized citizens, ethnic minorities, refugees, populations in diaspora, and inhabitants of borderlands all have ties to more than one nation, and often both resist and accommodate the norms of their host culture, evolving an "adaptive constellation of responses to dwelling-in-displacement" (Clifford 1994, 310).

Recognizing that recent advances in transportation and communication have furthered the global implosion and brought distant places closer, Nina Glick Schiller, Linda Basch, and Cristina Szanton Blanc use the term *transmigrants* to describe individuals who have "multiple and constant interconnections across international borders" and whose economic, social, and political networks revolve around relationships in more than one nation-state (1995, 48). Instead of viewing individuals in motion as uprooted, shiftless, helpless, and immoral, theorists suggest instead that we recognize the constant flux in human attachments to spaces and places (Daniel and Knudsen 1995; Malkki 1992, 32; Schiller, Basch, and Blanc 1995, 48).

Despite postmodern theoretical advocacy of "nomadology," the study of ongoing human movement regardless of historically constructed borders (Malkki 1992, 38), most of the world still thinks in terms of national citizenship. Although statistical information provides no substitute for qualitative ethnographic data, figures and percentages do map out significant international flows of people. Statistical data reveal both the categories through which local record-keepers conceptualize identity and the difficulty of keeping track of such huge numbers of people.

Numerous scholars lament the lack of reliable data on labor migration from South and Southeast Asia to the Middle East (Athukorala and Wickramasekara 1996, 556; Nair 1999, 212; Shah 1995, 561; Stahl 1991, 163). Many countries rely on "guesstimates," while insufficient administrative resources and multiple avenues of undocumented migration lead to "widely different estimates of the stock and flow of labour migrants in the Arab region" (Shah 1994, 4). For example, the Gulf War highlighted the inaccuracy of Sri Lanka's migration figures. In 1990 government officials estimated that sixty thousand Sri Lankans worked in Kuwait, but a head count showed that rescue efforts had aided closer to one hundred thousand people.

Guesstimates vary on how many foreigners work in the GCC countries. Nasra Shah estimates that there were 5.14 million non-nationals in the labor force in 1985 (1994, 21) Another source suggests that there were over seven million foreign workers in GCC countries in 1996 (*Migration News* 1996b). Indicating the difficulty of tracing the mass movement of people, yet another source estimates that in 1996, Saudi Arabia hosted 6.2 million people from 190 countries, including workers and their dependents (*Migration News* 1996a), a figure that suggests that the total number of foreigners in the GCC countries might have exceeded nine million in 1996.

In several GCC countries, foreign workers outnumber local workers: "Foreigners make up 90 percent of the work force in the United

Arab Emirates (UAE), 83 percent in Qatar, 82 percent in Kuwait, 69 percent in Saudi Arabia and around 60 percent in Bahrain and Oman" (*Migration News* 1996b; compare Shah 1994, 21). The term *foreigner* in this case deserves special discussion. Many GCC countries strictly limit the period a worker can stay in the country and make it difficult for workers to bring their families with them (Brochmann 1990, 61). GCC countries also enforce strict prohibitions against immigration, and people who have lived and worked for years or even decades in a country still count as foreign, as do their native-born children (Shadid, Spaan, and Speckmann 1992, 71). After the Gulf War the GCC countries began to worry actively about their dependence on foreign labor and created policies to discourage legal and illegal migration and to increase the proportion of citizens in the local work force (Addleton 1991; Looney 1992). These policies, however, have had only marginal success.

The composition of the foreign labor force in the GCC countries has changed over time in conjunction with political and economic dynamics. Jonathan S. Addleton (1991) notes an increase in the proportion of South Asian workers; in 1975 migrants from other Arab countries made up 65 percent of the migrant workers in GCC countries, but in 1985 that percentage had shrunk to 30.1 percent, while South Asian migrants made up 43 percent and Southeast Asian migrants made up 20.3 percent of the workforce. In 1985 Asians[2] accounted for over three million migrants (Addleton 1991, 510, 523; Shah 1994, 21). Research also suggests that a number of Asian countries send most of their migrant workers to the Middle East. For example, between 1976 and 1992, Bangladesh, India, Pakistan, and Sri Lanka sent over 90 percent of their migrant workers to the Middle East; Indonesia, South Korea, the Philippines, and Thailand also sent significant numbers of workers to the region (Stahl 1991, 183–84; Shah 1995, 608; see also table 3). Since 1985, this shift toward Asian labor has continued; Prema-Chandra Athukorala and Piyasiri Wickramasekara suggest that the changing labor composition depends in part on political polarization in the Arab world as a result of the Gulf crisis and note that "Asian workers may now receive preference over non-national Arabs

---

[2] Here "Asia" refers to South and Southeast Asia, where "South Asia" includes India, Pakistan, Bangladesh, Sri Lanka, and Nepal; "Southeast Asia" includes the Philippines, Indonesia, Thailand, and "other East Asia" (Addleton 1991, 522).

Table 3. Estimated number of migrant women going abroad from selected South and Southeast Asian countries to the Middle East, 1996

Country	Estimated percentage of women in migrant labor force	Estimated number of migrating women	Estimated percentage of country's migrants going to the Middle East	Estimated number of women migrating to the Middle East	Estimated percentage of Asian women going to the Middle East
Bangladesh	.5	1,000	99	1,000	0
Indonesia	68	136,000	83	113,000	28–25
Philippines (land-based)[a]	58	279,500	42	117,500	29–26
Thailand (1994)	10–25	17,000–42,500	77	13,000–33,000	3–7
Pakistan	1	1,500	99	1,500	0
India (1995)	10–17	41,500–70,500	97	40,000–68,500	10–15
Sri Lanka	79	128,000	95	121,500	30–27
Estimated total		604,500–659,000		407,500–456,000	

[a]Figures do not include seamen working on ships.
Source: Dimzon 1997, 84: International Labor Organization 1996; SLBFE 1997, tables 39 and 40; Stahl 1991, 183–84.

such as Jordanians, Palestinians, Yemenis and Sudanese because their countries sided with Iraq in the war" (1996, 539).

Feminization of the Labor Market

Worldwide, the proportion of women in the migrant labor force has risen gradually from roughly 15 percent in the 1970s to over 50 percent in many countries in 1996 (International Labor Organization 1996). The gender breakdown of migrant laborers differs from country to country. In some countries, such as Sri Lanka, the Philippines, and Indonesia, women make up over half of the migrant workers, while other countries send mostly men abroad (Shah 1995, 567). Actual labor flows may differ from official figures, however. Shah suggests that Indian data "probably underestimate the number of female migrants" (1995, 567). P. R. Gopinathan Nair concurs with this assessment, noting that "previous surveys of returned migrants in Kerala had found the proportion of women to be negligible. However, we found that women comprised nearly one-sixth of the returnees" (1999, 215). This lack of reliable data makes estimating the numbers of female migrant laborers difficult.

Despite their dubious quality, the best available statistics do reveal the increasing proportion of female migrants in labor flows from Sri Lanka, Indonesia, and the Philippines. In 1981 52 percent of the Sri Lankans working abroad were female; by 1992, women made up 68 percent of the migrants, and in 1994 they made up 79 percent of the migrants (Korale 1983; SLBFE 1997, table 32). Statistics on Indonesian women show similar changes; women made up 41.5 percent of the migrants in 1983 but constituted 83 percent of the migrants in 1997 (Ministry of Manpower 1997, 3). Likewise, Filipino women made up 12 percent of the migrants in 1975; that percentage grew to 26 percent in 1990, and to 58 percent in 1996 (Dimzon 1997, 85).

Asian women, most of whom work as domestic servants, make up 69 percent of the GCC countries' expatriate female workers (Shah 1994, 8). Of the women from Kerala who had worked in the Middle East, "all had worked in low-paid manual services, mostly in the household sector, as housemaids" (Nair 1999, 215). From Sri Lanka, consistently over 90 percent of the women traveling to work in the Middle East went as housemaids (Herath 1993; SLBFE 1997). Of an estimated 407,500 to 456,000 female workers going to the Middle East in 1996, approximately 25–28 percent came from Indonesia, 26–29 percent from the Philippines, 10–15 percent from India, 3–7 percent from Thailand, and 27–30 percent from Sri Lanka (see table 3). These figures suggest that the total stock of Asian women working in the Middle East in 1996 numbered between 1.3 and 1.5 million.

In 1987 62 percent of Kuwaiti households had maids, up from only 13 percent in the late 1970s (Shah 1995, 592). Sharif, a representative of a Saudi Arabian manpower recruiting agency whom I interviewed in Sri Lanka, felt that Arabic societies had come to rely on domestic servants' assistance, and that families in the Middle East required housemaids as status symbols. He said, "Without a maid, a house feels incomplete. After a bride gets married, she wants a housemaid. Sometimes it's even written into the marriage license itself, that she wants a house with X number of bedrooms, and a maid! It's like having a TV or a fridge. This demand won't stop. It is increasing every year." Government officials, manpower recruiting agents, and scholars predict that the current demand for housemaids will continue with no foreseeable decline.

Sri Lankan Statistics

To gather data on migration, the Research Division of the Sri Lanka Bureau of Foreign Employment (SLBFE) set up a research unit at the Katunayake International Airport near Colombo for monitoring departing migrant workers. Initiated in a limited way in 1990, the survey operated from January 1992 until mid-1995, when airport security measures and airline objections forced the unit to close. The project significantly improved the reliability of statistics for a limited period of time, but since neither the airlines, the airport authorities, nor immigration officials now keep records of travelers, the SLBFE has difficulty collecting accurate data (Rodrigo 1998, chap. 2, p. 4).

Estimates have varied widely on the total number of Sri Lankans currently working overseas. In 1994 the Ministry of Labour set the figure at 300,000 while the SLBFE put the figure higher, at 500,000. In 1996 the SLBFE estimated the number of Sri Lankan overseas contract workers at 580,000 (SLBFE 1997, table 37), and in 1999 *Migration News* reported that it stood at 800,000 (1999). Despite government efforts, much remains unknown about the size and characteristics of this massive movement of people.

During the late 1970s and early 1980s, Sri Lankan migrants generally traveled to oil-producing countries in the Persian Gulf. Even after employment opportunities in Singapore, Malaysia, Italy, and Hong Kong arose in the late 1980s, the GCC countries Saudi Arabia, Kuwait, and UAE continued to employ roughly three-quarters of the migrants from Sri Lanka (see table 4). During this same time period, migration patterns within Sri Lanka changed. In the late 1970s most migrants came from urbanized districts near the capital, but by the mid-1990s they came from areas all over the island (Gunatilleke 1995, 677; SLBFE 1997, table 30). Both the source and the destination of migrant flows diversified over the period.

Sri Lanka has a higher literacy level, lower population growth, and better sanitation than other countries in South Asia (Shah 1995, 614–16), and it compares favorably with Indonesia, the Philippines, and Thailand in terms of a number of basic indicators, such as economic growth, life expectancy, and infant mortality (Central Intelligence Agency 1998). Drawing a statistical picture of the average housemaid, Malsiri Dias and Nedra Weerakoon-Gunawardene found her poor, married with two or three children, educated to the fifth or sixth standard (sixth or seventh grade, in the American system), and not employed in the formal labor market (1991, 49). Similarly, on Indian migrants who had worked in the Gulf, Nair remarks that "in general, the women who returned were older, poorer and less educated than their male counterparts" (1999, 215). Although Sri Lankan living standards equal or exceed those of other countries in South and Southeast Asia, the flow of migrant women comes disproportionately from disadvantaged sections of the population.

Dias and Weerakoon-Gunawardene connect migration abroad with limited economic opportunities available to low-income women in rural Sri Lanka (1991). Female unemployment in Sri Lanka, at 21 percent in 1993, more than doubled male unemployment figures (Gunatilleke 1995, 673; Shah 1995, 571). At the same time, the majority of women who went abroad as housemaids were "housewives not actively seeking employment in the domestic labour market" (Gunatilleke 1995, 676), so the significance of female unemployment figures remains unclear. Nevertheless, scholars concur that high local unemployment provides a "push" factor that motivates labor migration to the Middle East.

Most migrant women work abroad in the prime of their working lives. Table 5 shows that roughly 85 percent of the migrant women from Sri Lanka were between the ages of twenty and forty. In 1996, a total out-migration estimated at 580,000 people represents roughly 3

Table 4. Out-migration of Sri Lankan migrants by country of destination, 1992–94

Country	1992 Total	Percentage of 1992 Migrants	1993 Total	Percentage of 1993 Migrants	1994 Total	Percentage of 1994 Migrants	Total 1992–1994	Percentage of 1992–94 Migrants
Saudi Arabia	41,083	33.0	51,413	39.8	45,005	34.6	137,501	35.9
Kuwait	32,368	26.0	30,362	23.6	33,273	25.6	96,003	25.0
UAE	22,409	18.0	19,901	15.4	17,982	13.8	60,292	15.7
Lebanon	3,145	2.5	4,389	3.4	7,953	6.1	15,487	4.0
Oman	8,715	7.0	5,520	4.3	4,523	3.5	18,758	4.9
Bahrain	6,225	5.0	5,684	4.4	5,624	4.4	17,533	4.6
Jordan	3,511	2.8	3,329	2.6	4,830	3.7	11,670	3.0
Qatar	1,655	1.3	3,114	2.4	4,121	3.2	8,890	2.3
Maldives	2,490	2.0	2,309	1.8	2,391	1.8	7,190	1.9
Singapore	1,775	1.4	2,065	1.6	1,975	1.5	5,815	1.5
Others	1,118	1.0	990	.7	2,350	1.8	4,458	1.2
Total	124,494	100	129,076	100	130,027	100	383,597	100

Source: SLBFE 1997, table 31.

Table 5. Sri Lankan female migrants by age, 1994

Age	Number	Percentage
Up to 20	5,721	5.3
21–25	18,883	17.3
26–30	22,208	20.4
31–35	29,959	27.6
36–40	22,066	20.3
41–45	8,407	7.7
46–50	1,419	1.3
51 and older	85	.1
Total	108,698	100

Source: SLBFE 1997, table 33.

percent of the national population, estimated at 18.1 million in 1995. Estimating 408,000 women abroad out of a working-age (15–64) female population of 5.4 million people means that 8.9 percent, (or one in eleven), of working-age Sri Lankan women worked abroad in 1996 (SLBFE 1997, table 37; Sri Lanka National Department of Census and Statistics 1996).

Figures from 1983 to 1994 indicate that approximately three-fourths of the Sri Lankans traveling to work abroad were married (Eelens, Mook, and Schampers 1992, 6; SLBFE 1997, table 34). This percentage exceeds the average in a comparable section of the general population (Dias and Weerakoon-Gunawardene 1991, 48), and this pattern differs from many other migrant flows, which often consist of unmarried men. 90 percent of the married women left children at home when they went abroad, and 20 percent of these children were under the age of five (Eelens, Mook, and Schampers 1992, 6). The migrant population had larger households and more children than the national average (Brochmann 1990, 93; Dias and Weerakoon-Gunawardene 1991, 48). This information on marital status, offspring, and household size suggests that family structure has a significant role in influencing migration.

Demographers concerned with future population growth speculate that increased age at marriage for single migrants and the repeated temporary separation of husband and wife for married migrants could lead to lower fertility rates and population growth among migrant communities. In addition, higher standards of living due to increased income levels could cause birth rates to decline (Lappé, Collins, and

Rosset 1998, 35; Schaeffer 1997, 233), and published sources do point toward slightly improved standards of living among a migrant population (Dias and Weerakoon-Gunawardene 1991, 48). However, if standards of living remain at roughly pre-migration levels, and if migrants have already had several children before going abroad, the migration may not affect fertility to any significant extent (Korale 1983). While not of immediate concern, these issues do pertain to the long-term effects of labor migration on the Sri Lankan population.

Demand for Muslim labor in the Middle East exceeds demand for workers of other religions (Gunatilleke 1995, 679). Arabic employers often request Muslim housemaids, and the percentage of Muslim[3] migrants exceeds the percentage of Muslims in the Sri Lankan population as a whole. While Muslims make up only 7 percent of the Sri Lankan population in general (Herath 1993; Jacobs and Papma 1992, 200), Muslim women make up 22–23 percent of the housemaids (Dias and Weerakoon-Gunawardene 1991), and Muslims make up as high as 27.8 percent of the total migrant population (SLBFE 1997, table 36). The percentage of Tamil-speaking Hindu women going abroad seems disproportionately smaller than their population percentage, but the political instability caused by the civil war in the North and East of the island complicates sampling by excluding large areas from the official statistics. Religion and ethnicity clearly influence migration patterns.

Ideologies of Development: Official Assessments of Success and Failure

Oil, money, and migrants move globally—and so do ideas. Indeed, sexist folk concepts about the value of women's labor can shape both academic and popular discourse on gender and work. Moreover, Western development ideology dominates assessments of migrants' "success" and "failure." This section examines the priorities, criteria, and timelines researchers propose in such assessments, and compares them to local standards, goals, strategies, and ambitions. Western categories and assumptions shape evaluations, whether or not they fit the local situation and worldview.

---

[3] In general speech in Sri Lanka, "Muslim" refers to Tamil-speaking Muslims; "Tamil" refers to Tamil-speaking Hindus.

Seeing Women's Work as "Work"

Ongoing research on women and work reveals the slow and some-times painful processes by which academics and non-academics change their conceptions of the value of women's labor in the local, national, and international economies. Economists and statisticians often fail to count female-gendered tasks as "work," or to count un-paid housework as employment. For example, R. B. M. Korale writes, "In the case of females, the majority of returned migrants were house-wives when they migrated, and were not really economically active females" (1989, 12). He justifies this statement by noting that women in the role of the housewife were not actively seeking work. D. M. Ariyawansa reports that in 1988, 93 percent of the migrant women were "housewives" before going abroad (1988). Like many others, he stumbles over how to classify these women upon their return: Does the reentrant qualify as a housewife again, or is she unemployed/un-deremployed merely because she labors for her family instead of for foreigners? (See Nair 1999 and Mahawewa 1993 for similar semantic difficulties.)

Research on female labor migration and domestic service highlights the importance of viewing housework and child care as work, whether performed at home or abroad (Constable 1997). A commodity on the global market, rendered for strangers, regulated by national and inter-national laws, women's work leapt to the Sri Lankan national con-sciousness; domestic workers formerly missed in employment surveys became "our army of housemaids" (M. Gamburd 1995b). The sale of domestic services on the global market forces both rural villagers and social scientists to recognize that the tasks housewives usually per-form for free in fact make significant contributions to household fi-nances and the national economy. This recognition in turn suggests the necessity of rethinking economic analysis to incorporate both waged and unwaged labor (Sacks 1989).

Women's perceived economic inactivity in the literature reflects not their daily performance but rather the "self-interested tailoring of de-scriptions and appearances by dominant powerholders" (James Scott 1990, 54), in this case scholars and policymakers, who define and dis-cuss "work" in such a way that women's contributions disappear. Mary Steedly writes, "By moving (slightly) against the grain of official discursive practices [we can] make explicit the necessary exclusions by means of which all narratives ... are engendered" (1993, 31). The

myth of the housewife's economic inactivity supports cultural ideologies that devalue women's labor; challenging this myth reaffirms
the worth of women's work (Collier and Yanagisako 1987a; Joan Scott
1988).

Evaluating Success and Failure

Ethnographic materials from Sri Lanka suggest that economists and
political officials use Western, middle-class values in assessing the
"success" of various categories of migrant workers. These values do
not fully capture the rationales, goals, and ambitions of Naeaegama
migrants. David G. Mandelbaum's statement, made thirty years ago,
still holds true:

> Whereas Myrdal states ... that the masses in South Asia do not calcu-
> late rationally in terms of costs, returns, and maximum profit, he is ne-
> glecting their own social calculations which are as rational in their vil-
> lage milieu as the economist's calculations are in his milieu. (1970, 639)

This section explores the values and assumptions implicit in several
critiques of migrants' economic strategies and behaviors.

The Sri Lankan government actively supports labor migration because jobs abroad reduce local unemployment while bringing much-
needed foreign exchange into the country. At the same time, officials
critically note that migrants spend the majority of their remittances
on consumption instead of investing in productive resources or commerce that would stimulate the economy. In a similar vein, R. E.
Looney notes that the Kuwaiti practice of hiring servants has not led
to increased Kuwaiti participation in the labor market. Instead, "foreign labour was used in menial tasks to substitute for Kuwaiti inputs
which were then consumed in leisure activities" (1992, 180). He suggests that "the real interests of Kuwaitis might be better served" by
restricting foreign labor and making citizens participate in economic
activities (1992, 181). In both of these examples efficiency, investment,
and productivity outweigh consumption, leisure, and pleasure in the
economic assessment of "real interests."

Sri Lankan government officials hope to draw migrant workers' remittances into the formal banking system and therefore offer Non-
Resident Foreign Currency (NRFC) accounts with attractive interest
rates. Mid-level and skilled-level migrants, overwhelmingly male, take

advantage of these accounts, but most poorer migrants, largely female, keep their savings in cash or invest in consumer items. Scholars often criticize returning migrants for purchasing and bringing home gold jewelry, cassette recorders, radios, televisions, and other electrical goods, which the social scientists see exclusively as items for conspicuous consumption. Closer analysis, however, reveals the economic strategy behind these purchases. Jewelry and expensive electrical goods act as a form of savings; worn, used, and displayed in times of prosperity, the items can be sold if needed and do not depreciate as quickly as the Sri Lankan rupee. In addition, friends, neighbors, and relatives are less likely to borrow and more likely to return consumer items than cash. Not merely for show, these "luxury" items provide a form of savings safer and more logical than money in hand or in the bank (see also Brochmann 1992, 232–35).

Godfrey Gunatilleke suggests a scheme for assessing the success and failure of Sri Lankan migrations to the Middle East (Gunatilleke and Perera 1987; Gunatilleke 1992). He divides migrants into the three premigration employment categories of principal earner, supplementary earner, or non-contributor to the household finances. In this case housewives are counted as unemployed, and seen as not contributing to household finances or having a meaningful economic role in the family. Focusing on four areas of potential improvement to the migrant's life (economy, quality of life, human relations, and community status), Gunatilleke proposes a complex mathematical scoring system for calculating the success or failure of the migration. Income-generating investments, such as businesses, bank savings, and the education of children, score higher than non-income-generating investments, such as building a house and buying household items. However, houses receive added priority because they improve the migrant's quality of life.

Gunatilleke finds that most of the "successful" migrants are of the first category (principal earner), whereas the majority of the total migrants are of the third (non-contributor to household finances). Asserting that sustainable improvements arise only through income-earning investments, Gunatilleke notes, "Households that are used to subsistence-level income flows do not find it easy to manage the new household budgets or to think in terms of a well-designed plan of consumption, savings, and future investments" (1992, 242). The author further notes that the successful migrant (always referred to by the male pronoun) "moderates" consumption, and "disciplines and regulates" money use (1992, 245). According to this system, women almost always "fail" in their migrations.

Gunatilleke suggests that detailed planning supported in a joint effort by all members of the household makes for a successful migration:

> The success lay in the way in which migrants defined their goals realistically, setting for themselves objectives that were commensurate with the incomes they expected to earn, and, given the constraints and limits of each earning opportunity, arrived at a package of investments and expenditures which increased the welfare of the migrant and his [sic] household. (1992, 243)

Success also requires that families continue to generate income in Sri Lanka in order to save foreign earnings. While ideally Naeaegama families hoped to maintain an income in Sri Lanka while the migrant worked abroad, in reality many families turned to migration in the first place because local incomes could not provide adequately for their families. Wealthier villagers who sent men abroad to work lived up to the scholars' standards more often than did poorer families who sent women abroad as housemaids. Instead of recognizing the village families' different starting points and modifying expectations accordingly, scholarly assessment weighs all families by the same standards and invariably finds the poorer families lacking.

Although Gunatilleke claims to take human relations and quality of life into consideration, he suggests that those who use money for consumption, weddings, and funerals "fared worse" (1992, 244) than those who make permanent, durable increments to their well-being. Although in 1994 Naeaegama villagers shared the goals of individual investment and accumulation that Gunatilleke identifies, they went abroad with a wider range of priorities and objectives, including feeding hungry relatives and preserving social networks by giving gifts, defraying medical costs, and contributing to ceremonies. Where family solidarity equals social security, distributing money among relatives constitutes planning for retirement and insuring against disaster. A family that saves money for a house while refusing relatives money for basic needs clearly comes closer to Gunatilleke's definition of success, but at the expense of severing vitally important social ties in the village. Such considerations caution against any easy assumption that economic well-being transparently equates with successful migration.

Numerous studies note the seeming lack of social mobility or permanent improvements in the quality of life in migrant families (Hettige 1992, 156; Brochmann 1992, 222). Where foreign earnings support daily consumption, many families grow dependent on having a migrant abroad at all times (Brochmann 1987, 1990). Naeaegama villagers also note with resignation the high proportion of foreign earnings channeled to daily consumption, and recognize the difficulty of saving money to buy land, build a house, or invest in business. Scholars lament the many half-completed construction projects they see in villages around the country, and suggest that most migrant women's remittances will bring about only short-lived improvements in quality of life.

A longitudinal assessment of improvements challenges this conclusion, however. In Naeaegama many construction projects half-finished in 1994 had been completed by 1997. A number of families had also invested in income-generating activities, improving their business ventures in small but significant ways. When a family struggled to pay off debts and support daily consumption with a migrant's salary, construction and entrepreneurial endeavors proceeded at a pace so slow as to appear, at first glance, stagnant. Nevertheless, persistent efforts accumulated into substantial long-term development. Dias and Weerakoon-Gunawardene also note that women often had to spend four to six years abroad before they could significantly improve their individual and family status (1991, 187). These observations suggest that poor families might require considerably longer periods of time than rich ones to accomplish their goals.

Sexist gender norms, rigid economic rationality, and culturally insensitive development ideologies shape discussions of women's labor and migrants' accomplishments. Dominant perceptions of the meaning of "work," and scholarly time lines, criteria, and formulae for "success," often conflicted with the rationales, goals, and strategies of families in the village of Naeaegama. (Chapter 5, in which I analyze village concepts of "improvement" and the logic of how people spend their remittances, explores these issues further.)

Conclusion

With the transnational movement of commodities, capital, people, and ideas, one cannot analyze local experiences without reference to global dynamics. Sri Lankan migration to the Middle East takes place in the context of the international demand for oil and the global influence of OPEC in controlling the price of petroleum, one of the most valuable and most widely traded products on the international market. The power and wealth of the GCC nations in the Persian Gulf draw migrants to the region, creating unequal labor relations similar to the colonial domination that spurred an earlier South Asian diaspora. The migration of labor to the Middle East is thus unique neither in the displacement of citizens nor in the unequal power relations of the countries involved.

Several patterns visible in migration to the Middle East do differ from previous power relations and movements of people, however. Migrants from all over Asia work in the Middle East. In contrast to colonial patterns, geography no longer maps power and poverty; in this case, third-world workers now labor in the seats of power. In some GCC countries, migration has reached the stage that foreigners significantly outnumber nationals, a situation that highlights the nation as an "imagined community," an arbitrary cultural construct created by a collective act of will. Unlike most migrants from Asia, many Arabic guest workers have significant ties to their host countries, but also keep roots at home. Such transmigrants challenge our commonsense assumptions about citizenship and national borders, suggesting that scholars—and all citizens—should consider alternative concepts of identity in an increasingly interconnected and interdependent world.

Continued migration is key to the well-being of many Sri Lankan families and to the nation's economy, but dependence on the unstable dynamics of the larger global market is risky, as the Gulf War illustrates. Labor administrators estimate that Sri Lanka lost one hundred million rupees in foreign exchange during the Gulf War, due to the loss of remittances. Sri Lanka also suffered from the worldwide increase in the price of petroleum products and the loss of a major export market for tea. Transnational ties join economies much more closely than ever before. As the shifting composition of the workforce in the GCC countries indicates, political issues of alliance and conflict affect the international distribution of jobs. With nearly 10 percent of Sri Lanka's working-age women employed in the Middle East, a significant part of Sri Lanka's financial well-being relies on continuing prosperity in the Persian Gulf.

The feminization of migrant labor provides another striking aspect of the migration patterns in question. Around the world, more and more women have entered the workforce, taking over many of the most poorly paid, difficult jobs (Harrison 1997). Sexist ideologies that view women's work as supplemental and unskilled justify low wages (Fernandez-Kelly 1983). At the same time, women's entrance into the labor market may provide a basis for changing negative gender stereotypes. Female labor migration and domestic service abroad have already challenged older ways of thinking about women's work, revealing the need to incorporate both paid and unpaid domestic work into economic calculations. Similarly, as the discussion of success and failure indicates, local practices challenge and contest the assumptions inherent in development ideology and rational economic thinking, questioning to what extent these concepts adequately explain individuals' identities and behaviors.

2   Administrative Structures: Getting a Job Abroad

Humans are creatures who live by the rules that they themselves create. These sets of rules, which many anthropologists refer to as "culture" or "discourse," shape how people interpret the world and guide what they think, say, and do. Any body of rules, either formal or informal, reflects the social and historical context in which it originated and the political interests of those who created it. Rules, norms, and values differentially benefit and disadvantage the various people they affect. In the processes of living their everyday lives, people make rules, break rules, and develop more rules for resisting rules.

When studying social structures, anthropologists often ask how formal networks of human relations channel power and authority. Foucault coins the term *governmentality* to refer to "the institutions, procedures, analyses and reflections, the calculations and tactics that allow the exercise of . . . power" over a population (1991, 102). He focuses in particular on the social structures and systems of knowledge that regulate "the conduct of conduct" (Gordon 1991, 2). Such regulation, or "governance" (Rose 1999, 15, 17), involves both governmental organizations and a range of private institutions.

Foucault identifies particular tactics and strategies that allow institutions to wield power over individuals and groups of people. Effective administration requires classifying and codifying groups *as* groups or creating what Nikolas Rose refers to as "governable spaces" (1999, 31).

The numerous bureaucratic techniques that channel official power over citizens include the "construction of a vast statistical apparatus through which this domain could be inscribed, visualized, tabulated, modelled, calculated" (Rose 1999, 33). Although the people included under any particular label may originally have little or no sense of group solidarity, the government's act of naming and administering the group can create a new sense of identity.

Defining group boundaries helps institutions to manage the people within the groups. Government "need" for information justifies the surveillance of large populations, analysis of the resulting information, and subsequent interventions meant to modify citizens' behaviors. Many government rules shape everyday behaviors; as Rose puts it, "the quotidian lives of the masses become gridded by regulatory codes" (1999, 113). Through rules regulating education, public health, economic transactions, geographical movement, and the like, institutions exert power over individuals and groups. Having codified the population, the government and other institutions solidify these social groupings by using them in administration, thus convincing people of the reality of the constructed identities and reinforcing official views of proper conduct.

Public and private institutions play a large role in creating the bureaucratic procedures and legislation that define identities and regulate behavior. Arturo Escobar suggests that institutions centered around an activity or process legitimize the "reality" of the activity, make it highly visible, and channel the exercise of power around it (1988, 431). With organizations come experts. Escobar sees professionalization as "a set of techniques and disciplinary practices through which the generation, diffusion, and validation of knowledge are organized, managed, and controlled; in other words, the process by which a politics of truth is created and maintained" (1988, 430). Experts monopolize authoritative knowledge about the subject in question.

Although cultural rules, discourses, and social institutions regulate behavior and shape self (and group) identity, individuals do not unquestioningly accept every rule and hierarchy. People also continually challenge, resist, and alter systems. Although some critics condemn Foucault for minimizing the influence of individual acts (see Diamond and Quinby 1988; Dirks, Eley, and Ortner 1994; Mascia-Lees, Sharpe, and Cohen 1989), others see in his discussion of resistance a "permanent provocation" in the face of authority (Gordon 1991, 4). This dual character of individuals as simultaneously rule-making and rule-following leads systems of governance to see people "as both self-governing individuals within a self-governing political community and clients to be administered, governed, and normalized with respect to governmental objectives" (Dean 1994, 209).

This chapter examines the growth of organizations, experts, legislation, bureaucracy, and accepted practices around the migration of labor to the Middle East. The Sri Lankan government's most prominent structure regulating migration, the Sri Lanka Bureau of Foreign Employment (SLBFE), controls and administers official policy on migration. Other formal and informal organizations also play a role in getting a job abroad, including licensed manpower recruiting agencies, local subagents, and informal personal connections.[1] Together these structures form a semicoherent system of governance that encompasses the diverse interests and points of view of the various actors in the system. Instances of fraud and corruption highlight cases where individuals within the system both comply with and resist the bureaucratic regulations and negotiate the power dynamics of economic advantages. Examining the official and unofficial structures surrounding women's experiences of migration raises provocative questions about agency, resistance, knowledge, and power.

The Sri Lanka Bureau of Foreign Employment (SLBFE)

Among the public discourses surrounding migration, the unquestioned legitimacy of the nation-state deserves attention. Governments teach patriotic citizens to recognize and defend lines drawn on the earth that separate the "territory" of the "nation" from foreign countries (Anderson 1991). The concepts of territory and nation, and the behavioral patterns associated with them, are all culturally constructed—to a large extent arbitrary but intensely meaningful and not optional. The system of rules arising around our concepts of national territory affects international migrants, who cross historically and culturally defined borders between political entities.

The extensive migration of labor from Sri Lanka to the Middle East began in the mid-1970s. Official responses followed quickly there-

---

[1] Mr. Ruhunage of SLBFE, Dr. Mananwatte of the Ministry of Labour, and Mr. Aponso and Mr. Madanayake from ALFEA were very generous with their time and insights, on which I have relied in this chapter. I also interviewed a number of job agents and subagents whose names I have changed to protect their privacy.

after; the government identified the emerging flow of labor as an object of regulation and created institutions to study, legislate, and administer migrants. In 1976 the government organized the Foreign Employment Unit in the Department of Labour to find employment for people abroad. After the free-market government elected in 1977 privatized many governmental functions, responsibility for managing foreign employment passed to private agencies, which the government monitored and controlled according to the Foreign Employment Act no. 32 of 1980. The expansion and reorganization of existing Sri Lankan embassies in the Middle East, and the opening of new embassies in UAE (1979), Saudi Arabia (1981), and Kuwait (1981) and new consular sections in Jordan and Lebanon to safeguard and assist Sri Lankan citizens abroad showed further institutional response to migration.

As the magnitude of migration to the Middle East grew, the government dissociated the regulation of foreign employment from the Department of Labour, creating the Sri Lanka Bureau of Foreign Employment (SLBFE). The Bureau of Foreign Employment Act no. 21 of 1985 established the SLBFE to:

1. Develop markets and promote opportunities abroad;
2. Support, license, and regulate agencies;
3. Ensure standards on contracts;
4. Train migrants;
5. Collect data on migration;
6. See to the welfare and protection of Sri Lankans abroad;
7. Give information and guidance to the families of migrants;
8. Make investments for Sri Lankans living abroad; and
9. Facilitate reintegration of returnees.

(SLBFE Act 21 of 1985, section 15)

This new section of legal code and the new branch of government it chartered arose to regulate and control migration. The social category of "the Middle East migrant" took shape alongside these developments.

In the early 1990s critics charged the SLBFE's 125 staff members with inadequately fulfilling the Bureau's envisioned role, claiming that unregulated agencies overcharged and cheated clients; employers often reneged on the minimal requirements in contracts with their housemaids; and little, if any, training for migrants took place. Critics suggested that foreign employment had not been regulated by the

Bureau in any significant fashion (see Dias and Weerakoon-Gunawardene 1991) and that the government needed to reinforce and revamp its institutions to control the private job agencies and to assist migrants abroad more effectively.

In February 1994 the government proposed a number of significant amendments to strengthen the SLBFE. The Bureau, funded through migrant registration fees collected through job agencies, planned to increase its charges, regulate job agencies more stringently, and train, register, and insure migrants more strictly. The SLBFE also planned to assist migrants by arranging bank loans to cover migration charges, setting up savings and banking schemes, and initiating programs to enhance entrepreneurship among returnees. Abroad, the government planned to enhance its enforcement of labor laws and upgrade embassy emergency welfare facilities. Generally speaking, the government prepared to step up its efforts through the SLBFE to administer the flow of citizens and their finances.

The Sri Lankan government employed a number of bureaucratic techniques to supervise, count, and regulate the migrant population. Foucault suggests that in the modern world, power often flows through technologies of "bio-power," or control over bodies. Bio-power operates on two levels. First, bio-power operates on the level of the individual body: children and adults learn in institutions such as schools, factories, or prisons to behave in orderly, efficient ways; their socialization makes them physically useful and politically obedient. Second, bio-power operates on the level of whole populations. Rules control, for example, public health and sanitation, construction, and transportation; policies regulate everything from childhood inoculations to restaurant inspections, construction permits, and vision tests for driving licenses. No aspect of life remains free from expert knowledge and control (Foucault 1979). Analysis of several programs implemented by the SLBFE suggests how government policies regulate and control the migrant population.

By 1997 the SLBFE had nearly doubled its 1994 size, with 250 staff members and thirteen branch offices outside Colombo. Some but not all of the initiatives proposed in 1994 had come on-line. In April 1995 compulsory registration for migrants came into operation. Shortly thereafter the SLBFE organized an administrative unit at Katunayake International Airport to monitor departing migrants. As a result, compliance with regulations soared; the total number of registered migrants jumped dramatically from 60,000 in 1994 to 172,000 in 1995

(SLBFE 1997, table 1), and the number of registered agencies grew from 250 in 1993 to 477 in 1995 (SLBFE 1997, table 28). Although the unit only functioned from mid-1995 to early 1996, it greatly enhanced compliance with regulations, as did public service announcements in the media that effectively disseminated information about migrant training, registration, and insurance. All the Naeaegama migrants I spoke with knew of these policies and programs. Pressure on agencies combined with a very thorough public awareness campaign created general knowledge of and conformity with the rules.

The government extended its role to systematize (and profit from) relations between job agencies and the migrants they sent abroad. The SLBFE required agencies to submit fees and documentation when a migrant went abroad. With the revenue thus generated, the SLBFE funded various programs for migrants. Beginning in October 1994, registered migrants automatically received Jathika Suraksha, the SLBFE's Foreign Employment Insurance Policy, which offered a life insurance and disability policy, medical benefits for the family left at home, and repatriation if killed or stranded abroad. Further incentives for registration included tickets to a raffle with cash awards for all registered migrants and scholarships for children of registered migrants. The government took steps to familiarize migrants with the official bureaucracy and encouraged their participation in programs.

The SLBFE supervised and controlled not only bureaucratic structures and practices but also the housemaid population itself, by instituting a national training and certification program. Women who had worked abroad before (the majority of the Naeaegama migrants) did not need to participate in the program, but administrators contended that first-time migrants lacked skills and experience and justified the program by arguing that training would protect and prepare the maids, in the process ensuring the reputation and reliability of Sri Lanka's migrant labor force.

In December 1993 the SLBFE began training women who would train future housemaids. Selected by the Ministry of Labour, the participants had never been to the Middle East themselves, but all had passed their O-level exams, the British and Sri Lankan equivalent of tenth-grade education in the U.S. In contrast, women in Naeaegama had for over a decade transferred information about how to live and work in the Middle East through informal female networks. The government training program set the knowledge of "experts" over firsthand experience, privileging one form of authority and dismissing the other.

By 1997 the free, week-long program functioned smoothly in the country, available in a number of convenient locations. The SLBFE provided Rs. 11 / (Rs. 15 / in 1997 rupees) (a daily travel stipend) and a free lunch as incentive to attend.[2] The training program included instruction in six major fields. First, the SLBFE estimated that the rural women and poorer urban women who made up 75 percent of the migrants would have little experience with modern household technologies; thus, women learned about vacuum cleaners, kitchen appliances, and bathroom fixtures. Second, the program provided some minimal language instruction in English and Arabic. Third, it offered information on the religious and cultural laws and customs of the Arabic countries, including special clothing requirements and restrictions on women's freedom. Fourth, the program counseled migrants on their rights and duties, suggested procedures to follow in the event of an emergency, and advised on homesickness, first aid techniques, family planning, and sexually transmitted diseases. Fifth, the program provided guidance on exchange rates, remittance procedures, bank accounts, and insurance policies. Finally, the program gave instruction in airport departure and arrival procedures, forms, airport taxes, customs, and security. By systematizing and disseminating official knowledge about migration, the government sought to create a housemaid population that was both lawabiding and productive.

Local Naeaegama views on training differed from official perspectives and priorities. One suit-and-tie clad Colombo bureaucrat I spoke with animatedly portrayed the shock and confusion of an inexperienced rural housemaid arriving in a new house where she found the carpets unfamiliar, the kitchen unintelligible, the bathroom a mystery, and the employers insistent on her starting work immediately. In contrast, Naeaegama housemaids rarely expressed anxiety about lack of training. Those departing for the Middle East for the first time felt that they could learn what they needed from returned housemaids in the village, from their employers, or from neighborhood housemaids abroad. Indeed, rather than valuing the training, several women cyni-

---

[2] Rampant inflation in Sri Lanka makes comparing prices from different years difficult. In this chapter, unless otherwise noted, monetary figures have been adjusted for inflation and are stated in 1994 rupees. In 1994, Rs. 50/= U.S.$1. To avoid encumbering the text with exchange values, I have only noted the U.S. dollar equivalent for particularly salient figures. For more information about inflation, exchange rates, and purchasing power, see appendix B.

cally remarked that extra skills would mean extra work. Though some returnees joked about initial difficulties with their housekeeping skills, they expressed more interest in having the government streamline emergency procedures abroad and increase minimum salaries. Women worried about finding honest job agencies, paying high rates of interest to moneylenders, providing adequate child care in their absence, and saving enough money to invest in a house and land. Although Naeaegama migrants agreed with many government initiatives, official programs and plans did not always echo local priorities.

Foucault suggests that power always spawns resistance, that codes of conduct generate patterns of counter-conduct, and that subjugated systems of knowledge challenge authoritative discourses. While power may appear as an unchanging monolith, in actuality it re-creates itself from moment to moment, in countless instances of interpersonal negotiations (Foucault 1978). Shifts in the balance of power bring about social change. Within the discourse surrounding migration, contradictions arose not only between official and local visions of migrant needs but also between different institutions involved with regulating migration. These latter instances highlight the danger of assuming that the state presents a seamless monolith of power and authority, free from internal frictions.

Several ongoing government initiatives concerning banking, labor contracts, and wages have revealed conflicts of interest within the institutional structures surrounding migration. In 1997 the SLBFE was negotiating an agreement to streamline and regulate credit arrangements for migrant women. L.K. Ruhunage, the head research officer at the SLBFE, felt that since migrants provided Sri Lanka with much-needed foreign exchange, the country should provide migrants with low-interest loans. Even government-run banks, however, refused to extend credit without collateral to high-risk borrowers. The SLBFE was engaged in negotiating a loan system that Ruhunage hoped would deliver migrants from the clutches of village moneylenders. This initiative, if successful, might lower interest fees but would also bring formerly informal financial relationships under the scrutiny of the formal banking system (see chapter 3).

The government also hoped to negotiate standardized labor contracts to institutionalize and regulate legal arrangements surrounding women's work. In 1997 Sinhala- and Tamil-speaking housemaids signed contracts written in English and Arabic with their job agencies, and signed different contracts, written in Arabic, with their employers. The SLBFE advocated a single contract, written in all relevant vernaculars, to be signed by the maid, her employer, and the job agent. Other parts of the system disapproved of the plan, however. First, local job agents worried that standardized three-way contracts would hurt business and cause delays. Second, diplomatic personnel expressed concern about keeping track of and enforcing the contracts without additional staff, especially in countries without embassies. Third, most GCC host countries did not cover expatriate workers in their labor laws, and had not adopted International Labor Organization standards on migrant workers (Rodrigo 1998, chap. 3, p. 5). The SLBFE realized that it could only enforce such contracts with the help of the job agencies, embassies, and host countries. Effective laws required a level of enforcement then impossible.

Sri Lankan authorities also had a long-term plan to negotiate labor agreements with countries that hosted migrants. Despite fears that regulations might turn employers toward Philippine or Indonesian housemaids instead of Sri Lankan labor, the government requested and received a wage increase for Sri Lankan housemaids in Kuwait. Bargaining from a position of relative disadvantage, however, the SLBFE had not tried to raise wages in other countries, such as Saudi Arabia, and took no steps to enforce the agreement in Kuwait. In 1997 several international trade unions were coordinating multinational efforts by manpower-exporting countries to protect the interests of migrant laborers. If successful, such initiatives could shift the balance of power within the international system.

In summary, a governmental structure grew up to accommodate migration. Internationally, Sri Lanka opened new embassies in the Middle East; nationally, it formed the SLBFE. These institutions counted, trained, registered, insured, and ministered to migrant women. The massive bureaucracy—with its accompanying bureaucrats—saw to the professionalization of the housemaid population through training and registration. Within the system of governance, however, conflicts of interest between major institutions regulating migration left many policies open for debate and negotiation.

Licensed Manpower Recruiting Agencies

Potential migrants obtain employment in the Middle East in one of two different ways: through licensed agencies or through "tickets" sent by informal personal connections. A range of institutions and practices surround job agencies, including local subagencies, rural and Colombo-based agencies, and foreign manpower-recruiting agencies.

The character of "the wicked, exploitative, Muslim job agent" plays a major role in the horror stories that circulate about the migration of female labor to the Middle East. Whereas common images present homogenized caricatures of job agents, in reality agents and subagents come from a diversity of backgrounds, experiences, and religious affiliations and take a variety of approaches to their occupation. While agents exercise power over the migrants they send abroad, they also experience regulation by both the SLBFE and the Association of Licensed Foreign Employment Agencies (ALFEA), an organization that mediates between agencies and the SLBFE. Requiring agencies to obtain licenses generates money and information for the SLBFE and enhances its control over the migration process.

Mansoor, a brisk, well-informed, and well-organized man who ran an agency in the Muslim business section of Colombo, described the licensing process. Mansoor's framed business registration, printed on larger-than-legal-sized paper, with a large stamp, hung on the wall over his desk. His SLBFE permit, a framed sheet of paper with a red seal, graced the wall over the fax machine. Mansoor said that in 1997 job agents made a Rs. 73,000/ cash deposit (Rs. 100,000/ in 1997 rupees), and two guarantors signed bonds for another Rs. 73,000/ apiece, with the money serving as security that an agency would not defraud or abuse clients. Applicants also presented a character certificate signed by a justice of the peace. Offices had to have a telephone, a fax machine, a typewriter, and a minimum floor space. Each year the agency paid Rs. 7,300/ (Rs. 10,000/ in 1997 rupees) to renew its license, and the SLBFE required the labor license number on all business transactions and advertisements (see also Rodrigo 1998, chap. 3, p. 3). The government regulated agents through a combination of economic leverage, bureaucratic requirements, and symbolic certificates of authority.

In 1996 464 licensed manpower recruiting agencies operated in Sri Lanka (SLBFE 1997, table 28). The parliamentary Act that established the SLBFE also called for the formation of an Association of Licensed Foreign Employment Agencies (ALFEA) and required every licensee to become a member (SLBFE Act no. 21, 1985, section 54). ALFEA resolved disputes between members, formulated a code of conduct and ensured its enforcement, and represented agencies in official negotiations with the SLBFE and the government (SLBFE Act no. 21, 1985, section 55). As government regulations increased the number of registered agencies, ALFEA's influence grew, even as power struggles factionalized its membership.

Naleem, a thoughtful and humorous retired schoolteacher, worked in an agency in an air-conditioned house on a quiet, residential lane leading down to the seaside in Colombo. The agency originally specialized in sending male migrants abroad but had recently branched into the housemaid trade. Naleem expressed some qualms about his job. He felt that his agency made unreasonable profits by "squeezing poor people for every penny they had." Most of Naleem's uneasiness centered around sending housemaids abroad. He noted that sponsors often specified characteristics that they wanted in their housemaids. Naleem had received requests for "fair," "good looking," and "healthy" housemaids and said that this sort of description made him uncomfortable. He jokingly went on to list other traits sponsors might specify, such as "virgin," "tall," or "big-bottomed," and felt that other agents did not share his worries about sexual abuse and prostitution. Calling himself "too old to learn new tricks," Naleem mentioned that he was considering a career change.

Naleem's agency worked closely with a Saudi Arabian one, and Sharif, the partner agency's business representative in Sri Lanka, Indonesia, and the Philippines, worked out of Naleem's office. Through a translator, Sharif interviewed laborers and housemaids seeking jobs in Saudi Arabia. Unlike Naleem, Sharif did not dwell on migrants' vulnerability but instead focused on how job agencies facilitated women's opportunities to earn money abroad. He cited the benevolent supervision and control employers imposed on their maids as a check on women's bad judgment and promiscuity. Sharif, a college-educated engineer familiar with multiple facets of his family's international business, found fault instead with the inefficiency and corruption he saw in government institutions surrounding migration, particularly the senseless hurdles for businessmen and unnecessary delays and fees for obtaining passports for migrants.

While Colombo agencies dominated the manpower recruiting business, in the mid-1990s some agencies opened in rural areas. Ruby Overseas Services occupied an old mansion off the main coastal highway about three miles from Naeaegama. The raised porch area blended seamlessly into the front room, which served as the office; a fax machine and a telephone accompanied a couch and a coffee table. Mendis, the agency proprietor, ran the main business and a branch office with the help of his mother, wife, and brother. Mendis had met a contact while working in Kuwait and set up a job agency in Sri Lanka in 1994. His negative experience with his former partner ("a very crafty crook") motivated him to set up his own licensed agency and office in Kuwait. He claimed that he saved money and time by operating both ends of the business himself. Proud of his entrepreneurial accomplishments, Mendis said that at age thirty, he was the youngest person to have a job agency in Sri Lanka.[3]

Agents portrayed themselves as hardworking businessmen with entrepreneurial spirits who had taken risks that had paid off. Only Naleem said that he felt unethical sending women abroad. The other job agents I spoke with noted both the profits and the costs of running an business and emphasized that they provided needed services for reasonable fees. They turned their discussion of unethical behavior toward other actors in the institutional structure surrounding migration; Sharif condemned corruption in Sri Lanka, while Mendis critiqued dishonesty in Kuwait. These different perspectives reveal conflicts and contradictions within the structure governing migration.

Subagents

Subagents form another level of the institutional structure surrounding migration. For an extra fee, subagents help migrants with paperwork, passports, medical checkups, and transportation to the airport. Many caricatures portray subagents as misleading and overcharging gullible migrants. Sharif called subagents "a bunch of crooks," depicting them as crafty city slickers preying on confused rural women at the bus and train stations in Colombo, or rural con-men wheeling and dealing passports and "selling" housemaids to unscrupulous and unlicensed agencies. Officials at the SLBFE coupled images of exploitative subagents with equally unflattering images of rural women as lazy, helpless dupes. These freely circulating negative images have colored policies made on migration issues.

In practice, subagents help women find jobs and help agencies find workers in a timely fashion. The subagent's position in the official

[3] In 1997 Mendis was pursuing possible garment-factory business connections in Bangkok.

structure, however, remains liminal. Although many agencies keep a
registry of subagents whom they contact when they need recruits,
legally, subagents cannot charge a fee to mediate between a migrant
and an agency, nor can agencies send people to recruit in the rural areas. One pragmatic official suggested that the SLBFE should begin licensing subagents in order to professionalize, supervise, and control
their practices.

Byron, a well-respected and well-known Naeaegama subagent, has
worked with four Colombo agencies. Tall and thin, Byron came to the
interview at Siri's house dressed in Western trousers, a button-down
shirt, and sunglasses. That day Siri, much to his wife Telsie's embarrassment, wore his usual casual sarong. Most of our official interviews
took place on the front porch, but Byron's respectability afforded him
access to the more prestigious living room, and Telsie served him
milk-tea in our best china. A well-educated former military man in
his late forties, Byron had served as a subagent since 1982. Far from
the wicked character of stories, Byron was well-liked in the local
community.

Although many felt that subagents creamed off a great deal of the
migrant's profit while doing little of substance, Byron portrayed himself as hardworking and knowledgeable, as a source of necessary information, and as a valuable asset to the local migrant. In addition to
facilitating the actual migration process, Byron sometimes vouched to
the moneylender that a potential client had secured a job abroad. He
advised women on how to remit their money to the village. On occasion, women sent money to Byron, especially if he had acted as guarantor for their loans, or if they wanted to be sure money reached several recipients. Byron also helped cash checks for relatives who could
not sign their names, or who did not have an identity card to show the
bank. For these services, Byron claimed that he charged only a modest fee of Rs. 2,000/ or 3,000/. Byron's business depended on word of
mouth, and in 1994 roughly 15 percent of the women from the
Naeaegama area who had worked abroad had gotten at least one of
their jobs through him, which suggested general satisfaction with his
services.

The subagent's position in village society has grown out of older
patterns of behavior in which high-status people and respectable
women interact with the outside world through male intermediaries.
Nearly every government, university, and business office has a "peon" to
run errands, and women often send their sons and husbands to deliver

messages or do the marketing. In the mid-1980s many women, circumscribed in their movements by ideologies of honor, decency, and propriety that frowned on their solitary travel, relied on go-betweens like Byron to arrange jobs abroad. Experienced and knowledgeable, Byron traveled to the city, provided women with forms and paperwork, and guided first-time migrants (usually accompanied by male family members) to and through the airport. Like other middlemen, Byron acted as a local contact with a larger, sometimes inscrutable world deemed inappropriate for female contact. Subagents have found themselves caught between official structures of governance, which condemn them, and local discourses on female respectability, which call for them.

How a Sponsor Hires a Housemaid

A number of actors and agencies in the home and host countries help sponsors find housemaids, and housemaids find jobs. Each Sri Lankan agency maintains good working relations with a limited number of overseas manpower recruiting agencies. For example, Mansoor worked mainly with four agencies in Kuwait and one in Lebanon. Government regulations require that Sri Lankan agencies only do business with agencies registered and licensed in their own countries, and to the best of its ability the SLBFE monitors transactions between agencies. For example, Mansoor showed me a "demand letter" from an agency in Kuwait, asking for one hundred housemaids and ten houseboys. After the SLBFE gave Mansoor official clearance to recruit, he advertised in the newspaper and on the radio and informed his subagents that he needed workers.

Women wishing to work abroad first need to obtain passports. Subagents like Byron help first-time migrants negotiate the government bureaucracy. Byron also provides his clients with application forms from the agencies with whom he works. These forms request "bio-data" about the applicant's age, marital status, number of children, education, work experience, language ability, and other particulars. Byron takes a woman's passport, several photographs, and application papers to Colombo, and checks about job openings with his contact agencies. Women with more experience often bypass the subagent and bring their photographs and passport directly to the job agency. Colombo agencies send a copy of the passport, the pictures, and the housemaid's bio-data to their partners abroad.

Sponsors seeking domestic servants contact agencies in the Middle East and look at the bio-data on available housemaids, including their experience and religious affiliations. Employers expect that experienced maids will know the work and speak Arabic but might be less compliant. Many sponsors also prefer Muslim or Christian women, and in response to this demand, most Buddhist housemaids list themselves as Christian on their application papers, and some Hindu housemaids claim that they are Muslim. Agency fees in Sri Lanka and the Middle East reflect the high demand for Muslim housemaids in the Gulf States. In 1997 in Saudi Arabia, sponsors paid agencies U.S.$750–800 for a Muslim housemaid and U.S.$450–500 for a non-Muslim housemaid. The U.S.$300 recruitment bonus earmarked for Muslim maids rarely made its way intact to the housemaid in Sri Lanka, but Muslim women paid Sri Lankan agencies less for their jobs than their Sinhala counterparts did (M. Gamburd 1999). Having seen the photographs and bio-data of the women available, sponsors choose the housemaids they want.

From this point procedures vary in different countries, but the general outline remains the same. In exchange for a down payment on the agency fee, the agent in the Middle East gives the sponsor a copy of the housemaid's passport. The sponsor obtains official clearance to hire a domestic worker, declaring his income and assuring the government officials that the family has adequate accommodation for a maid. The sponsor then returns to the agency with the housemaid's visa and pays the remaining agency fees. The agency sends a copy of the visa to Sri Lanka. The visa includes the housemaid's name and passport number as well as the employer's name, nationality, address, and phone number.

As soon as a sponsor takes the housemaid's passport to get her a visa, the agent in the Middle East faxes the Sri Lankan agency. That agent contacts the subagent or contacts the housemaid directly, telling her to get a full body physical examination. The medical exam includes X rays (for chest ailments, especially asthma and tuberculosis), a urine test (for pregnancy, drug use, and diabetes), a VDRL test for syphilis, and (for Saudi Arabia) an HIV test. If the maid fails the medical exam, the agency sends the visa back to the agency in the Middle East where the sponsor chooses another maid. If the woman passes the medical exam, she brings her medical certificate, training certificate, and agency fees to the agency. The Sri Lankan agent, acting for the sponsor, signs a contract with the housemaid. The agency sends copies of the contract, the visa, the maid's passport, medical and training certificates, and Rs. 3,800/ (Rs. 5,200/ in 1997 rupees) in foreign employment charges to the SLBFE for final approval. The SLBFE returns Rs. 2,555/ (Rs. 3,500/ in 1997 rupees) to the agency as a commission.[4]

The agent gives the housemaid her airline ticket, her medical report, her passport, and her visa. In Naeaegama, Byron often accompanied his clients to the airport on their first trips abroad; more experienced housemaids went alone. The agent in Colombo relays flight information to the agent in the Middle East, who arranges transportation in the host country. From the time the maid gives her passport to the agency to the time she steps off the plane can be as little as three weeks or as long as five months. Once a sponsor's visa arrives in Sri Lanka, the housemaid will be abroad within two weeks.

A vast array of regulations control the movement of people around the world. Passports and visas index citizenship and the right to work in particular countries (Anderson 1994, 323). Government institutions and private agencies direct the movement of workers. Medical examinations classify the bodies of female migrants while bio-data forms categorize women according to their religious affiliations, experience, appearance, and skills. Participants in the system view these techniques of control, surveillance, regulation, and administration as normal and unremarkable aspects of labor migration.

Fee Structures and Fraud

Constraints on migration come not only from institutional governance and local ideologies of respectability but also from national and international economic dynamics. One characteristic of globalization is that one cannot adequately explain local dynamics without reference to larger-scale phenomena. Exploring structures and practices related to finding positions abroad for Sri Lankan men and women helps explain why over time wages have dropped and agency fees have risen, why a job for a janitor costs more than a job for a doctor, why jobs for men cost more than jobs for women, and why jobs for women cost three times more than the officially regulated price.

Changing international economic dynamics cause shifts in agency fees and wages. In 1985, when oil prices dropped, Arab employers lowered commissions paid to Arabic job agencies. At the same time, high

---

[4] This figure composes the entirety of the agent's legal profit.

demand for the limited number of jobs in the Middle East created competition between different labor-exporting countries and between agencies in Sri Lanka. With seemingly endless supplies of male and female
workers hoping to travel abroad, local and international agencies offered jobs to those willing to accept the lowest wages. Adjusted for inflation, women's salaries brought them five times as much in 1980 as
they did in 1994. Agencies bargained away workers' rights, privileges,
and salaries in order to secure scarce jobs. And in order to pay competitive commissions to Arab recruiters, agencies in Sri Lanka charged
higher fees from prospective migrants. Although from 1976 until 1985
the employer paid the laborer's airfare, passport, and medical costs, by
1994 migrants footed most of these charges as well as job agents' commissions; fees increased more rapidly than inflation.[5] The combination of international economic dynamics with Sri Lankan population
growth, unemployment, and national policies, then, affected both fees
and wages.

Men pay different agency fees, depending on the sort of job they seek.
Only the top 5 percent of Sri Lankan migrants, such as doctors, have
their way paid by their employers. The remaining 95 percent, including everyone from janitors to engineers, pay for their positions. International jobs requiring little skill and training cost the most, due to
their scarcity and the surplus of applicants. For example, in 1997, because engineers were in high demand abroad and in low supply in Sri
Lanka, an engineering job paying U.S.$533 a month cost only the
equivalent of one month's salary in agency fees. In comparison, because garden laborers were in low demand abroad and in great supply
in Sri Lanka, a gardener's job paying relatively low wages (U.S.$106–33)
cost the equivalent of six to eight months' salary in agency fees. Sri
Lankan agents said that they often paid their Saudi counterparts as
much as 1,500 or 1,600 riyals (U.S.$400–25) to secure a laborer's job
for a client; they paid much lower commissions for engineers (see table
6). In 1997 Naleem noted that gardeners' wages had recently dropped,
but many Sri Lankan men still eagerly applied for the scarce positions.

High agency fees are not the only hurdles faced by men seeking jobs
abroad. In 1994, to pay Rs. 30,000/ to Rs. 60,000/ for a job, poor vil-

---

[5] For example, in 1978 one Naeaegama migrant paid an agency Rs. 675/ (Rs. 4,500/
in 1994 rupees) for a job in the UAE, where she earned Rs. 3,200/ (Rs. 21,500/ in 1994
rupees [U.S.$430]) a month. In contrast, in 1994 migrants regularly paid agencies Rs.
13,000/ for jobs that paid Rs. 5,000/ (U.S.$100) a month. The former paid one-fifth of
one month's salary; the latter paid 2.6 months' salary for their jobs.

Table 6. Job profiles for engineer and garden laborer in Saudi Arabia

Job profile	Engineer	Garden laborer
Salary	2,000 Saudi riyals (U.S.$533)	400–500 Saudi riyals (U.S.$106–33)
Commission to Saudi Arabian agent	less than 1,000 riyals (U.S.$267)	1,500–1,600 riyals (U.S.$400–425)
Commission to Sri Lankan agent	Officially no more than Rs.10,700/ (U.S.$178)	Officially no more than Rs.5,200/ (U.S.$87)
Subagent commission		Rs.5,000/(U.S.$83)
Ticket price	U.S.$300	U.S.$300
Total fees paid	Rs.25,000/–Rs.30,000/ (U.S.$416–500)	Rs.50,000/–Rs.55,000/ (U.S.$833–916)

Source: Interviews with job agents.
Note: All monetary figures in this table are in 1997 values. My sources quoted prices and charges in a number of different currencies, reflecting the international aspects of labor migration.

lagers often considered borrowing money at 100 percent interest from local moneylenders (see chapter 3). Many who took money on credit found repayment charges prohibitive—for example, owing Rs. 60,000/ for Rs. 30,000/, or 120,000/ for Rs. 60,000/. Poor men could rarely find individual moneylenders, let alone banks, willing to lend them such large sums of money without collateral. Given the high risks involved with migration, such as the possibility of early termination, illness, or a misleading job description, most Naeaegama families found sending men abroad too expensive and too risky; only the wealthy and the well-educated had either the money, skills, or political affiliations necessary.

Expenses and procedures for procuring jobs abroad differ for men and women, with jobs for men usually costing two to five times as much as jobs for women. High Middle Eastern demand for housemaids coupled with high Sri Lankan demand for female foreign employment lead to relatively low agency fees (because jobs abound) and relatively low wages (because applicants abound). Housemaids I interviewed in Naeaegama in 1994 paid agencies Rs. 13,000/ to 16,000/ on average. Employers paid them an average wage of U.S.$100 a month and also provided free room, board, airfare, and medical facilities. Housemaids who borrowed from local moneylenders to cover their agency fees often owed as much as Rs. 35,000/ (U.S.$700) when they left the country, a debt they would work six to eight months to repay.

While government rules attempt to regulate and standardize the recruitment system, official and actual fees usually differ. Agents and subagents I interviewed disagreed over why Sinhala maids paid at least Rs. 9,200/ more than the official cap of Rs. 3,800/ (Rs. 5,200/ in 1997 rupees) for jobs abroad. Colombo agents blamed local subagents for driving up prices; Byron, the Naeaegama subagent, claimed that he charged only a modest commission, and in turn he blamed the agents for jacking up the prices. Mendis, the local Naeaegama agent, claimed that he charged housemaids only Rs. 4,380/ to go abroad, a figure Rs. 580/ more than the official rate and less than half of what housemaids said they generally paid. Another source suggested that some agencies charged women Rs. 5,000/–Rs. 10,000/ as commission. Agencies also occasionally passed along to migrants a charge of Rs. 1,500/ to cover ticket costs not reimbursed by the agency in the Middle East. Extra charges and commissions such as these drive actual agency fees much higher than official limits.

At various points in the system, middlemen and middlewomen clearly charge more than the officially sanctioned rates. When questioned, however, sources at each step attributed the extra charges to people elsewhere in the system. One insider cynically described the process of getting a man a job abroad:

> The managing director of a company in the Middle East gives his personnel manager money to hire ten new workers, covering their airline tickets and all other expenses. The personnel manager then calls a recruiting agency and says, "Get me ten people; I don't have money for their tickets." The job agent there calls his Sri Lankan connections and asks them all what sorts of commissions they can pay him for ten jobs in the Middle East, for which he can't pay the airfare. The Sri Lankan agencies bid, some saying $200 for you, others saying $250, and the bargaining continues until the agent in the Middle East chooses the highest price. So some poor worker in Sri Lanka ends up paying $400 commission for the agent in the Middle East, plus the price of the ticket, plus the passport and medical fees, and the fees for the SLBFE. It adds up to $1,000 or so. The middleman takes all the profit, and the laborer borrows money on interest to go abroad to work.

Note that this speaker, associated with a job agency, neglected to mention any extra charges added by his own stage in the system. A separate system exists alongside the official structures of governance; most of the participants recognize the unofficial rules but deny that they themselves play by them.

Opportunities for fraud and corruption have arisen not only among foreign and local agencies but also at several points in the Sri Lankan bureaucracy. Sources suggest that medical exams required for migrants actually cost Rs. 180/, but medical offices often charged as much as Rs. 880/. Laboratories frequently returned a portion of their profit (Rs. 300/) to the agency as a commission for sending the worker to that particular lab. Despite these shady arrangements, most certificates accurately reflected a housemaid's health. Since agencies lost significant sums of money if housemaids came back before the end of their first three months abroad, they dealt harshly with doctors issuing faulty medical certificates. On a similar note, agents suggested that there was little fraud surrounding the training certificates required by the SLBFE, since they were easy to obtain and free.

Passport forgery has provided another venue for corruption. One agent described "a real racket" surrounding fraudulent ages, names, photographs, and religious designations. Several sources independently confirmed that women paid Rs. 6,000/ to Rs. 7,500/ in bribes to acquire an altered passport. Since Saudi Arabia required all guest workers to be over thirty years of age, many younger women bought passports with altered ages or used other people's photographs for their passports. Some women, particularly Tamil-speaking Hindus, had passports made with Muslim names. Patricia Lawrence, an anthropologist working in eastern Sri Lanka, said that Tamil-speaking Hindu women from the area had been arrested as suspected members of the separatist guerrilla movement, the Liberation Tigers of Tamil Eelam (LTTE), because they had travel documents that falsely portrayed them as Muslims.[6] Mansoor maintained that a dozen bodies remained unclaimed at the public morgue because their relatives did not recognize their false names.

From many disparate sources, I have pieced together a tentative, unofficial fee structure for migrant housemaids (see table 7). With the many service industries springing up to facilitate migration, an elaborate legal and illegal system has arisen that redistributes the profits of migration.

Both male and female migrants pay more than the official rates for their jobs abroad. People at each link in the system claim that they

[6] Letter to author, 17 July 1999.

Table 7. Fees and expenses for a housemaid's job abroad

Service	Price in 1994 rupees	Price in U.S. dollars
Medical exam	180/–880/	U.S.$3.60–17.60
Passport	220/–1,100/	U.S.$4.40–22
Legal agency fees	3,800/	U.S.$76
Extra agency fees	0–10,000/	U.S.$0–200
Extra ticket charge	0–1,500/	U.S.$0–30
Subagent fees	0–3,750/	U.S.$0–75
Low and high fee range	4,200/–21,030/	U.S.$84–420.60
Prices women report paying	13,000/–16,000/	U.S.$240–320

themselves always deal according to the official rules but point out how other middlemen and middlewomen overcharge migrants. Although a number of bureaucratic institutions attempt to control the migration process, their surveillance techniques do not always bring about the conformity they seek. The social structure governing migration in no way represents a coherent, monolithic entity. Instead of living obediently by official dictates, many individuals and organizations invent ingenious systems for bending and breaking the rules, often working at cross-purposes from one another. Any analysis of system and authority must take into account both official and unofficial patterns of behavior, noting the power dynamics that shape them.

Troubles and Troubleshooting

After housemaids arrive in the homes of their employers, conflicts and disputes arise with enough frequency to warrant a formal regulatory structure. The procedures for dealing with complaints offer benefits and disadvantages to housemaids, sponsors, job agencies, and the governments in the sending and receiving countries.

Statistical records reveal patterns in documented troubles between housemaids and their sponsors. Maids most commonly complain of lack of adequate communication with their families in Sri Lanka, nonpayment of wages, and harassment (SLBFE 1997, table 27). Sponsors commonly complain that their maids are too old or too lazy to work, gossip, have inadequate hygiene or bad attitudes, or speak insufficient Arabic. Less common but more serious employer complaints consist of child abuse, sexual misconduct, and theft. For relatively minor disputes, some job agencies in the Middle East have Sinhala-speaking representatives who mediate conflicts. Sharif felt that this sort of follow-up work, although expensive, gave his agency a good name in both countries. If mediation fails, the agency or the individuals take the case to the police. Agencies also give departing housemaids the phone number for the Sri Lankan embassy or consulate in their host countries in case of emergencies.

During the first three months of a housemaid's stay with a sponsor, either the housemaid or the sponsor may terminate the arrangement at the agency's expense. After this trial period, the agency does not cover the cost of finding the sponsor another housemaid or finding the housemaid another job. If the sponsor rejects the maid or if the housemaid asks to return home, the agency pays for a ticket (U.S.$300) and refunds fees to the sponsor of U.S.$400, for a total loss of U.S.$700. Several agents estimated that 2 percent or 3 percent of the women who went abroad came back early. If four or five housemaids return during a one-month period, it can bankrupt a small agency.

Agencies strongly encourage housemaids to stay with their jobs; in line with this policy, they do not refund agency fees paid by dissatisfied housemaids. Mendis explained that if his female assistant at his agency office in Kuwait gave a sympathetic ear to housemaids' complaints, it only encouraged the housemaids to call back again and again. He said that his secretary "understood" that homesick women often told lies about the character of their sponsors in order to get themselves a ticket home. If free medical services cured a woman's physical complaints, she would say she had "devil problems" (*yaksha doosha*), psychological illnesses curable through spiritual healing (*tovil*) found only in Sri Lanka (see also Ong 1987, 1988). Mendis took a skeptical view of such complaints; he and other agents said that they required such "lazy" women to pay the price of their tickets home. Since removing a housemaid from an unsatisfactory job hurts an agency financially, having the agency handle women's complaints about problems presents a conflict of interest.

Officials in the government system also voiced skeptical opinions about housemaids' complaints. One bureaucrat maintained that non-Muslim housemaids spent only Rs. 4,500/ for passport, medical fees, and Bureau charges; he believed that Muslim women went abroad for free. In contrast, the Sinhala women I interviewed in Naeaegama said that they paid at least Rs. 13,000/ for a job; Muslim women I interviewed said that they paid about Rs. 3,750/ for a job. Misconceptions about the official and unofficial costs of migration support assumptions that women will lightly give up jobs abroad because they can cheaply and easily find others. Financial worries and misconceptions lead job agents and bureaucrats to doubt women's motivation to stick with difficult jobs and work hard to please their sponsors.

In their efforts to keep maids in their original sponsors' houses, job agents minimize the reasons women give for wishing to return to Sri Lanka. Their descriptions of migrant women's cavalier attitudes toward leaving their jobs reflect neither the gravity of the harassment some women report nor the relatively large sums of money that many women spend to get a job. Negative stereotypes of migrant housemaids as lazy liars, combined with mistakenly low estimates of the level of financial commitment women make when seeking a job abroad, allow agents to trivialize women's complaints and dismiss as frivolous their efforts to leave bad jobs.

Tickets: Informal Personal Networks

A woman seeking a job abroad generally chooses one of two strategies. She either locates employment through a job agency or gets a "ticket" through informal personal networks. Many migrants, both male and female, from Sri Lanka and other countries find jobs abroad through this "chain migration" (Shah and Menon 1999, 361). The effectiveness of such networks varies, depending on the nationalities of the participants and the skill levels of the jobs sought (Shah and Menon 1999, 371). In this section I explore the institutional structure surrounding sending tickets to friends and relatives.

Frank Eelens and Toon Schampers suggest that "it is quite likely that in Sri Lanka the ever-increasing costs of recruitment will ultimately make it impossible for poor people to secure a job in the Middle East" (1992, 36). Although agency fees have remained high, a thriving trade in tickets provides affordable employment for a growing number of Naeaegama women. In 1997 Byron mentioned that his subagent position had grown less lucrative. As women learned more about the process of migration, they no longer felt the need for his services. Instead of finding jobs with agencies, many women took ticket jobs arranged directly with Arabic sponsors by other village women, thus bypassing subagents, agents, and moneylenders. Within the space of "regulated freedom" (Rose 1999, 22) mapped out by the governing institutions, women developed tactics to find cheaper and more reliable employment. Women's emerging strategy of obtaining jobs through informal personal networks shows resistance to systems of power and control in official structures of governance and discourses on gender. The emerging system, of course, has its own rules and structures.

Arranging a ticket usually proceeds as follows. A woman working abroad finds a job for a friend or relative with a household in her employer's network of friends and family. The mediating contact has the potential housemaid mail a copy of her passport to the potential sponsors, who arrange a work visa for her. The future sponsor purchases an airplane ticket and faxes a copy of the visa to the airline office in Sri Lanka. The future housemaid picks up both the ticket and the visa from the airline office. Housemaid and sponsor connect in the airport by comparing copies of the visa or with the help of the mediating contact.

Ticket jobs benefit the woman who arranges the ticket, the housemaid who receives it, and the employer. Ticket jobs take as little as two weeks to arrange, much less time than agency jobs require. The sponsors pay U.S.$300 for airfare but save U.S.$200 by avoiding agency fees. Women going abroad save anywhere from U.S.$60 to $440. In 1994, with passport fees, agency fees, medical exam fees, and transportation to the airport, women often paid Rs. 13,000/–Rs. 16,000/ (U.S.$260–320) for a job abroad. Agencies require payment for the job up front, forcing most first-time migrants and many return migrants to take loans to cover the agency fees. The accepted 100 percent interest rate meant that in 1994 women paid back sums approaching Rs. 26,000/–Rs. 32,000/. In contrast, with tickets, women usually pay the mediating contact the equivalent of two months' salary (Rs. 10,000/ or U.S.$200). The mediator usually waives charges for relatives and nearly always allows other recipients to pay the set fee out of their first two or three paychecks, without interest, thus forestalling indebtedness to a moneylender. Some women voluntarily purchased insurance from the SLBFE for an extra Rs. 2,340/ (Rs. 3,200/ in 1997 rupees). This increased their migration cost to about U.S.$250, still less than half of what an agency job and interest would have cost them (see table 8).

Official opinion varies on the legality of tickets. Naeaegama women going abroad through personal connections in 1997 did not need training certificates or medical exams. Many, but not all, registered with and bought insurance from the SLBFE, thus situating themselves within the official structure. A representative of ALFEA, however, claimed that women who set up jobs for their friends acted

Table 8. Comparative charges for agency and "ticket" jobs

Service	Agency job in 1994 rupees	Agency job in U.S. dollars	Ticket job in 1994 rupees	Ticket job in U.S. dollars
Finder's fee	13,000/–16,000/	U.S.$260–320	10,000/	U.S.$200
Interest charges	13,000/–16,000/	U.S.$260–320	0	U.S.$0
Insurance	0	U.S.$0	2,340/	U.S.$47
Total expenses	26,000/–32,000/	U.S.$520–640	12,340/	U.S.$247

as illegal agents or subagents and felt that the government should step in to regulate their activities. While describing the practice of sending tickets, he overstated the price asked by the mediating contact as three months' salary (U.S.$300) rather than two months', as I found in Naeaegama. He also claimed that women paid only the official price of Rs. 3,800 (Rs. 5,200/ in 1997 rupees) for agency jobs, and he failed to take into account transactions with moneylenders. Using these figures, the official claimed that ticket jobs cost more than agency jobs. Pointing out the dangers of going abroad without signing a contract or having the security of an agency to mediate disputes, the official roundly condemned ticket arrangements and the women who made them.

Migrant women hold different opinions about tickets. Sinhala and Muslim women whom I interviewed in 1997 used different migration strategies for a number of practical reasons. Due to high demand for Muslim housemaids in the Gulf countries, Sri Lankan agencies charged lower fees for Muslim women than for Sinhala women. Muslim women paid 25 percent to 50 percent less for agency jobs than non-Muslim housemaids did. Further, most Muslim women did not borrow from moneylenders. They usually paid Rs. 3,750/ to Rs. 5,500/ for a position abroad, U.S.$140–75 less than their Sinhala counterparts paid for tickets. Muslim women tended to go abroad through registered agencies that provided a number of services to aid and shelter the migrant, while Sinhala women tended to go abroad through tickets.

Women found good reasons beyond economics to explain their choice of job procurement strategy. Sinhala and Muslim women emphasized not only the financial benefits but also the psychological advantages of their chosen job procurement strategies. Sinhala women in Naeaegama felt more comfortable taking ticket jobs than taking agency jobs because a "known person" (a friend or relative) could assess the character of the employers, evaluate the working situation, and report the size of the family. Agency jobs provided no such information. In contrast, Muslim women said that they would not feel comfortable finding another woman a ticket because they would take the blame if anything went wrong. The Muslim women considered agency jobs cheaper and more reliable than ticket jobs, citing the insurance policy, the telephone numbers to call in case of emergencies, the mediation services, and the promise to find the housemaid another position if required. Both groups of women emphasized the advantages of their chosen strategies.

Conclusion

As migration has grown over the years, it has changed from an isolated event to a constant occurrence. A number of institutions have arisen to regulate and administer the new movement of people and money. By exploring the norms and values inherent in some of the local, national, and international organizations that serve migrants, I have asked how the procedures and practices surrounding migration create identities and circulate discourses that regulate behavior (Dean 1994, xiv). Tactics of governance employed by government structures and private enterprises count, register, license, train, and certify migrants and job agents. These techniques lead to the ever-increasing knowledge and power held by the bureaucracy. Organizational adjustments to migration include the professionalization of the field, with an accompanying set of new norms and rules shaping practices and a new concept of "the migrant" growing out of these emerging discourses.

At the same time, migrant women and other actors challenge the official structure, creating rules and practices of their own. Although the governing bureaucracy seeks to establish a "regime of structured times, spaces, gazes and hierarchies" (Rose 1999, 22), resistance at all levels of the structure makes it clear that the ideas and procedures the bureaucracy hopes participants will accept as automatic are in fact still open to debate, contention, and modification. Forces within the system operate continuously to destabilize the dominant narrative, challenging "all those claims made by others to govern us in the name of our own well-being, to speak for us, to identify our needs, to know us better than we can know ourselves" (Rose 1999, 59). Insightful analysis of the players in the game, and the contradictions among various parts of the system, creates a space both for resistance to regulation and for alternative approaches to migration.

3 Moneylenders:
Crucial Resources
and Crippling Interest Rates

Money makes the world go 'round and makes women go 'round the world. Often women borrow money to pay the agency fees that secure their employment abroad. Many villagers and social scientists think of moneylenders in the abstract as a category of "evil enemies."[1] Nevertheless, ethnographic data reveal their centrality to a complex local economic network. Moneylenders simultaneously provide crucial resources to migrant women and siphon off a large share of the migrants' profits through crippling interest rates.

This chapter compares case studies of two Naeaegama-area moneylenders. Both women ran similar moneylending operations but came to their occupations through dissimilar routes. The first, Elsie, conceived her female patron-client network through her involvement in the declining coconut fiber industry. The second, Lakshmi, began lending money with capital she earned while working as a housemaid in Bahrain. The two women also spoke of their economic activities in very different terms. A number of factors influenced their divergent points of view, including their personalities, family structures, ages, castes, and ideas about gender roles and the proper use of money. This chapter also discusses some theoretical approaches to class, particularly those that explore how class interacts with other aspects of iden-

[1] See Rudner (1994, 35ff.) for a discussion of stereotypes of Indian moneylenders.

tity. Situating moneylending in a historical context of female economic networks and patron-client relationships reveals how gender
identities interact with changing local attitudes toward capital and
class.

Class

Many current discussions of class take place within the Marxist intellectual tradition. Marx discusses society in terms of *relations of
production*, which in capitalist societies are relations between people
and people (labor) and people and things (machinery, capital). He argues that class emerges where the relations of production involve a
differentiated division of labor. People with nothing to sell besides
their labor find themselves at a disadvantage. Marx distinguishes between the wages that laborers need to reproduce themselves and their
families and the exchange value of the labor they perform. Employers
pay laborers less than the value of the work they do. Marx refers to the
difference between wages paid and the value of the work performed as
surplus value. Employer exploitation of surplus value brings about
class struggle, through which the members of the working class, associated through their position in the division of labor, develop a sense
of group identity, growing into a self-conscious, politically active force.
When he wrote 150 years ago, Marx suggested that the capitalist mode
of production would eventually polarize society into two main classes,
the property-owing bourgeoisie and the oppressed proletariat. Marx
foresaw the proletariat rising up in revolt, overthrowing the existing
power structure, and ushering in a new age of socialist utopia (Marx
1978, 1971).

Many Marxist scholars have worked to modify Marx's theories in
light of the past 150 years of economic and political history. Retaining Marx's central insights on conflict and exploitation, they have applied his theories in creative ways to conceptualize social structures
and group relations in settings with which Marx was not concerned.
Marx himself recognized that forces other than class played a major
role in motivating political and economic behavior; he hoped that as
the working class consciously recognized its oppression, it would set
aside other divisive allegiances, such as religion and nationalism. Most
Marxist scholars currently recognize that class takes no clear prece-
dence over other forms of social segmentation (Becker 1989, 128). Gen-

der, ethnicity, race, and nationality play an important role in class relations and economic forces. In Naeaegama, where gender identities,
family ties, caste solidarity, religious allegiance, ethnic affiliation, and
electoral politics all shape economic relations, an analysis of class
must necessarily integrate the multiple cross-cutting hierarchies of
village life.

Discussing class in relation to other forms of identity goes beyond
merely recognizing separate bases of affiliation, such as gender, age, or
caste. More crucially, it notes how these different identities relate to
and interact with each other. Karen Sacks argues that we cannot expect to find a generic "working-class" individual; instead, age, race,
marital status, ethnicity, and gender affect who labors at which jobs.
For example, Sacks notes that in the nineteenth century unmarried
women of European descent worked in New England textile mills; in
the twentieth century this work is done by unmarried women in
Southeast Asia. In the United States today, married Euro-American
women do "front office" work, younger African American women do
"back office" work, and teenagers run fast food shops around the nation (1989, 542). This complex segmentation in the labor force calls
for sophisticated analysis.

Gender not only marks but also creates segmentation in the labor
force. For example, Erik Wright suggests that gender ideologies that
define housework and child care as discrete activities done by women
produce the working-class jobs of housemaid and nanny: "It is not just
that gender sorts people into these jobs; if gender relations were dramatically more egalitarian, the jobs themselves might not exist" because their characteristic duties might not have been bundled together
in the first place (1997, 243). Just as gender roles create jobs, so labor
relations reproduce and transform gender identities. For example, the
"family wage," designed to support not just an individual but his
whole household, reinforces the ideal of the male breadwinner and
marginalizes women, who earn only "supplemental wages," from the
paid labor force (Wright 1997, 244). Gender and labor relations overlap and interact in multiple and complex ways.

Like gender, race and ethnicity also interact with labor relations and
class identity. Eric Wolf argues that race and ethnicity rank workers,
creating within the working class cultural divisions used to recruit,
control, and exploit labor. Although "capitalism did not create all the
distinctions of ethnicity and race that function to set off categories of
workers from one another" ([1982] 1997, 380), it nevertheless profits

from and reinforces these categories, simultaneously disguising underlying similarities in class position. Wolf argues that often racial and ethnic identities are "not 'primordial' social relationships [but rather] historical products of labor market segmentation under the capitalist mode" ([1982] 1997, 381). These examples suggest that capitalism increases diversity, or at least the appearance of diversity, rather than necessarily unifying the working class.

Diversity and divisiveness exist not only in the working class, but also in the middle and upper classes. Scholars find that middle- and upper-class social structures vary not only between different societies but also within particular societies. Economic relations may limit possible social structures but do not fully determine patterns of human interaction. The monopoly of economic power does not lead inevitably to one single form of social organization and one dominant ideology. For example, patron-client relations such as those central to money-lending practices in Naeaegama have much in common economically with employer-employee relations in the West but operate according to different historically shaped cultural norms and standards. Long-term patron-client relations imply loyalty and responsibilities not necessarily paralleled in Western concepts of contracts, labor, and wages. While often exploitative, patrons are not necessarily heartless, and many cultural regulations oblige them to treat their clients well. Rather than making sweeping assumptions about class relations based on economic structures, scholars now investigate how particular formations of power and hierarchy operate on a case-by-case basis.

The absence of unified classes on the group level is paralleled by the ambiguity of class identity on the individual level. Discussing relatively objective material and economic relations, Wright defines *direct class location* as how "one's relationship to the process of exploitation [shapes] one's material interests" (1997, 26). Other forces, particularly family ties, also affect material and economic interests. For example, a teenager who works for minimum wage at McDonald's but has wealthy parents would occupy two different, contradictory class locations, creating a *mediated class location* (Wright 1997, 27). Similarly, a Naeaegama woman who works abroad in a low-status job as a maid for extremely low wages, yet has the capital and the prestige of a moneylender upon her return, would occupy a contradictory class location. Transnational migration requires a contextual discussion of such contradictions.

Class location, the objective condition of exploitation, does not lead directly to a particular form of individual class consciousness; nor does it lead inevitably to collective political organization agitating for class interests. Each individual owes allegiance to a number of different and often contradictory forms of identity, which gives rise to the "multi-faceted nature of consciousness" in which class forms but one component (S. Hall 1996, 433). Furthermore, scholars who take Marx seriously now recognize that individuals with similar economic interests may or may not unite in self-conscious groups with explicitly economic political aims (Wright 1997, 380; S. Hall 1996, 423). The diversity within classes, and competing forms of identity, work against either a united working-class consciousness or a unified and effective "hegemony" asserted by the ruling class (Roseberry 1989, 46).

The transnational movement of ideas adds another layer of complexity to the concept of class. Discussion of class consciousness and class identity must address not only indigenous consciousness arising from local relations of exploitation but also "class" as a form of identity transplanted from the West. Pierre Bourdieu discusses class in modern France not only as a social grouping by wealth and employment but also as a function of taste and judgment, with associated mind-sets, values, and predispositions that legitimize social differences (1984). European and American tastes, behaviors, and values affect people all over the world. In Naeaegama, many people who explicitly identified themselves as middle class did so to indicate their identification with a "modern," Western worldview.

Analyzing class in Naeaegama provides many challenges. People's class locations, their direct or mediated relationship to material conditions of exploitation, are relatively straightforward. Questions of class consciousness and class identity prove more complex. Villagers who identified themselves as middle class seemed to hold a diversity of views ranging from a vaguely positive attitude toward modernization and the West all the way to a capitalist, individualist mind-set deriving status and prestige from property, business ventures, white-collar jobs, and education (Srinivas 1962). Some who never used the term "middle class" nevertheless expressed views and opinions that corresponded to this mind-set. Wright defines *class formation* as "collectively organized social forces within class structures in pursuit of class interests" (1997, 379). Naeaegama residents did not have a strong working-class or middle-class formation. Despite the lack of self-conscious group identification through unions or economically motivated political parties, some of the local money-related relationships and conflicts could be categorized as emerging forms of social consciousness based on class location. When I speak of "class" with respect to Naeaegama, in most cases I refer to class location, not to "class" in a classical Marxist sense, which includes class consciousness and class identity.

In Naeaegama, several diverse systems have simultaneously shaped individual taste and judgment. Individuals and families move between forms of social expression, searching to find, and to legitimize, the system or systems offering them the most upward (or the least downward) mobility. In 1997 many of the same people who identified themselves as middle class also relied on traditional displays (such as giving to the temple or contributing to rituals) to mark their social standing in other systems of identity. Social mobility depended not only on progress and development within a given system but also on the relative dominance of different, competing systems in the local, national, and international arenas.

I see migration, a significant aspect of increasing local integration into the global economy, as one of the driving forces behind social change in Naeaegama. Uwe Becker argues, "Because of capitalism's power to penetrate, it can justifiably be seen as the central motor of social development in the modern world" (1989, 138). Although few theorists now believe that economic forces directly determine social structures, most scholars acknowledge that economic change can affect tastes, values, and concepts of identity. As shown later, patterns of labor migration interact with preexisting gender hierarchies, historical ideologies of money, and traditional female economic networks to affect changing moneylending practices.

Lending Money for Migration

A mix of old and new norms and practices governed moneylending in Naeaegama in the 1990s. As discussed in chapter 2, a number of services and social structures grew up around labor migration. At the village level, many women had a need for ready cash. Those villagers just at or below subsistence level could not borrow at the moderate 10 percent interest rate offered by banks because banks refused to lend to those who had no collateral. Banks required security in the form of land deeds or jewelry, in case the borrower died, or had an accident, or could not pay the loan back for other reasons. Excluded from bank services, the vast majority of villagers turned to relatives and local moneylenders to cover migration fees.

Most moneylenders charged 100 percent interest, requiring a payment equal to 20 percent of the principal per month over the course of ten months. On smaller sums lent over a shorter term, they often charged 10 percent or 12 percent per month. High interest rates served a number of purposes. First, moneylenders needed to earn enough from interest to offset losses from unpaid loans. Second, local inflation depreciated their working capital, and money earned through interest supplemented a lender's principal. Third, the devaluation of the rupee also reduced the value of the lender's capital. With ready cash in short supply in Naeaegama, those with financial assets rarely banked them; instead, money circulated rapidly from those who had to those in need, returning more slowly, with interest.

A number of current moneylenders, and their moneylending procedures, have roots in older networks tied to the coir (coconut husk fiber) industry. The southern coast of Sri Lanka has engaged in the trade in coir products for thousands of years, a trade which continued and intensified under colonial rule and through independence, with a gradual decline starting in the 1960s due to the increased manufacture of synthetic products (Risseeuw 1991). The Halaagama caste and several other castes specialized in producing coconut fiber products (Risseeuw 1991, 217), which circulated in the local, regional, and international economies.

In late 1960s Naeaegama, many women's financial networks centered around making coconut rope. Gathered and soaked in pits for at least six months, the dense coconut husks began to decay. Dried and pounded (by hand or by machine), husks disintegrated until only the coconut fiber remained. Women wove this fiber by hand or by machine into lengths of rope, while men stuffed it into mattresses or bound it into brooms. Women with some extra capital often paid poorer neighbors in kind for pounding the dried husks or lent them machine-processed fiber, taking payment in the form of a certain number of woven skeins of rope. The lender then purchased the extra rope the borrower had woven out of the remaining fiber, reselling her collected stock for a profit to outside dealers. Often women who ran this sort of fiber business also lent small sums of money to the women to whom they lent fiber and from whom they bought rope. These informal female patron-client financial networks pervaded the coconut rope trade in the Naeaegama area.

In Naeaegama, women made up the majority of moneylenders, perhaps stemming from the tradition that women handled household fi-

nances. Women in the richest families in the village, who might or
might not work in the coconut fiber industry, often made loans to their
poorer neighbors. To protect herself from not being paid back, each
moneylender lent to a relatively set group of trusted clients. Someone
needing a loan but lacking fixed relations with a moneylender approached the source through someone already established in the
lender's sphere of interest, or borrowed through a middle woman, paying a commission for that person's guarantee of repayment. Money
moved most often through these informal networks.

In 1994, in the area surrounding Naeaegama, approximately a dozen
sources lent money on a scale to fund Middle East migrations, giving
Rs. 10,000/ to 20,000/ at a time.[2] Many first-time migrants got their
jobs through agencies and borrowed money to cover the fees. High
agency fees and interest rates meant that many women worked
roughly eight months of their two-year contract just to pay for the
placement services. Women regularly spent between Rs. 12,000/ and
Rs. 16,000/ to get an agency job. After borrowing "a little extra" for
household needs and preparations for migration, and having agreed to
pay 100 percent interest to the moneylender, they often owed Rs.
28,000/ to Rs. 40,000/ upon their departure. With an average monthly
salary between Rs. 4,000/ and Rs. 5,000/, and with families depending on their remittances for some aspects of their daily subsistence,
women estimated that it would take them between six months and a
year to clear their loans. Moneylenders and job agents thus acquired
the reputations of exploiting migrants and siphoning off the lion's
share of their profits. Lenders, however, saw their business as hazardous and their rates as just and justified, and noted the value of their
service to women who would not otherwise be able to afford a job
abroad.

Still, in 1994 several factors threatened to affect moneylenders' practices in the future. As more women went abroad on tickets provided
through informal personal connections (as discussed in chapter 2),

[2] In this chapter monetary values are not uniformly standardized; instead, for any
rupee figure not from 1994, both nominal values (rupee values informants report) and
real values (equivalents in 1994 rupees, adjusted for inflation) are given. This shows
how dramatically inflation has affected the value of the rupee over the years. In 1994
Rs. 50/ was equal to U.S.$1. To avoid encumbering the text, only U.S. dollar equiva-
lents for particularly salient figures are noted. For more information on inflation, exchange rates, and consumer prices, see appendix B.

fewer borrowed money to pay fees to get jobs through agencies. Migrant women's new employment strategies cut out both the job agent and the moneylender. Furthermore, by 1997 a number of other families, many involved in migration themselves, had amassed enough capital to lend to prospective migrants, though not to more than one migrant at a time. In 1997 demand for money on credit remained high, and interest rates showed no sign of dropping. If the supply of money in the village continued to grow, however, interest rates might drop in the future.

Ideologies of Gender, Debt, and Patronage

A pervasive but subterranean undertaking among women with some financial means, moneylending rarely came into open discussion during my interviews. Borrowers euphemistically identified their sources by place of residence rather than by name, referring to the prominent moneylender Lakshmi as "someone at the junction," for example. Asking moneylenders about moneylending proved even more difficult than interviewing migrants about their sources. Gendered ideologies about money, traditions surrounding the discussion of debts, and customs governing patron-client relationships combined to minimize local discussions of monetary transactions.

Most moneylenders tried to avoid speaking openly about their lending. Of those people whom migrants identified as moneylenders, only one, Lakshmi, admitted she currently lent money on a large scale. Contrary to evidence in migrants' work histories, the other moneylenders all initially said that they lent very little or nothing at the present, though they had lent "small sums" in the past. This nearly universal reticence reflected several elements in local ideologies of money: a certain disrespect for making money by charging interest, fear of theft if financial reserves came to public knowledge, and an unwillingness to make explicit the local lines of financial dominance and obligation. Prior to the migration of labor to the Middle East, moneylenders rarely lent large sums at one time. Nevertheless, unpaid debts to moneylenders proved a major force in hostile land transfers (particularly inter-caste transfers) as richer (often higher-caste) patrons took deeds as collateral for unpaid debts.[3] Debts had thus long formed

---

[3] See chapter 6 for more information on caste and debts.

a major axis of local power, though neither borrowers nor lenders spoke freely about them.

Gender ideologies have also affected the silence around money-lending. Although women usually controlled household finances, a "good" woman did not lend this money, except "on occasion," "to friends." Wide knowledge of the financial activity of a successful lender earning a great deal of money challenged the image that her husband provided the family's income. Lenders were often women with either very wealthy husbands or profligate husbands giving no aid to the household. Compounded with the shame surrounding money-lending, and the shame of the borrower for being indebted, the need to minimize the image of women's financial activity in many cases preserved the official silence around moneylending.

The following sections compare the financial activities and self-portrayals of two local moneylenders: Elsie, a former coconut-fiber trader, and Lakshmi, a former Middle East migrant. Both women developed a network of clients to whom they lent money, and both justified the high interest they charged by explaining the risks they took. Despite their similar class locations, they had widely diverging world-views. Their personal histories, family situations, castes, and ages in part explain their very different ideologies of gender, class, and money.

The Coconut Fiber Industry: Elsie

Elsie, a gray-haired woman in her sixties belonging to the lowest caste in the village area (Para, or Untouchable), lived at the far corner of Naeaegama on the border of a Para caste village. Allegedly one of the illegitimate children of a deceased, wealthy, Halaagama landowner in the area, she (and one of her brothers) lived in neighboring large cement houses.[4] Elsie and her four siblings grew up with wealth and all had considerable fortunes. The Halaagama in Naeaegama did not, to my knowledge, harass these wealthy families as they did some of their poor lower-caste Berava neighbors (see chapter 6). Nor did they socialize with them freely. Elsie's caste status colored her relations with other villagers.

In the 1960s and 1970s Elsie played a large part in the local coir fiber industry. Elsie was one of half a dozen entrepreneurial Naeaegama

---

[4] Children of mixed-caste marriages usually take on the caste identity of the lower-caste parent.

women who distributed fiber to and collected rope from groups of women in the area. Elsie bought cartloads of soaked and aged coconut husks and distributed them to her Halaagama, and Para, caste clients to pound and weave into rope. After several mills opened in the area, she bought processed fiber and distributed it to a steady network of women, who spun it into rope. The women either bought the fiber from Elsie or took it on loan, promising a certain number of rope skeins in exchange. Elsie and other fiber merchants marketed their products through distributors, local men who peddled ropes and brooms by bicycle. Although men sometimes paid up front, they often gave Elsie her profit after they had sold their wares and thus counted among Elsie's circle of clients. Like other women with enough capital to buy coconut husks or processed fiber, Elsie often advanced cash as well as fiber to her female and male clients, amassing considerable wealth in her role as middlewoman.

In her study on the coir industry, Carla Risseeuw notes that exploitation and resistance in relationships between fiber merchants and their clients appeared in subtle forms, alongside intimacy and even affection. Clients often did domestic work for the merchants and provided them with village gossip. In return, merchants found odd jobs for their clients to do when they needed work and supplied them and their families with extra food in times of need. At the same time, clients routinely shortened the lengths of the ropes they wove and increased the weight of their goods by adding sand and water: "Today a woman undertakes every possible form of resistance to her trader. She prefers to be independent if she has the financial means thereto, to fool and cheat the trader if she hasn't, and finally to please him/her if she is economically exceptionally vulnerable" (Risseeuw 1991, 267). Traders in turn subtly increased the work they demanded and decreased the pay they gave. Both sets of women "realize the exploitative nature of the work-relationship, but also ... deny it on the surface" (Risseeuw 1991, 266). While Elsie made a profit distributing fiber and lending money, her relationships with her clients rested on long years of personal interactions and contained many layers of conflicts, rights, and obligations not found in more straightforward sorts of employer-employee interactions.

During an interview, Elsie remarked that the coconut rope and fiber business had decreased and that currently "everyone was going to the Middle East." Elsie shifted her own economic activities in response. When pressed, a number of Naeaegama migrants identified Elsie as their source of borrowed money. When Sita and I brought up the topic of moneylending with Elsie, she said that while she used to give money to Middle East migrants, currently she only lent "small sums." Migrant women I spoke with, however, suggested that Elsie still lent money actively, and Sita confirmed that Elsie had lent money for at least twenty years, starting with small sums of Rs. 50/ and Rs. 100/, and building up to sums on the order of 10,000/ and 20,000/ for Middle East migrants.[5]

Once started on the topic, Elsie spoke relatively freely about moneylending, admitting that she charged 100 percent interest. She noted that since people had few other sources of money and could not get lower-interest credit from the bank without some form of valuable asset as security, they were willing to pay the interest she asked. In Sri Lanka, people sign official contracts on postage stamps, and agreements involving large sums of money have to be signed over large-denomination stamps to hold in a court of law. Elsie asked borrowers to sign a contract on a stamp when they borrowed money but said that she never took deeds or jewelry as collateral. Elsie's discussion revealed her familiarity with banking procedures and legal formalities, two spheres quite distinct from the more informal, personal aspects of older patron-client relations.

Elsie felt that the risks involved in lending money without security justified the high interest rates she charged. Elsie cited an example, stating that she lost a large sum of money lent to Kanti, a housemaid caught in the Gulf War, despite having asked a Para caste neighbor woman to act as the guarantor of the loan. At the time of her premature return from Kuwait, Kanti had only repaid part of the principal (Rs. 13,000/ [Rs. 19,500/ in 1994 rupees]) on a loan of Rs. 16,000/ (Rs. 24,000/ in 1994 rupees) borrowed on the promise to repay Rs. 32,000/ (Rs. 48,000/ in 1994 rupees). In the intervening two years Kanti had made no attempt to repay the rest of her debt. Elsie related this story with heat and passion, noting with condemnation that despite five trips abroad and other jobs in Sri Lanka, Kanti's family showed no "improvement." The woman serving as Kanti's guarantor had also failed to cover the debt. Despite Elsie's precautions, her investment had not paid off, and her profits from other loans had to compensate for her losses. Elsie claimed that her business had suffered greatly due to the effects of the Gulf War.

---

5 Adjusting for inflation, Rs. 100/ in 1974 was worth the equivalent of 800/ in 1994.

Returning from an errand, Elsie's husband Punyasiri joined our conversation. Punyasiri's gradual takeover of the conversation revealed a
great deal about family gender dynamics and ideologies of women's
work. After Punyasiri arrived, Sita and I found it very difficult to speak
directly with Elsie, since Punyasiri answered all our questions himself and broke in to retell any story Elsie started. Eventually Elsie, silenced, retreated to the kitchen. Punyasiri, a retired bridge repair
worker, narrated several further stories about moneylending and then
launched into an account of his own life. When Punyasiri arrived, I
asked if he dealt with loans as well, and he and Elsie both laughed and
said no. Nevertheless, with moneylending cast into the limelight by
the ethnographer's evident interest, Punyasiri monopolized discussion of his wife's avocation, a claim to knowledge Elsie never openly
challenged.

Punyasiri said that most of the money he and Elsie lent came from
a loan of Rs. 50,000/ from Elsie's younger sister. Borrowing at a low
rate of interest, they lent the money out again at a higher rate themselves. I asked Elsie how many people they lent to. Punyasiri answered
that he lent to three or four people at a time, dividing the Rs. 50,000/.
He said that once the money returned, he could give the interest and
the principal out to someone else, but if someone did not pay him
back, then there was no profit in it. The information about the source
of Elsie's principal surprised Sita and me, especially considering how
long Elsie had lent money in the village. Whether truth or exaggeration, the statement minimized Elsie's own financial success. Despite
Elsie's considerable contributions to the family income and her
family's supply of the original capital, her husband overpowered her
completely during our conversation, even when discussing the moneylending activities in which most evidence suggested Elsie herself specialized.

Punyasiri portrayed himself as an active participant in the effort to
retrieve loaned money from a second migrant caught in the Gulf War.
Through the police and the courts they reached a settlement whereby
the returned migrant agreed to pay back Rs. 400/ (Rs. 540/ in 1994 rupees) a month until she had paid off the principal of the loan. Having
paid three months at Rs. 400/ and another two at Rs. 200/ (Rs. 270/
in 1994 rupees), the migrant ceased payments. Punyasiri noted that
the court could often force the borrowers to sell jewelry, land, or other
valuables to return the money, but since this family owned nothing of
value, there was little recourse. Although in a number of instances I

felt that Punyasiri sought to claim his wife's accomplishments as his own, I suspect that he did indeed represent the family interests in court, since such an action would have conformed with local gender norms that kept respectable women of any caste out of the public eye.

Elsie's attitude toward moneylending reflected local gender norms about women's work. A coconut fiber distributor in the previous generation, Elsie adapted her small-scale patron-client moneylending relations to meet the new economic demands of the Middle East migrant, perhaps with the help of a loan from her sister. Nevertheless, describing her life, Elsie said that she had "no job" and had never held one but that she did housework. To portray herself and her husband in accord with local gender norms, Elsie underplayed her economic activity. Ideally, wives of well-employed husbands did not work, which in turn justified Elsie's claim that moneylending did not count as "work." Not a profession many claimed with pride, moneylending remained "merely a sideline" to Elsie's main task of housekeeping, no matter how lucrative the trade had proven.

Elsie's discussion of moneylending also revealed issues of taste associated with wealth and respectability. By disavowing her role as moneylender, Elsie implicitly claimed a higher status in the community, that of a housewife whose family wealth did not require her to work. Paradoxically, the wealth generated by Elsie's work brought the family to a financial level at which, were the breadwinner male, his respectable wife would not labor outside the home. The tastes associated with her family's class location did not condone working women, which again led to the claim that moneylending did not count as "work." Local ideologies of class and gender, together with the silence surrounding debt, made it difficult for Elsie and Punyasiri to speak of moneylending as a business or to conceive of female moneylenders as capitalist entrepreneurs.

Housemaid and Businesswomen: Lakshmi

Migrants in Naeaegama and Polwatta often said that "someone at the junction" had provided their loan. When pressed, many identified Lakshmi as their source. Although Elsie and Lakshmi ran similar moneylending operations, they held very different ideologies about gender and class. Lakshmi's position at the junction represented more than her spatial location near the main road; as an independently wealthy woman with a great deal of knowledge about working abroad, she mediated between village women and the new views and new opportunities migration encompassed. While other moneylenders, including Elsie, hesitated to speak of their profession or identify it as a business, Lakshmi spoke openly and freely about her entrepreneurial activities. Her confidence and self-assurance sprang from her heterodox views of women's work, debt, and the proper use of money.

When Sita and I interviewed Lakshmi, she quickly settled us on her roadside porch with tea and cookies from the shop adjoining her house, which her brother ran. A consummate storyteller in her late 30s, Lakshmi spoke in quick, idiomatic English. Plump (a rarity in the village area) and beautiful, Lakshmi sported pink nail polish on her toes and fingers and sand-dollar studs in her ears. Since few older women painted their nails or wore anything but round gold ear studs, Lakshmi's uncommon personal adornment marked her with subtle indications of her experience abroad. Her household, situated in the center of the business district at the junction, bustled and hummed with an energy level unlike any in Naeaegama or Polwatta. A center not only of money but also of advice, Lakshmi colored the area with her commanding presence in a way at odds with older images of respectable femininity.

Gender Ideology and Family Structure

Like Elsie, Lakshmi came from a wealthy family, but unlike Elsie, Lakshmi belonged to the Halaagama caste. While both women had middle-class backgrounds, Elsie had a low-caste status, and Lakshmi came from the dominant caste. The two women also had different family structures and marital statuses, and the differences correlated with Lakshmi's heterodox ideas about gender. Some of Lakshmi's disrespect for men sprang from her unsuccessful marriage. At the age of nineteen, instead of waiting for her parents to arrange a match, Lakshmi eloped. Although her husband came from a good family and occasionally held good jobs, the cumulative portrait she painted showed him as an unreliable spendthrift incapable of providing for his family. Fed up with poverty, in 1983 Lakshmi left her two daughters with her mother and went to work in Bahrain. After nine years in the Middle East, she returned to Sri Lanka and lived in her large cement house at the junction with her mother, daughters, and various brothers, nieces, and nephews.

After the first six months of her work abroad, Lakshmi remitted nothing to her husband, an alcoholic gambler. Nor did Lakshmi share her wealth with her husband upon her return to Sri Lanka, though he clearly coveted access to her money. Six weeks after I interviewed Lakshmi in 1994, my research associate Siri informed me that Lakshmi's husband, drunk, broke, and "mad for money," came to her house and hit her with a bottle, cutting three of her fingers in a fight before other members of her household chased him away. Despite their long separation, in 1994 Lakshmi had not legally divorced her husband. Claiming that "the children need a father," she retained the official place as wife for the sake of appearances but refused to act the customary part. In 1997, however, sensitized to probate laws by her mother's death, Lakshmi divorced her husband to protect her children's inheritance in case of her own demise.

Remarks Lakshmi made about her brothers and her daughters indicated her strong preference for women. Lakshmi said that her six brothers had made her life difficult as a child, and she grew to hate boys. When she got married, she prayed and said "*epaa*" [I don't want any] to sons and "by grace or luck" had had only daughters herself. Many villagers looked on the birth of a female child as the beginning of a grave financial responsibility, but despite the dominant discourse favoring sons, women often privately expressed the longing for a daughter. In hoping only for girls, Lakshmi staked out an unusual turf. Despite her harsh words about her siblings, however, Lakshmi seemed to have a close and compatible working relationship with her six brothers, especially those who lived locally. With money she earned abroad, Lakshmi invested heavily in her brothers' business ventures, and several still owed her money. Her brothers' protective presence allowed Lakshmi to live respectably while separated and divorced from her husband in a village where people viewed most women living alone with suspicion.

Differences in family structure and marital status shaped some of the differences between Elsie's and Lakshmi's expressed views of women's work. Like Elsie's business ventures, Lakshmi's financial initiatives fund her family's material well-being. Unlike Elsie, Lakshmi did not have a husband whom she respected. She and her family not only denied her husband the role of family breadwinner but also refused him access to Lakshmi's money. Lakshmi relied on the support of her family, especially her brothers, to resist her husband's demands. Although dependent on her brothers' protection, Lakshmi maintained the upper hand in their interactions, mainly through her financial investment in their business ventures. While Elsie conformed to local gender roles that highlighted her husband as the head of the house and the breadwinner, Lakshmi disparaged and divorced her spouse, talked about her work as work, and publicly asserted her control over her money.

Working Part-Time for Expatriates

Whereas Elsie developed her moneylending business through her involvement in the coconut fiber industry, Lakshmi earned her capital while working as a housemaid in Bahrain. The story of Lakshmi's nine years of work contrasted markedly with the stories told by other migrant women. Most housemaids had little opportunity to shape the trajectory of their migration once they arrived in the Middle East. Lakshmi's career path became atypical when, after two years of working for an Arabic household in Bahrain, she got a series of jobs with British and American expatriates. These jobs paid two to three times better than regular housemaid jobs, provided separate living quarters, and gave her evenings and weekends off, in which Lakshmi pursued part-time work in the neighborhood. For most housemaids, confined to their sponsors' houses, harder work just meant harder work, but for Lakshmi, after she started working for Westerners, hard work and ingenuity translated into money.

Narrating her experiences abroad, Lakshmi portrayed herself as resourceful, trustworthy, indefatigable, and always ready to take on more work for wages. For example, during her stay with an American family, Lakshmi worked part-time at a British neighbor's house and baby-sat for an Irish banker and his Indian wife who lived across the street. Lakshmi, who loves children, said, "That baby was a pain, but the money was coming." Although always rushed and tired, she wanted to earn as much as she could. When the American family prepared to leave Bahrain, the British neighbors needed a servant, and they secured a visa for Lakshmi. In similar fashion, during the following six years, Lakshmi found new jobs as needed when subsequent employers left Bahrain. Valuing her mobility and freedom to take on part-time work, Lakshmi even gave up a stable job with a work permit and visa when one employer began arbitrarily restricting her holidays, freedom of movement, and communication. She worked in a total of seven households during her time abroad, traveling to England several times and returning only once to visit her family in Sri Lanka. Unlike Elsie, who claimed that she "had no job," Lakshmi explicitly and consciously tied her financial success while abroad to her own hard work and initiative.

Lakshmi said she earned at least one hundred dinar per month for the seven years from 1985 to 1992, for a total of about 1,000,000 (U.S.$22,000–$25,000).[6] In addition to money, Lakshmi also acquired clothing, jewelry, and furniture. Lakshmi claimed that she had brought back dresses "from now to forever," and Siri's wife Telsie later confirmed that Lakshmi's cupboard "looked like a shop"; if anyone wanted a fancy sari to wear to a wedding, they could borrow one of the sixty or so there. Lakshmi brought back Rs. 150,000/ (225,000/ in 1994 rupees [U.S.$4,500]) in gold, in the form of bangles and chains and earrings for herself and her children. She also brought back two television sets, a VCR, a stereo, three refrigerators, a gas cooker, an electric keyboard, and a blender. Lakshmi's accumulation of money and material possessions indexed her wealth. While many migrants sold their jewelry and consumer goods soon after returning to Sri Lanka, Lakshmi's moneylending operations and her investment in her brothers' businesses allowed her to maintain her high standard of living and her influence in the village.

Money Flows

Both Elsie and Lakshmi charged interest on borrowed money, ran similar risks from bad debts, and used the court system to pressure defaulters. Unlike Elsie, Lakshmi not only lent money but also pawned jewelry and took property deeds as collateral on loans. The two moneylenders also differed in their relationships with their clients.

Lakshmi spoke much more openly about the intricacies of her financial ventures than Elsie did. In 1994 Lakshmi asserted that nearly

---

[6] Estimated at an average of U.S.$300 per month for 84 months, Lakshmi earned $25,200 during her time abroad. 100 dinar per month for 84 months comes to 8,400 dinar, or Rs. 840,000/ in 1991 rupees. Adjusting for inflation, this sum would provide the purchasing power of Rs. 1,133,907/ in 1994 rupees, or U.S.$22,678 at 1994 exchange rates. Like all Sri Lankan citizens, however, Lakshmi faced high inflation and a devaluing currency; this combination eroded her wealth. In 1991 1 dinar converted at Rs. 100/, while in 1994 1 dinar was valued at Rs. 125/. In 1991 U.S.$1 exchanged at Rs. 40/, while in 1994 U.S.$1 exchanged at Rs. 50/ and in 1997 for Rs. 60/. See appendix B for more information on exchange rates and inflation.

all of the Rs. 400,000/ (Rs. 600,000/ in 1994 rupees [U.S.$12,000]) she brought back from Bahrain had been given out on loan. To keep up with inflation, she needed to earn a high return on her investments. She charged between 10 percent and 20 percent interest per month. Lakshmi clearly thought of her principal as productive capital, and when people repaid their debts, she said she lent the money out again immediately, "without even buying five hundred grams of fish." She saw the interest as her income. Although some villagers superstitiously suggested that money made from interest would net the lender no lasting benefit, Lakshmi said, "If they return the money with just Rs. 5/ then at least I can buy a loaf of bread." When I asked about the interest rate, Lakshmi said, "That's the rate. People seem happy to borrow for that." High interest rates cushioned moneylenders from inflation and bad debts.

Lakshmi's file of documents revealed a great deal about her loan strategies. Eleven letters with signatures on stamps promised to repay sums varying from Rs. 2,000/ (U.S.$40) to Rs. 17,000/ (U.S.$340) for a total of Rs. 107,000/ (U.S.$2,140). The bulk of Lakshmi's money, however, had gone to a small number of extremely poor women who had not signed contracts. One migrant, Lakmini, owed Lakshmi Rs. 45,000/ (U.S.$900). Lakmini's sister Jayanthie had recently sent Lakshmi Rs. 40,000/ (U.S.$800) from the Middle East and still owed her Rs. 25,000/ (U.S.$500). Taken aback by the huge sums involved, Sita asked rhetorically what these sisters did with all the money they borrowed. Throwing up her hands, Lakshmi laughingly remarked, "And their father works as a gatekeeper at the railroad crossing, too. Some people *sellan karanavaa* [play games]. It's no use, they aren't improving." Altogether, a small number of repeat migrants owned Lakshmi roughly Rs. 200,000/ (U.S.$4,000).

Lakshmi considered these deeply indebted women, her main clients, foolish for borrowing such large sums of money despite their many trips abroad. Speaking of one migrant who owed her Rs. 65,000/ (U.S.$1,300), Lakshmi remarked, "Silly girl, she doesn't bank!" Although I cannot generalize about these women's motives, a separate interview with Lakmini shed light on why she herself incurred such high debts and also suggested why Lakshmi confidently expected repayment. Most migrants struggled to minimize the size of the loans they took from moneylenders, borrowing only what they needed to pay the agency fees to procure a job abroad. In contrast, Lakmini and her sister took large loans and spent the money on food and consumer goods while they were in Sri Lanka, promising Lakshmi that they would repay her with interest during their next contract abroad. While expensive, this strategy allowed the sisters to retain control over their money, spending it directly, instead of entrusting their family with money they remitted from abroad. Using this method they effectively kept their earnings away from their father, a notorious alcoholic. Lakmini's and Jayanthie's ability to return repeatedly to the Middle East acted as the security Lakshmi needed to assure her that they would repay their debts; Lakshmi's loans allowed Lakmini and Jayanthie to control the use of their money. Although "silly" from a financial perspective, the strategy suited the sisters' family situation. Nevertheless, only a small percentage of migrants borrowed in this fashion.

Unlike Elsie, Lakshmi lent money with property deeds as collateral. She had obtained ownership of a small piece of cinnamon garden by collecting on a bad loan and stood to obtain several more properties in a similar manner. For example, Lakshmi had lent a client Rs. 75,000/, holding two deeds worth a total of Rs. 120,000/; the borrower had agreed to pay Rs. 150,000/ within a year. Eighteen months after the original loan, the family still owed, with interest, Rs. 180,000/ (U.S.$3,600), and Lakshmi had taken the case to the courts. Since collecting property for bad debts proved difficult, time-consuming, and expensive, Lakshmi would have preferred the money to the hassle and the land.

In 1994 it looked as if Lakshmi's hard-earned savings, lent out on 100 percent interest, held the potential to double and redouble exponentially. In 1997, however, Lakshmi suggested that bad debts had greatly diminished her capital. Wearing a gold ring, earrings, and chain at the time of our interview, Lakshmi said that "all" of her jewelry was in the bank; she had borrowed money against her assets to cover her operating costs. Further discussion revealed that a number of families were due to return money soon. Although Lakshmi appeared genuinely worried about her business ventures and declared herself "bankrupt," Sita, with her firsthand knowledge of village finances, viewed this statement with skepticism.

Class Organization and Class Consciousness

Two issues arise from the discussion of "class consciousness." The first issue centers on the specific self-consciousness of a member of a class as a group, represented by organizations working for class interests. Marx predicted that class struggle would inevitably shape a self-conscious, politically organized, revolutionary proletariat. Contemporary theorists have elaborated on Marx's insights, recognizing the complexity of individual identity and group alliance and noting that economic exploitation may not lead automatically to a vocal or articulate political organization based solely on class interests. Instead, Wright uses the term *class formation* to refer to "cooperative social relations within class structures" or historically contingent alliances between social groups. He argues that class formations can be strong, weak, unitary, fragmented, revolutionary, counterrevolutionary, and so on, depending on the circumstances (1997, 379, 380).

Naeaegama villagers did discuss conscious ideologies of class identity and class politics. Many wealthier village families called themselves middle class, and most citizens had heard the rhetoric of the small but active communist parties that contested in local and national elections. Village discussions of class identity also reflected other social positions, however. For example, a very interesting discussion of "class" (in the living room of a leftist political organizer) highlighted Marx, exploitation, and class struggle. In this particular case, however, other contextual elements might have affected the organizer's choice of political philosophy; as a Halaagama man married to a Para caste wife, the man might have let his low-status marriage influence his preference for class over caste as a unit of identity. Villagers showed varying appreciation of class solidarity, and their awareness reflected other aspects of their identities.

The second issue of class consciousness centers on how individuals understand and conceptualize economic activity and how their beliefs and ideologies justify, support, and inspire their actions. Values connected to class issues (such as positions on private property, income tax, charging interest, hard work, and diligence) affect class practices (such as daily work habits or participation in strikes) that further class interests. Class consciousness, beliefs and effects of beliefs on the individual level, may or may not overlap with collective political organizations, such as unions or political parties (Wright 1997, 382–84).

Lakshmi's narratives often exhibited class consciousness of this second type. While Lakshmi never spoke of "class" explicitly, many of her statements revealed a strong work ethic and an inherently capitalist attitude toward money. When I asked Lakshmi what factors she felt had contributed to her success, she first talked about the poverty she experienced during her marriage, when she and her daughters sometimes lacked essentials such as food, clothing, and soap. To have a good life and be able to afford the things that she needed, she went to the Middle East. Lakshmi then spoke at length about how hard she worked in Bahrain. Returning from part-time baby-sitting at 2:00 A.M., she started work again at 5:30, washing cars in the cold and dark. At the house where she worked full-time, she did the washing, ironing, cooking, and child care. She took on part-time jobs whenever her friends went home on vacations. In all her nine years working abroad, she never took any extra holidays. Showing us three burn marks from falling asleep at the ironing board, Lakshmi emphasized how hard she had pushed herself to earn her fortune. Her "rags to riches" narrative emphasized many "Western," middle-class values.

Lakshmi not only lived by these values herself but also emphasized similar themes of hard work and diligence when she gave advice to migrants. If women complained about the conditions abroad, Lakshmi "made courage" by telling them that it was much harder to live in Sri Lanka: "There the water comes from the tap, you don't have to fetch it from the well. There you don't have to grind spices or pound rice flour. There all you have to do is eat and earn." Lakshmi lent a childhood friend Rs. 17,000/ to go to Saudi Arabia. Soon after, she heard from the friend, who complained that her employer's house was too big, the work was too hard, and she wanted to come home. Lakshmi said that she told the friend, "Think of the hard work people do here, like breaking rocks, for much less money." She told her friend to do her work slowly and leave what she could not finish. When the friend said that she still wanted to come home, Lakshmi replied, "Then sell your house and give me my money!"

Lakshmi believed that anyone should be able to work abroad to pay back a loan and that with a little fortitude they should be able to save and "improve" in Sri Lanka. She saw lending money as a service, for which she charged a reasonable fee. Those unable to free themselves from massive debts despite multiple migrations she saw as "silly," or "playing games"; those reluctant to continue working abroad she counseled to persevere with determination. Although not heartless in collecting on loans, Lakshmi felt no guilt when those who could not conform to her payment schedule found themselves landless or crippled by debt; in her frame of reference, those who lacked resolve deserved to fail, and those who encountered bad luck could always borrow again in the hopes of getting a better job the second time around.

Lakshmi's advice both challenged and reinforced larger gender and class relations surrounding migration. By urging women to keep control of their own finances and not to send money to their husbands, Lakshmi worked against existing gender hierarchies in the village. By encouraging housemaids to work diligently and save thriftily, assuring them that hard work would pay off, Lakshmi reinforced the hierarchies in employer-employee relations. Few housemaids found themselves in such enviable work situations as Lakshmi had. Lakshmi's Western sponsors in Bahrain encouraged entrepreneurship and industry by leaving her free hours in which to work part-time. In the Arabic households where most maids worked, however, women had no such mobility, and all their extra work benefited their employers under cover of the basic wage. By counseling housemaids to be diligent and obedient, Lakshmi paradoxically asked women not to demand the very freedom and mobility that had contributed to her own spectacular success. Lakshmi's injunctions enforced the authority of the employer without necessarily increasing the earning power of the housemaid.

Conclusion

Discussion of class proves challenging and complex, due to the diversity within classes, the multiple class locations individuals can occupy, and the many-faceted nature of individual identity. Economics is just one of many forces that shape ideas; ideology does "not precisely mirror, match or 'echo' the class structure of society" (S. Hall 1996, 434). Stuart Hall argues that "ideologies are not transformed or changed by replacing one, whole, already formed, conception of the world with another, so much as by 'renovating and making critical an already existing activity'" (S. Hall 1996, 434). The two local moneylenders discussed held widely different views about women's work and the use of money despite their similar business practices. Although one cannot generalize from a sample of two, some of the contrasts might indicate a generational shift in gender and class ideologies.

Many diverse factors influenced Elsie's and Lakshmi's attitudes toward moneylending and gender, including family structure, marital status, age, and life experiences. In a village where many people spoke only indirectly about moneylending, the older and more traditional

Elsie modestly understated her business ventures, presenting herself as a housewife and her husband as the family breadwinner. In contrast, the younger and more Westenized Lakshmi spoke openly about moneylending. Her lack of reticence seemed to stem from two sources: her pride in her undisguised role as breadwinner and her unabashedly capitalist attitude toward money and work. Lakshmi's estrangement from her husband, close relations with her brothers, and financial prestige and security combined to shape her heterodox views on gender and moneylending. Only time will tell if Lakshmi's views represent a peculiar anomaly or the wave of the future. Her charismatic presence, economic and symbolic capital, and woman-centered advice certainly influenced many people in the Naeaegama area.

Elsie and Lakshmi represented a category of people often seen as exploiting the migrant women whom they financed. Job agents and moneylenders took a cut of the funds that flowed through their hands so that the migrant herself supported a long chain of people, each one taking a portion of her earnings. Elsie and Lakshmi benefited from existing socioeconomic inequalities, which the interest they charged perpetuated. While some migrants returned time and time again to work abroad without much improvement to show, Elsie and Lakshmi prospered visibly. At the same time, migrants without collateral to offer for a bank loan had nowhere else to turn for money; the jobs Elsie and Lakshmi financed offered the glimmering hope of an escape from poverty. Lakshmi portrayed herself as providing information and financing to facilitate migration. In a context of subsistence economics and perpetual poverty, the services Elsie and Lakshmi provided proved both useful and usurious.

4 Agency: Women's Work Experiences Abroad

Agency

Anthropologists often set *agency*, "the human capacity to act" (Ahearn 2000), in juxtaposition to *structure*, the social norms and values that regulate human behavior. Practice theorists investigate the interaction between agents and structures, noting that structures shape human actions but that at the same time human actions recreate and transform the structures that govern them (Ortner 1984; Sahlins 1981). As ordinary people in the course of their daily lives comply with, question, modify, and resist the culturally constructed discourses that shape thoughts and actions, these standards shift and change (R. Williams 1977).

To begin to understand human agency, social constructionists examine the cultural construction of meaning (S. Hall 1996; Dirks, Eley, and Ortner 1994). Although instinct and biological imperatives govern the behaviors of most animals, humans live by the rules that they themselves create. Phrased slightly differently, genetic predisposition to culture requires humans to develop and pass on learned patterns and strategies for living in the world. Systems of meaning and knowledge that guide behavior rest on classifications and categories shared by members of a culture. These systems are most evident in the vocabulary of a people's language (Douglas 1966; Friedrich 1989; Gramsci 1988). Language is not a fixed, objective, closed system, a neutral medium, or a pure tool contained in a grammar book or a dictionary. Instead, language is a practical material activity embedded in socially shared and reciprocal relationships. Edward Sapir writes:

> Language is a guide to "social reality." ... It powerfully conditions all our thinking about social problems and processes. Human beings do not live in the objective world alone, but are very much at the mercy of the particular language which has become the medium of expression for their society.... The "real world" is to a large extent unconsciously built up on the language habits of the group.... The worlds in which different societies live are distinct worlds, not merely the same world with different labels attached. (Sapir 1949, 162)

Language forms "a distinctively human opening of and opening to the world ... a constitutive faculty" (R. Williams 1977, 24) through which we understand and act in the world.

Action often takes place in a context of power and hierarchy. In the process of creating cultural classifications, humans identify differences and decide which differences "make a difference" or distinguish items into categories. While many of the classifications we make (red vs. blue, wet vs. dry) have little to do with power and authority, other classifications (good vs. evil, believer vs. pagan, freedom fighter vs. terrorist) carry political implications about how we should evaluate and react to individuals and events. In the process of creating categories, we also create hierarchies, judging some items of higher value than others. By accepting the categories and taking them for granted as common sense, people acquiesce to the hierarchy implicit in the system of classification (Bernstein 1981). But since humans create categories, they can also change them, creating different classification systems with different hierarchies, serving different political interests.

Pierre Bourdieu coins the term *habitus* to refer to learned dispositions that both structure and are structured by human actions. These dispositions operate below the level of conscious knowledge, yet remain open to revision, challenge, and modification. Community members re-create, but do not merely duplicate, these culturally constructed viewpoints in the process of acting. "The conditioned and conditional freedom [that the habitus] secures is as remote from a creation of unpredictable novelty as it is from a simple mechanical reproduction of the initial conditionings" (1977, 95). Bourdieu also calls the habitus "the durably installed generative principle of *regulated improvisations*" (1977, 78; emphasis added). The process of regulated improvisation and bounded innovation ensures change and continuity, generating both the transformation and the reproduction of social structures. In situations of rapid change, the cultural categories that shape action often lag behind events, and people may find that their patterned dispositions run counter to the necessities of new circumstances.

In talking about power, hierarchy, and inequality in everyday interactions, many theorists identify symbolic forms of oppression as well as those that employ physical force (Bourdieu 1977; Gramsci 1971). Systems of "lived dominance and subordination" (R. Williams 1977, 110) shape most people's subconscious habits and everyday actions. Foucault sees "power" as immanent in all relationships. Transitory, "produced from one moment to the next" (1978, 93), power suffuses society like a network of capillaries in a body, permeating institutions, bodies, and thought; it is constantly moving, constantly contested, and yet the "concatenation" of its local manifestations creates the effect of permanence and inertia (1978, 92–93). This chapter explores the micropolitics of domination and resistance, as housemaids and sponsors challenge and reaffirm the seemingly stable structures of authority and inequality in the Middle East.

Lakshmi: Power in the Family

Stories related to me by returned migrants indicated that women encountered foreign systems of power and meaning in their employers' homes.[1] Within the mutually accepted bounds of the sponsor-housemaid relationship, employers and employees used both official and unofficial strategies to negotiate their particular associations. Formal and informal disciplinary techniques operated to control housemaids; these limiting sanctions worked against the informal but powerful authority that housemaids acquired through their central position in the household. Complex dynamics operated to keep house-

---

[1] Since I did not undertake research in the Middle East and have not interviewed any sponsors personally, the following discussion of conflicts and negotiations between housemaids and their employers relies exclusively on the housemaids' side of the story.

maids at once marginal insiders and intimate outsiders in the homes of their sponsors, as the following story demonstrates.

While working in Bahrain for Western expatriates, Lakshmi, the moneylender introduced in the previous chapter, found herself caught in a dispute between the couple she worked for. Lakshmi got along better with the Boss than the Madam.[2] One night the Madam and the Boss quarreled over a business party, which the Madam did not want her husband to attend. She said that if he went, he would have to take the children along. The Boss asked Lakshmi to baby-sit. The Madam then stormed off and locked herself in the master bedroom so that her husband, still in his work clothes, could not shower or change. Lakshmi guided the Boss toward clean towels, soap, and shampoo in the children's bathroom and ironed a clean shirt from the laundry. Soon after the Boss left for the party, his wife came out of the bedroom, said that she would take care of the children, and sent Lakshmi to her quarters.

Lakshmi related the story above as background for a longer story, concerning an injury, to explain the Madam's lack of sympathy with Lakshmi's request for time off. Several days after her employers' quarrel, Lakshmi hurt her arm on her day off. The next morning she set up the family's breakfast with one hand, waiting to tell the Boss about her troubles. Carrying his shoes, the Boss came to breakfast, hurrying to catch a flight out of the country. Lakshmi polished his footwear while he ate and never had a chance to discuss her injury. After his departure, Lakshmi explained her predicament to the Madam, who accused her of maneuvering for an extra day off. Although the Madam allowed Lakshmi to visit the doctor, she refused to grant any sick leave despite the sling on Lakshmi's arm. Lakshmi scrubbed the five bathrooms and looked after the rest of the house one-handed; the Madam grudgingly allowed her to skip the ironing for several days. Lakshmi felt sure that the Boss would have treated her differently.

Lakshmi's stories point out two contradictory dynamics. The first story emphasizes how her control of domestic tasks made her powerful in her employers' household. The second points out Lakshmi's vulnerability to her employers' grudges and goodwill. Preexisting roles for housemaids and sponsors set broad bounds for individual behavior

---

[2] Housemaids regularly refer to their female employer as "the Madam" or "Madam" and their male employer as "the Boss" or "Boss." Here I have adopted the English terminology they used.

within a structure of power and hierarchy that all parties implicitly acknowledge. Within these bounds, actors engage in "regulated improvisations," where personal affiliations, practical skills, and access to material resources come into play. In Lakshmi's stories, as in the stories of most housemaids, employer-employee dynamics overlapped with more subtle and more personal politics. Although official hierarchies trumped informal insubordination, housemaids playing their cards correctly could achieve a significant degree of power and autonomy in the homes where they worked.

Discipline

Recognizing that live-in domestic servants become deeply and personally integrated into the private lives of their employers, sponsors create and maintain a social space between themselves and their housemaids to preserve and emphasize social prestige. Elaborate etiquette regulates dress codes and forms of address, restricts socializing and mobility, and demarcates accessible and inaccessible space. This etiquette, accepted as normal by both housemaids and sponsors, draws on and reinforces classifications that distinguish household workers from family members (see also Hansen 1989, 1990; Gill 1994; Rollins 1985, 1990; Sanjek and Colen 1990). The intricate rules for respectful behavior constitute techniques and tactics of domination that Foucault terms *disciplinary power* (1994, 219). Such power functions most effectively in situations short of direct confrontation and conflict; when employers cancel a housemaid's contract or punish her physically, or when the housemaid quits, different power dynamics come to the fore. Disciplinary power operates as employers socialize servants to accept as normal the system of beliefs and behaviors that perpetuate inequality.

James Scott argues that household workers often live a dual life, enacting one set of behaviors and voicing one set of ideas in the company of their employers, and another in private with their own families and friends. Examining situations of dominance and resistance, Scott identifies offstage "hidden transcripts" (uncensored talk among subordinates) that voice very different positions from those expressed during the obsequious dialogues of the "public transcript," which both dominant and subordinate players use when they interact. Scott questions the extent to which workers actually believe the public transcripts about boundaries and power hierarchies that their employers construct and suggests that in their hidden transcripts workers recognize their oppression (1990).

While housemaids doubtless tailor their comments to fit the audience, how self-consciously they challenge the disciplinary strategies their employers use is less clear. Barriers of class, race, ethnicity, and nationality separate master from servant, but at the same time, housemaids, their sponsors, and their sponsors' children develop emotional intimacies that challenge the maintenance of clear-cut cultural and personal boundaries between master and servant. Despite awareness of their subordinate positions, housemaids often freely and gladly give their employers the loyalty and diligence they demand. Personal relationships obscure a straightforward narrative of resistance and critique.

The housemaid's work includes child care, cooking, cleaning, and laundry. Most housemaids live in a separate room in their employers' houses; lodging, board, and necessary sundries such as shampoo, soap, toothbrush, and clothing come as part of the wage package. Many Arabic households require their housemaids to wear long gowns to cover their legs and scarves to cover their heads. A housemaid's schedule rarely offers vacations, days off, or scheduled free time. In a survey of returned housemaids, Grete Brochmann found that "49 percent of the respondents say they have a work day of more than 16 hours," and "72 percent of the housemaids did not get *any* days off during the whole contract period" (1990, 132, 133). Employers rarely let housemaids out of the house unsupervised; Brochmann notes that a third of the women in her sample were not allowed to leave the house at all, whereas most of the remainder did so only in the company of their employers (1990, 136). Women did develop relationships with other housemaids in the neighborhood, however; for example, they would arrange to meet when "taking out the garbage" (Brochmann 1990, 140). These findings correspond with the experiences of Naeaegama migrants.

In the following case studies, each woman's experiences abroad depended both on dynamics specific to the housemaid and the family she worked for and on culturally constructed norms, habits, and values. Within general patterns typical of sponsor-housemaid interactions, housemaids and their employers negotiated how much freedom the housemaid had, what she wore, how much she worked, and what sorts of compensation she received. Comparing the work situations and daily schedules of two migrants who returned repeatedly to work in the same households abroad illustrates their duties, responsibilities, and the degree of freedom and authority they perceived themselves to have.

Indrani's Success Story

Housemaids and their sponsors have often come into direct and indirect conflict over issues such as the amount of work a housemaid did, the amount and distribution of her time off, the degree of respect she received from household members, and the extent to which sponsors restricted and supervised her socializing, mobility, and attire. Indrani, a dynamic mother of four in her forties, had one of the best job situations among the migrant women in the village. Her older brother Byron, the village subagent introduced in chapter 2, had helped her find employment in 1985. In 1997 she still worked for the same family in Doha, Qatar.

Indrani looked after the three children and did most of the cooking, sewing, and chores in her sponsors' two-story house. Although most Naeaegama housemaids reported that they did not receive pay raises from their employers, Indrani's monthly wages had increased from U.S.$110 to U.S.$150 per month over the years of her service, and her employers supplemented this generous salary with numerous gifts and presents. Using her remittances, Indrani and her husband took three years to build a new house on a plot across the road from Siri's land. Although new houses sprang up all over the village, Indrani's grew more quickly than others. Indrani had close, cordial relations with her employers, which enhanced her financial success.

Indrani described her typical workday. Rising at 6:00 A.M., she prepared breakfast for the family and sent the children to school. From 8:30 to 11:00 Indrani did housework. She started cooking lunch at 11:00, and the Boss and Madam came home to eat at 1:00 P.M. At 2:00 the children came home from school and ate. Indrani cleaned the kitchen, and then she and the other household members slept until 5:00 or 5:30. At 8:00 P.M. she and the children ate sandwiches for supper, unless there was a party. After 9:00 P.M. Indrani was free to write letters, sleep, listen to the radio, or watch television. The local television and radio stations catered to the housemaid population by broadcasting programs in languages spoken by guest workers in Qatar. Indrani devoted her whole day exclusively to tending her employers' family and had very little privacy or free time, yet she seemed to accept and even enjoy the situation.

Although Indrani's employers restricted her socializing and mobility, they clearly trusted Indrani personally. Indrani said that while some households locked their valuables, her employers were "very nice people" and did not. They allowed her to move about and socialize to a small extent, letting her visit the neighbor's house, for example, and talk on the telephone. When I asked why their trust did not extend to allowing Indrani to go out of the house alone, she said that they did not like it "because it was not her country." Indrani did travel with the family, however. During the three-month summer school holiday, her employers gave Indrani the choice of returning to Sri Lanka or traveling, all expenses paid, with them; between 1993 and 1997 Indrani went to Saudi Arabia and Syria instead of returning to Naeaegama. Instead of chafing against the restrictions her employers imposed, Indrani valued the opportunities they gave her.

Religious identity has lead to discord between housemaids and sponsors. As a rule, most Buddhist housemaids declare themselves Christian on their job application forms, since Arabic sponsors prefer Muslim and Christian housemaids to Buddhist and Hindu ones (see chapter 1). In a survey of returned migrants, Brochmann found that sponsors had forbidden about half of the respondents to practice Buddhist rituals but allowed "Catholics" to attend mass on Sundays, where they socialized with other Sri Lankan "Catholics" (1990, 134, 140). Naeaegama women did not mention socializing at churches, but Buddhist maids masquerading as Christians did instruct their families in Sri Lanka never to send them holiday cards with Buddhist images. Some maids announced their Buddhism openly, however, and said that their employers never pressured them on the topic. Indrani, a Buddhist, told her employers that she was a Christian. She went with the family to the mosque, but she, like other housemaids, said that her sponsors never asked her to convert.

Islamic traditions have often influenced housemaids' experiences in terms of daily schedule and clothing. During the month of Ramadan, everyone over eight years old in Indrani's employers' family fasted from 4:00 A.M. until after dark (6:00 P.M.). Although they permitted Indrani to eat, the family would not even drink any water. Indrani adjusted her cooking and sleeping schedule to accommodate the fast. In terms of clothing, Indrani noted that officially only Muslim women had to observe norms of covering their legs and heads, but some families made their housemaids conform to these same rules, both in private and in public. Customs and norms varied slightly from country to country and family to family (see also Brochmann 1990, 135). The Madam in Indrani's family wore short dresses in the house and let Indrani do so as well. Housemaids' intimate life, including their clothing and their eating and sleeping schedules, revolved around Islamic practices.

Indrani's long association with her sponsors brought her a great deal of personal power in the household. When she first went to work abroad, the eldest of the family's three children was only one month old. Indrani felt that she knew more about the children than their own mother did because she had taken the primary responsibility in raising them. All the children understood Sinhala, though they rarely spoke it. Indrani knew her employers' children loved her; they asked her again and again not to leave them and cried when she went to the airport. Indrani said that her Madam was like a sister to her. Sometimes the Madam did the laundry and washed Indrani's clothing too. Indrani's friends among the neighborhood housemaids laughed when they found this out, and they envied Indrani's fortune in having found such a good place to work. The ties of affection that developed over twelve years of service made Indrani more a member of the family than hired help.

Indrani's description of her relationship with her employers portrays a warm, caring, and generous interaction. Her salary of U.S.$150, though low in international terms, seemed lavish by Sri Lankan and Middle Eastern standards, especially when complemented by generous gifts (as described later). Indrani appeared not to chafe against restrictions on her mobility and religious practices, and, although very busy, she did not complain about her workload. Instead, she seemed to see her life abroad in terms of her close personal relationships with the children and their mother, her earnings, and the travel opportunities her work abroad had brought.

Rupawathie's Ambivalence

Individuals improvise relationships within the general disciplinary structure set up around "housemaids" and "employers." These "regulated improvisations" benefit some women more than others, depending in part on the luck of the draw and the chemistry of individual personalities. Like Indrani, Rupawathie negotiated with her sponsors over the amount of work she did, the time off she got, and the restrictions on her socializing, mobility, and attire. Unlike Indrani, Rupawathie seemed less than pleased with her situation abroad.

Like Indrani, Rupawathie had worked with the same family abroad
for an extended period—in this case nine years. A quiet and unas-
suming mother of three, Rupawathie first went to Jordan in 1984 on a
ticket from her brother-in-law. Her employers had six grown children
and owned olive, grape, and apple orchards. The house had five bedrooms and three baths when she first went to work, and the family
later constructed an addition. Rupawathie's quarters, which she found
luxurious, had a wardrobe, bed, and private bathroom. During her nine
years abroad she returned to Sri Lanka for two one-month vacations
and took two days of sick leave due to a back injury. At the end of her
stay, she earned U.S.$80 a month.

Although Rupawathie earned just over half what Indrani did, her
workload seemed greater. Rupawathie described her daily round.
About 6:00 A.M. she made tea and breakfast for the Boss. Then she set
another table for the rest of the family, who ate at about 9:30. After
cleaning the kitchen, she arranged the bedrooms, ran the washing machine, and dusted and vacuumed the whole house. The family came
home to eat lunch, which Rupawathie prepared, at about 2:00. After
clearing up the kitchen, she did the ironing. From 3:00 to 4:30 she
washed the family's five cars, and from 4:30 to 6:00 she watered the
plants and washed the ceramic tiles in the garden. Around 6:00 family
relations often came to visit, and Rupawathie served tea while making dinner. The family ate at about 9:30 and watched television while
she served fruits and cleaned up the kitchen. She went to bed about
10:30. Rupawathie found her job very tiring and felt her compensation
inadequate for her time and efforts. Unlike Indrani, Rupawathie did
not speak about close and affectionate ties with her sponsors.

Rupawathie's employers restricted her socializing and mobility.
They did not allow her to leave the house alone, and she never went
out with the family, even to the shops nearby. Her employers did not
let her talk to other Sri Lankans on the telephone or in the street. They
justified their position by explaining that their relatives had had problems with promiscuous servants; several housemaids "went out with
boyfriends" on their days off, and one got pregnant. Rather than resent
the restrictions on her freedom, however, Rupawathie saw her employers as "protective," which she considered a positive aspect of her
job. Since they never abused or harassed her, she never tried to find a
different position, notwithstanding the low pay and hard work.

Despite Rupawathie's portrayal of rather cool relations with her
sponsors, the family wanted her to return to Jordan after her final va-

cation. When she stated that she wanted to stay permanently in Sri Lanka, they said that she could have as much vacation as she wanted, but she must come back. Fearing that they would not let her leave at all unless they thought she would come back, Rupawathie avoided direct conflict by allowing her sponsors to renew her visa and buy her a return ticket. She said with a smile that once she arrived in Sri Lanka her husband burnt the visa and sent the ticket back to Jordan.

As insiders *and* outsiders in the households where they worked, housemaids experience both great intimacy and an underlying loneliness while living abroad. Most maids with whom I spoke described daily routines very similar to those of Indrani and Rupawathie; only the assessment of the difficulty of the work varied. Few maids complained about the food and accommodation they received, although many mentioned that they would have welcomed an occasional day off. Confined to the house or proximate neighborhood and denied a social space of their own, the maids interacted mainly with their sponsors' families and neighborhood housemaids, intimately integrated into the daily routine but always to some extent kept on the margins of family life.

Employers' practices and values also influenced how they treated housemaids. Indrani speculated that as outsiders in Doha, Qatar, her Palestinian employers understood cultural difference and discrimination, treating her better as a result of their own marginal position in society. As the first housemaid they hired, Indrani did not have to battle against preset family patterns of distancing servants. Bonding closely with the young children and cultivating a good relationship with their parents, Indrani found herself in a supportive and giving atmosphere. In contrast, entering a large household with grown children, one already experienced in dealing with servants, the more reticent Rupawathie negotiated a less open and affectionate work environment.

Maids step off the airplane into a more or less fixed role governed by local norms and hierarchies. Jean Comaroff argues that "the subject is constructed by external sociocultural forms.... [Relations of domination] become inscribed in the taken-for-granted shape of the world—in definitions of the body, personhood, productivity, space, and time" (1985, 5). The migrant housemaid, while abroad, molds and censors her behavior according to the signs, symbols, and practices by which her employers demarcate structures of authority and submission. At the same time, her centrality to smooth domestic functioning gives her a certain power to negotiate boundaries and resist her subordinate position. Within the broader patterns of behavior cultur-

ally suitable to housemaid and employer, individuals negotiate interpersonal relations. A maid's autonomy and authority depend on the
preexisting conceptions of the maid and of the household she joins as
well as on the continually shifting dynamics of daily life. Although
long tenure in a job often gives the housemaid confidence and leverage, she might still emerge disappointed with her situation, as Rupawathie's case shows.

Gifts and Conspicuous Consumption

Within the bounded and regulated framework of the housemaid-
sponsor relationship, individual housemaids and sponsors improvise
and devise acceptable behavior and etiquette. The norms and standards
of the labor structure leave a minimal range for negotiation centered
on women's socializing and mobility, their daily schedules, their work,
and their free time, as already described. Unlike many employer-
employee relationships, however, domestic service jobs in the Middle
East do not allow negotiation of wages and hours.

Most housemaids earn the local equivalent of U.S.$100 per month;
some jobs, especially those in Jordan and Lebanon, pay even less. With
the exception of the lucky few such as Indrani, most housemaids receive only insignificant raises, or no raises at all. In fact, the average
salary of U.S.$100 has held steady for nearly twenty years. Thus, due
to inflation, real wages have in fact dropped significantly between 1980
and 1997 (see chap. 1). As the previous case studies illustrate, housemaids have little leverage to negotiate better hours; confined to their
employers' homes and constantly "on call," they lack even the opportunity to make extra money by working overtime. Although employers lay claim to all of a housemaid's labor, housemaids retain control over the quality of their work. Domestic servants perform duties
crucial to the smooth functioning of a household, such as preparing
food and caring for children. While force or threat of force may make
servants go through the motions of their jobs, it will not inspire them
to be pleasant, diligent, caring, or loyal. With wages and hours set outside the realm of negotiation, housemaids and sponsors often come to
an unofficial understanding concerning other aspects of labor—effort
and attitude—and another form of compensation: gifts.

The anthropological literature contains a long and interesting debate on the dynamics of gift giving, starting with Marcel Mauss's slen-

der but provocative book *The Gift* (1990 [1925]). A cross-cultural investigation of gifts reveals the intricacies of gift giving in particular cultures, as well as certain overarching themes and trends. In many societies, a gift given between equals requires the deferred return of an item or service roughly equal to that given, which implicitly demands that those involved continue their exchange relationship (Cronk 1997). Many foraging communities have well-developed cultural leveling mechanisms to counter the power and influence of successful hunters who distribute food to others (Lee 1997); an Inuit saying suggests that "Gifts make slaves like whips make dogs," which concisely summarizes the social force of gift giving between equals. Conspicuous gift giving, such as the competitive feasts or potlatches once prevalent in the American Pacific Northwest, increases the prestige of the feast giver and obliges guests to equal or outdo the gift in a similar event at a later date (Cole and Chaikin 1990). In this case generosity indicates high social status, and recipients acquire a one-down position that they must escape by giving gifts themselves. In India, complex religious meanings inhere in some types of gift giving; for example, Gloria Raheja refers to "the poison in the gift" when analyzing the transfer of inauspiciousness in ritual gifts among castes (1988). In Sri Lanka, gifts given from patrons to clients and vice versa presuppose hierarchy and inequality but also contain obligations for ongoing interactions (Risseeuw 1991). Even the briefest survey reveals that, far from a casual expression of unconditional generosity or kindness, gift giving often indicates dynamic, ongoing negotiations of hierarchy and indebtedness. While the norms, meanings, and expectations surrounding gifts vary cross-culturally, they usually indicate complex links between givers and receivers.

Gifts from a sponsor to a housemaid might at first glance appear to be simple and selfless gestures of affection, but a closer examination shows the intricacy of such exchanges. Due to her central position in a household, a housemaid holds the considerable power to subtly make her employer's life miserable. Erik Wright notes that

> Exploitation ... does not merely define a set of statuses of social actors, but a pattern of on-going interactions structured by a set of social relations, relations which mutually bind the exploiter and the exploited together. This dependency of the exploiter on the exploited gives the exploited a certain form of power, since human beings always retain at least some minimal control over their own expenditure of effort. Social

control of labor which relies exclusively on repression is costly and, except under special circumstances, often fails to generate optimal levels of diligence and effort on the part of the exploited. As a result, there is generally systematic pressure on exploiters to moderate their domination and in one way or another to try to elicit some degree of consent from the exploited, at least in the sense of gaining some level of minimal cooperation from them. (1997, 12)

In the housemaid-sponsor relationship, the social and symbolic value associated with gifts creates obligations and relations very different in quality from those generated through wages alone.

Building on the idea that people rarely give gifts without at least an element of calculation, Bourdieu coins the term *symbolic capital* to discuss exchanges that take place outside the officially recognized economy (1977, 171). Bourdieu suggests that the "linguistic market" plays an integral role in many exchanges of symbols and meanings. Symbolic capital euphemizes or "misrecognizes" such exchanges "to prevent the [symbolic] economy from being grasped *as* an economy, i.e. as a system governed by the laws of interested calculation, competition, or exploitation" (1977, 172). Bourdieu's reliance on the market metaphor leaves him open to the accusation that he sees all exchanges as ultimately rooted in and motivated by market values and economic rationality, an assumption that might not hold true in particular cultures or particular cases. Nevertheless, the general concept of symbolic capital does shed light on gift-giving relationships between sponsors and housemaids, as the following analysis suggests.

Gifts

Labor relations between housemaids and their employers rely on wages and on gifts. Many women expect to receive both from their employers. Housemaids provide their services to their employers twenty-four hours a day, seven days a week; employers offer no official bonuses for diligence or overtime. Many maids I spoke to, however, felt that if they worked assiduously, their employers would reward them with gifts. Easily converted into cash both in Sri Lanka and in the Middle East, gold jewelry topped the list of women's favorite presents, followed closely by electrical appliances such as cassette players, televisions, and clocks.

Indrani counted herself lucky that her employers gave her everything she needed so she could save every penny of her salary. They also gave her lavish gifts, including an oven for Rs. 25,000/, new dresses, shoes for her children, and gold. At separate times Indrani had brought home a refrigerator, two color TVs (worth about U.S.$300 each), a cassette player, and a juice machine. She had brought toys for her children, a suit for her husband, and jewelry for her mother-in-law. Indrani reciprocated by bringing her employers small but thoughtful presents from Sri Lanka, such as pineapples, coconuts, or cloth for making dresses.

Rupawathie's case proves harder to analyze. Although in the course of her narrative she mentioned a number of gifts that her employers had given her, Rupawathie expressed considerable bitterness over what she perceived as her longtime employers' stinginess. Saying that she earned U.S.$80 at the end of her stay abroad, Rupawathie pointed out that some employers paid their maids U.S.$120 or more a month, especially after long service. Once, thinking that they would give it to her as a gift, Rupawathie asked her employers to get her a gold chain, but they deducted the price from her salary. The first pick of the old clothing from the house went to the Boss' younger brother; Rupawathie got what he did not want. She pointed to the girlish denim skirt and white cotton blouse that she was wearing as an example of the hand-me-down clothing she had acquired in this way. Rupawathie said, "They had five cars and after nine years of work, they didn't even give me a gold chain when I left. All they gave me were three imitation rings and a plastic soap box." In the family's defense, however, one must note that Rupawathie left her sponsors with the impression that she would return. Despite the relatively cool relations between Rupawathie and her employers, the lack of a generous parting present galled her, and the family's closefisted nature came up again and again in Rupawathie's narrative.

Gifts from sponsors to housemaids provide an appropriate mode of symbolic and material compensation for services above and beyond any formal, contractual rights and obligations. What constitutes "above and beyond," however, remains subject to negotiation between individual sponsors and housemaids. As intimate outsiders and marginal insiders in their sponsors' homes, housemaids gradually learn the explicit rules and unspoken but powerful norms that regulate their behavior. Gifts reward a housemaid's past loyalty and diligence and obligate her to continue such behavior in a manner that a contract could not. In a similar vein, withholding such presents indicates a sponsor's dissatisfaction with the personal aspects of the relationship.

In her case, Rupawathie clearly felt that her hard work deserved more recognition. (Without her employers' side of the story, their motives and actions remain unclear.) Although housemaids feel free to remind their employers to pay their monthly wages, they rarely request and never directly demand gifts. By its very nature, the exchange of affection, diligence, and loyalty for gifts remains indirect, unspoken, and unenforceable.

Prestige and Conspicuous Consumption

Gifts form a central component of interpersonal relations not only between housemaids and their employers but also between women and their social networks at home.[3] Goods brought from abroad served as signs of prestige, and the symbolic value of an item often exceeds its monetary worth. Either received as gifts or purchased in the Middle East or in Sri Lanka, consumer items such as gold chains, televisions, and cassette players operate as visible symbols of affluence in Naeaegama. The continued presence of such objects, easily sold for cash in times of financial need, indicates a household's continuing economic stability and provides a resource to fall back on if times get rough. The best consumer items and gifts combine the greatly prized qualities of high resale value, durability, ostentation, and obvious overseas origin.

Although her employers failed to give her many gifts, Rupawathie purchased a number of goods to bring to Sri Lanka. She bought a gas cooker from the Sri Lankan duty-free store and two boxes of foreign cigarettes from the Jordanian duty-free store. She brought cloth, apples, canned fish, toffees, and chocolates. She brought no alcohol, no television, and no cassette player, all items commonly purchased by or given to returning migrants. Just as we raised the topic of cassette players in our conversation with Rupawathie in Siri's living room, music from Indrani's house across the street invaded the quiet afternoon air, blaring from the stereo system purchased by Indrani's family. Laughing, Rupawathie speculated that someone in the household across the street must have felt the need to remind the world that they had a cas-

---

[3] Chapter 5 discusses conflicts over the control of women's remitted wages and the distribution of goods that they brought back from the Middle East. This chapter, though, focuses on the things women brought home and the meanings such objects carried in local contexts.

sette. In contrast, Rupawathie said that her family wanted to build a new house and stock a grocery shop in the front room, another conspicuous display of accumulated wealth.

Although consumer goods have operated as savings accounts, they have also—perhaps more importantly—acted as symbolic membership cards in the village arena of the newly wealthy. In certain cases conspicuous consumption has proved more significant than practical improvements. For example, upon returning to the village, one migrant built a small house, furnished it, and left materials to construct an outdoor toilet. After she returned to the Middle East, her alcoholic husband sold first the supplies for making the toilet and then most of the movable items in the house, including the wardrobe, the bed, the tables, and the chairs. The gold chain around his neck and the large cassette player, the most public of the consumer items his wife had purchased, were the last to go. Most villagers condemned this man's actions, but many people seemed to understand the abstract principle governing the order of his sales, namely that the symbolic importance of certain prestigious items exceeded the value of other, more useful, household accoutrements.

Gifts and consumer items circulate in a variety of overlapping systems of value and meaning governed according to diverse, culturally constructed rules and norms. Gifts not only augment women's salaries, they also acknowledge the importance of the personal relationships housemaids develop with the families they serve. Similarly, villagers prize foreign consumer items not only as valuable objects they can use and sell but also as symbols of their financial success and household prestige. Bourdieu's concept of symbolic capital, which suggests the integration of economic and symbolic exchange, opens a fruitful line of analysis. At the same time, one must avoid the assumption inherent in the term *capital* that one bottom line, namely economic rationality, ultimately governs all exchanges of both symbols and material goods. Some goods circulate with other-than-economic motivations through other-than-market systems.

Initiative and Networks: Emergency Situations

Improvising within preexisting structures, women have some leeway to negotiate their relationships with their employers. The preceding sections present instances where housemaids and sponsors worked within the framework of employment. The housemaids in the following case studies encountered difficult situations abroad and lost their jobs. The initiatives they took, the avenues they pursued, and the resources they drew upon in times of trouble reveal the nature of women's agency in adverse conditions.

Working abroad, a woman without relatives in a foreign country has little leverage or recourse in a quarrel with her employeers. Serious disputes lead almost inexorably to the termination of a woman's job and her return to Sri Lanka, despite the grave financial difficulties she encounters as a result. Noting that local police usually side with their countrymen, that agencies only mediate between sponsors and employees for the first three months of a contract and that the Sri Lankan embassy holds little practical sway, maids realize their lack of effective bargaining power.

Commonly circulating images portray housemaids as isolated, structurally marginalized, vulnerable individuals (see chap. 9). Despite the many factors that place women at a disadvantage, most of the women who related "trouble" stories presented themselves as active agents who drew on all their available resources—including informal networks of acquaintances, saved money, and family in Sri Lanka—to extricate themselves from bad situations. Contrary to representations of housemaids in the national press and much scholarly literature, not one of the migrants I spoke to portrayed herself as a helpless victim.

Priyanthi, introduced in the introduction, worked in five different households abroad. In the following story, which she related about her third job, she portrayed herself as a dynamic actor extricating herself from an unpleasant situation, not as a passive victim swept up by events. Priyanthi worked for a year and a half in Kuwait in a household where her employers took drugs. One day Priyanthi tossed out some pills she found under the bed sheets in the linen closet. About a week later, the Boss grew very upset when he could not find the pills. He yelled and shouted, threatened to hit Priyanthi, and demanded that she leave her job and pay for her own airfare home. Selling two gold bangles worth U.S.$400 (four months' salary) at a loss, Priyanthi bought herself a ticket to Sri Lanka. Despite the illegality of the substances involved, and the innocence of her actions, Priyanthi had no recourse in a situation that left her financially disadvantaged. Using her savings, she did manage, however, to leave Kuwait and return to Sri Lanka.

Common images of victimized housemaids depict them as women without the strong characters or past life experiences that might prepare them to handle events abroad. Yet Lakmini, a bigboned, slightly plump woman of about forty recently returned from the Middle East (introduced briefly in chapter 3), had a rich and varied employment history. With four children, an estranged husband, and only two years of formal education, Lakmini had held several jobs in Sri Lanka before going abroad: she had cleaned in a hospital, labored at a factory, and cleared cinnamon gardens. She saw migration as an opportunity to make more money than she could earn in Sri Lanka. Lakmini summed up her opinion of Arabic women, the majority of whom did not have jobs outside the home, by saying, "The Madam is always sleeping and I am always working." She did not mind working hard for pay but found infuriating the unpleasant, critical comments of women she perceived as idle and lazy. Despite high agency costs, Lakmini roved from job to job, quickly growing dissatisfied in household situations with too much work, too much danger, or too little pay.

A crisis precipitated Lakmini's return from the fourth household she worked in abroad. The Boss drank, and his wife had left him to go to her parents' house. The Boss's friends came over to party at his house in the evenings. Staying at the Boss's mother's house in his wife's absence, Lakmini came to clean in the mornings. During this time, a very valuable necklace disappeared, and the family accused Lakmini of taking it. Claiming that she had never even seen the item, Lakmini offered to go to the police station if the family wanted her to do so. Having searched her and her possessions and found nothing, the family accused Lakmini of passing the necklace off to an accomplice. Unable to prove her innocence, and uncomfortable in the hostile atmosphere, Lakmini wrote to her father, instructing him to send a telex requiring her to come home immediately. Leaving without six weeks' pay, Lakmini faced another indignity; as requested by her employers, the security guards at the airport searched every inch of her baggage and her person, finding nothing.[4] Despite financial loss and the invasion of her privacy, Lakmini successfully extricated herself from a very difficult situation.

Saved money, family networks, and strategic planning helped Priyanthi and Lakmini. Both women had worked abroad a number of times,

[4] My pen ran out of ink at this point; Lakmini gave me one of the fancy gold-colored pens she had brought from Saudi Arabia, saying that my notebook also would not be enough to write her whole story. When we finished the interview, she would not take the pen back.

and each told her story of difficulty in the context of a larger narrative of several successful contracts in the Middle East. Despite the unpleasant situations that Lakmini and Priyanthi faced, neither woman felt that the risks of going abroad outweighed the benefits of migration, and Lakmini even arranged to send her daughter abroad. Women balanced realistic assessments of their vulnerability abroad against their knowledge, skills, resources, and needs. Women's narrative self-presentation as active agents challenges the widely circulating image of migrants as passive victims.

Kanti: Escape from Kuwait

Images of guest workers stranded in the Middle East due to the Gulf War flooded the international media in August and September 1990. During that time period, seventy-five thousand Sri Lankans returned home, with a further twenty-five thousand displaced within the Middle East (Perera 1992). Although the Gulf War adversely affected many Sri Lankans, social networks, national solidarity, international aid, and ingenuity in the face of crisis brought most home safely. Thirteen women from the village, nearly 15 percent of the Naeaegama-area migrants, were working in Kuwait when Iraq invaded, and three more found themselves unable to return to good jobs.

When I raised the topic of the Gulf War, Kanti, a slender and energetic mother of three, retrieved her passport from the back room of her small house in Polwatta. Showing me various stamps and stickers on the document, she related the following story. The war started in the morning of 2 August and several days thereafter Kanti's employers gathered their possessions and joined a convoy of nine cars of friends and relatives fleeing to Saudi Arabia. The family brought Kanti (whom the youngest baby adored) and another servant along but left a third servant behind. Denied entry at the Saudi Arabian border, the whole convoy returned home.

When the three servants overheard their sponsors planning to leave them all behind on their next attempt to cross the border to Saudi Arabia, they decided to run away. At 3:00 A.M. on the night of 18 August, the three women packed their bags, climbed over the wall, and went to stay with some other housemaids, friends who had been left in their employers' house. Eventually twenty-eight Sri Lankans, including nineteen women and nine men, banded together. They lived for about ten days by collecting food and household items from abandoned houses in the neighborhood.

On 1 September an Iraqi broadcast on the television instructed guest workers to leave Kuwait. None of the Sri Lankans in the group knew how to drive, but they had access to a truck in the house garage. One of the men took five air conditioners gathered from neighboring houses and sold them to some Iraqi soldiers. With that money, the Sri Lankans paid a driver to take them to the border with Iraq. They spent the night at the border in a shelter they built from suitcases and covered with a canvas they found in the truck. They ate well from the nine bags of food that they had brought with them.

The next day, under the supervision of the Red Cross, in a truck provided by the Iraqi government, they left for Baghdad, taking the three hundred-mile journey in stages. In Baghdad they joined a huge crowd of people from many different countries. The same truck took the group to the Jordanian border, a journey of three hundred miles that took several days. The Iraqi army provided water, and with the gas cooker, food, and mattresses the Sri Lankan group had taken from Kuwait, they found the trip comfortable. The truck left them at the border between Jordan and Iraq, calf-deep in dust and sand. Kanti remembered that some people fainted from dehydration.

Kanti's passport contained an exit stamp from Iraq, dated 4 September 1990, and a visa from Jordan. From the Jordanian border the group was taken to a camp near Amman, where they stayed from 6 September to 15 September. The authorities collected everyone's passports, issuing claim numbers in exchange; Kanti pointed to a bright sticker on the front cover of her passport. The group also received a flight departure number to watch for on a bulletin board. Their informal leader, a man who had some money, had insisted that they all stay together. All twenty-eight group members crowded into three blue tents supposed to house only six people each. The group waited in line for food and had plenty of water for bathing and drinking. Some Americans came and took photographs. On the evening of 15 September their flight number appeared on the bulletin board. At the airport, the Red Cross returned their passports and issued boarding passes. They arrived in Colombo at 10:45 P.M. on 16 September and stayed near the airport that night.

Kanti returned to Naeaegama the following morning. She brought with her two suitcases of clothing and a small cassette player. She left without four months' pay. The United Nations promised to compensate all those whose employment was disrupted by the Gulf War, but they planned to draw the funds from the sale of Iraqi oil, which remained under UN sanctions. Negotiation over compensation dragged on for years, with the money only reaching the displaced workers in August 1997, seven years after the war began. Kanti pointed to the exit stamp from Iraq in her passport, saying that it alone proved to the authorities her right to compensation.

The dynamics of inclusion and exclusion in Kanti's story reveal deep-seated patterns of identity and affiliation. Under stress, Kanti's employers had to choose which of their housemaids to bring along with them in their flight to Saudi Arabia. Because of the baby's strong attachment to Kanti, they included her as a surrogate family member. Reunited and distrustful of their employers, Kanti and her companions escaped to the company of fellow Sri Lankans. Despite her employers' efforts to restrict her socializing and mobility, Kanti had built a small but useful network of informal relationships that provided vital shelter and companionship during the crisis.

Kanti's story of the ten days the group spent living off the fat of the land in Kuwait contains a strong element of antiauthoritarian jubilation and carnival (Limón 1989). Without the oppressive supervision of their sponsors, the Sri Lankans lived like lords, selling electrical appliances, eating foraged food, and helping themselves to air conditioners, mattresses, gas cookers, and trucks from abandoned houses. In their employers' absence, Kanti and her companions adopted a new and clearly pleasurable relationship to the houses in which they lived and the items that they used. Despite the obvious dangers and insecurity, the group creatively and successfully engineered their own exit from Kuwait, for an exhilarating but brief moment escaping the confines of their normal structural positions.

Although the international community reacted quickly, providing support and facilities for migrants caught in the midst of the Gulf War, economic upheaval extended for many years into the future, especially for guest workers. Kuwaiti citizens disrupted by Iraq's invasion received ample compensation very soon after the war, but Sri Lankans waited seven years to receive the promised payment. All the Naeaegama women caught in the Gulf War managed to return home safely, but they lost money, possessions, and jobs, and several faced financial difficulties in repaying outstanding loans.

Conclusion

Accepted cultural categories and meanings establish and legitimize hierarchies in the eyes of most members of society. Everyday human practices create social boundaries and embody them in individuals and institutions. Foucault writes, "Where there is power, there is resistance" (1978, 95). Since human actions shape behavioral patterns and habits of thought, actors disadvantaged by the system will struggle ceaselessly against those who create, maintain, and benefit from it. Raymond Williams captures the dynamic nature of hegemony when he states that "it has continually to be renewed, recreated, defended, and modified. It is also continually resisted, limited, altered, and challenged" (1977, 112).

James Scott examines situations of dominance and resistance in terms of public transcripts of authority, and hidden transcripts of subordinates, which voice radically different assumptions and perspectives (1990). Critics point out, however, that theorizing both self-conscious resistance and brainwashing hegemony creates a paradox. Resistance suggests that the oppressed preserve a space of mental clarity, where they recognize and analyze their oppression. Hegemony suggests that its worldview has convinced both the dominant and the subaltern of the justice of the prevailing social structures and economic conditions (Mitchell 1990; O'Hanlon 1988). The preceding cases reveal neither full-fledged resistance nor complete acquiescence to hegemony. Women simultaneously resist and accommodate the dominant discourse.

This chapter has explored the dynamics of agency and resistance in three historically contingent settings where migrant women and their employers reproduced, negotiated, and transformed structures of power and inequality. First, in everyday relationships between housemaids and employers, commonly accepted etiquette circumscribed migrants' behavior and shaped their identities as domestic servants, setting parameters for housemaids' workload, salary, clothing, religious practices, free time, social milieu, and mobility. Within the preexisting constraints, housemaids could and did improvise the details of their relationships with their employers. Personal ties, especially with their employers' children, and their work at the center of the domestic sphere often gave housemaids a great deal of informal power. At the same time, this intimacy also blunted a clear and self-conscious critique of the system. While the women I spoke with recognized and condemned certain aspects of the dominant ideology, they also unquestioningly accepted and even welcomed others.

Gifts and consumer items formed a second arena of negotiation and agency. The value of certain goods rested not only on their monetary worth but also on their symbolic importance. Consumer items indexed prestige and success in the village; wages paid workers for services; rendered in a contractual manner; and gifts acknowledged the importance of intangible personal characteristics such as loyalty, love, and diligence, and obligated the recipient to maintain a high caliber of social relations. In a work situation where all of a maid's labor already belonged to her employers, women sought through their attitudes and personal deportment to win gifts to supplement their meager salaries. Although often honored, this sort of informal understanding also proved fragile and unenforceable. Analysis of gifts from employers to housemaids (and of conspicuous consumption of prestige items in Naeaegama) reveals the complex strategies and intricate webs of cultural meaning that motivated actors' relations to material goods.

Stories women told about the troubles they encountered abroad offered a third arena for analyzing agency. In juxtaposition to images of migrant women as passive victims, women's narratives about difficult experiences overseas portrayed housemaids as active planners and strategic thinkers who drew on their available resources, such as saved money and networks of friends and family, to extricate themselves from trouble. Despite their low salaries and their isolation in their employers' houses, many migrants saved money, maintained close contact with their families, and made friends with other Sri Lankans working abroad. Inadequately supported by agencies, police, labor laws, and embassies, women occupied vulnerable positions in the global economy. Nevertheless, they showed character, knowledge, intelligence, and critical thinking, all characteristics lacking in the generic image of the migrant maid in trouble. Even as they faced difficulties and disadvantages abroad, they portrayed themselves as dynamic agents vigorously negotiating their futures in both everyday and extreme situations.

5 Control of Remittances: Prosperity and the Extended Family

When Domestic Workers Leave the Domestic Economy

In the 1960s cinnamon production and the coconut fiber industry employed most of the Naeaegama villagers, but since the early 1980s dramatic shifts in the local economy have occurred. Jobs in the armed forces, tourist industry, and local garment factories now employ significant numbers of local men and women, yet the migration to the Middle East overshadows all other forms of work. This change in economic orientation foreshadows transformations in village and national gender hierarchies, with a large range of local tensions and conflicts arising as women step into the role of wage earner. In this chapter I first examine the concept of "prosperity," the goal for many female migrants. Through case studies of married and unmarried migrants, I then explore how different families negotiate the control of remittances, and how these decisions create and reflect patterns of power and authority in the family.

In the early 1980s Sri Lankan social scientists speculated that salaried employment would bring women control over the money they earned, which would, at least in theory, heighten their standing in the family and community. R. B. M. Korale noted that the migration of labor provided women with a mobility "unimaginable a few years ago":

The economic necessities which fuel these migration flows will alter the social relationships within family units and in society as a whole. It is also expected that the desire for greater independence and participation in the social and economic process by women will be enhanced. The wealth acquired by females and the dependence of other household members on this income, will further buttress their social transformation resulting in greater social and economic rights being granted to females. (1983, 23)

Ten to fifteen years after this optimistic prophecy, new economic opportunities for women have transformed their social roles. This chapter examines both the ways in which women have gained authority and independence and the forces that have worked against dramatic upheavals in village gender hierarchies.

Bringing domestic work into the global economy has changed how women think of their work. Interviewed village women explicitly equated the job they did abroad "for the market" with their everyday activities in the home in Sri Lanka, recognizing the market value of their labor. At the same time, however, they recognized that work abroad gave them no other skills they could sell to enhance their earnings upon their return. Nor did domestic service challenge the gendered division of labor. Poorly paid and not well respected, jobs as domestic servants in Sri Lanka attracted only the most desperate returned migrants. In their study of Sri Lankan female migrants to Singapore and Hong Kong, Dias and Weerakoon-Gunawardene (1991) suggest that returnees stepped relatively easily back into their household roles of wives and mothers. During their work abroad, they do not adopt foreign customs or assume a different ethnic identity. Although they gained self-assurance, women did not go far in rejecting accepted customs, starting their own businesses, or taking on roles of community leadership. Dias and Weerakoon-Gunawardene claim that women take a passive approach to their return, fitting back into their households smoothly.

While Korale's optimistically predicted gender revolution has not yet come to full blossom, Dias's and Weerakoon-Gunawardene's pessimistic portrayal of passive women also oversimplifies changes in practices and ideologies in the village. Taking domestic work out of the domestic economy has sent a series of shock waves through village social hierarchies, giving migrant women leverage to bring about transformations in gender relations. This leverage stems not so much from changes in what work women *do* as from changes in what that work *means,* which is associated with shifts in women's employers, workplaces, and earnings. Despite the lack of major changes in their home environments, migrants have acquired a certain self-worth and dignity through their jobs which lend them assurance in their struggle for power. Through migration opportunities many poor women have ready access to gainful employment, while poor men have none. This situation threatens earlier patterns of male dominance in the village. Changes in women's social positioning have taken place not on a *tabula rasa* but in the context of preexisting gender hierarchies and cultural ideologies that devalue women's work to begin with. Women's new control over financial resources has not led directly to an increase in their authority and decision-making power. Instead, change has come about through slow and painful struggle.

The following sections focus on the contestation and renegotiation of gendered power structures. I examine three cases in which husband and wife struggled over the control of remittances and two cases in which unmarried migrants sent money to their parents. In these, like many, instances, the person who spent the money acquired as much or more power and authority than the person who earned it. Paradoxically, the "greater independence and participation in the social and economic process" that Korale predicted as a byproduct of migration appears as much or more in the individuals handling remittances as in the migrants themselves. The incrementally shifting habits and attitudes of ordinary people in their everyday world reveals the rupture and reinforcement of older village practices in flux.

"Prospering"

By the most frequently voiced village standards, the goal of migration is *diyunu venna* meaning to prosper, improve, or develop.[1] A num-

---

[1] A person, village, or country can *diyunu venna*, or acquire more wealth, knowledge, or assets. Saying *"minissu vaeDi diyunu venavaa"* means that people have become rich and prosperous, or *diyunu vecca minissu. diyunu raTaval* are developed countries. A rich or improved literature would be *diyunu sahitvayak*. One can improve in knowledge (*daeniima, vidyaava diyunu karanavaa / venavaa*) and learning (*igaenniima diyunu karanavaa / venavaa*). *karanavaa* [to do or make] is the active verb here, while *venavaa* [to happen or become] takes the passive role. Thus *diyunu karanavaa* implies an active agent while *diyunu venavaa* merely denotes that development has taken place. Denoting mental and meditative cultivation in religious writings, *diyunu* also refers to the development of institutions and communities. Although one can improve lands and gardens (*iDam, vatu diyunu karanavaa*), *diyunu* does not refer to development in the physical or biological sense—for instance, children reaching puberty, or trees and vegetation growing in a field. My thanks to Kusuma Karunaratne, W. S. Karunatillake, and Anne Blackburn for their private communications on the concept of *diyunu*. Any misinterpretations are strictly my own.

Fig. 3. A successful businesswoman, Polwatta. This entrepreneurial merchant spent
a number of years in the Middle East. With the help of her family, she set up a shop
in Polwatta upon her return. (Courtesy of the author.)

ber of situations qualify as prosperity, but housing provides the most
visible index of family accomplishment. Almost unanimously, women
and men say that migrants go abroad because they want to buy land
and build a house; acquiring such property counts as "prospering."

Over the thirty years between 1968 and 1997, the correlation between social status and housing quality in Naeaegama underwent a
shift. In 1968 only the wealthier (often high-caste) families in the village lived in cement or brick houses with tile roofs, whereas the poorer
families lived in clay houses with tin sheets, tar sheets, or coconut-
frond mats as roofing. House size and quality reflected social status
and wealth. After 1968, population pressure reduced the size of individual home gardens, though the wealthiest Halaagama villagers still
retained the largest land shares. Whereas a cement house once un-
equivocally indicated a wealthy Halaagama residence, in 1994 people
of all castes owned cement houses (often only half-finished) on relatively small plots of land. In 1968 the gradual rise and fall of family
fortunes roughly paralleled the grandeur of the house. In contrast, the

speed with which family affluence could change had greatly increased by 1994; some families went hungry in half-finished mansions while others stored color televisions under palm-frond roofs. Sporadic access to money through migration gave more people the means to improve their housing, thus making housing a less reliable marker of social status than it had been in the past.

Villagers often channeled remittances toward family consumption. While using "Middle East money" this way did not count as a waste in most villagers' opinions, neither did it count as prospering. Many families planned that after a woman went abroad, her parents or husband would continue to work, meeting most if not all of the immediate family needs. Unskilled men, however, found the jobs available for them in the village area labor intensive, unpleasant, poorly paid, and short-term. Under these conditions, many preferred not to seek out such opportunities actively, especially if their wives earned good salaries abroad. In cases where families depended on remittances for daily consumption, little or nothing remained of the migrant's wages but what she might have kept in a personal bank account or invested in jewelry.

The common trope (or figure of speech), "He sits idly, drinks, and wastes,"[2] expressed many women's frustration with idle husbands. Although they held repaying loans and sustaining a family without further debt as laudable objectives, working women often resented their spouses' indolence. Local, national, and international observers shared a critical attitude toward instances of voluntary male under- or unemployment, especially when the family "failed to prosper." (I explore men's perspectives on this issue further in chapter 7.)

Control of Remittances: Married Migrants

This section presents three case studies where married migrants remitted money to their spouses, and explores the power dynamics involved in decisions about who should use the money and how. While some of the events discussed are more dramatic than a random sampling of cases would provide, many of the issues over which these couples struggled also appeared in decisions faced by other village

---

[2] "*nikam innavaa, bonavaa, naasti karanavaa.*"

Fig. 4. A woman and her grandchildren, Polwatta. The woman on the right looks after her four grandchildren while their mother works abroad. With the money from her second trip to the Middle East, the mother started construction on the house in the background. (Courtesy of the author.)

families, and Naeaegama residents frequently referred to these cases as examples and illustrations when they spoke of migration.

Ranjani's House

A tall, thin woman with worry lines beyond her years, Ranjani lived with her grown son and daughter on the marshy back portion of her sister's small land plot. After eight years of work abroad, Ranjani lived in a house she described as "like a kennel where bitches have puppies,"[3] a tiny two-room clay hut with coconut-frond roofing. She said that some women would have drunk poison if what had happened to her had happened to them.

Receiving a piece of land in a government land distribution in 1980 (described in chap. 6), Ranjani and her husband Sarath started building a large house in 1986 with the money she sent home from working for two years in Saudi Arabia. Construction continued, funded by Ranjani's next job in Jordan. Tensions between the couple grew, however, over Sarath's alleged infidelity with a neighborhood woman and over how to spend Ranjani's remittances. Although Sarath asked that Ranjani not give any money to her parents, she sent them some secretly. Furious when he discovered her deception, Sarath fought with Ranjani's parents; her elderly father's leg broke in the brawl. In 1988, while Ranjani was still in Jordan, her husband sold their house and land for much less than its worth and bought a second house further from her parents' land. Upon her return from Jordan, Ranjani said her husband beat her to keep her from being too close to her family, but when he hit her, she ran to her parents. Sarath burnt Ranjani's identity card and her clothing, sold the second house at a loss, took the money, and left the village to live with his lover. Having allowed both the bank account and the land to be written in her husband's name, Ranjani and her family had no leverage to prevent the sales.[4]

After her husband sold their house and left, Ranjani returned to the Middle East. Working two years in Kuwait, she sent her money to her

[3] "*balu paeTav dannạ kuuDuvak vagee.*"
[4] In 1988 Sarath sold the first house, land, and Rs. 30,000/ worth of unused building materials (worth Rs. 61,500/ in 1994 rupees) for a mere Rs. 70,000/ (Rs. 143,500/ in 1994 rupees). He bought the new house for Rs. 47,000/ (Rs. 96,350/ in 1994 rupees). Sarath sold the second house for Rs. 30,000/ (Rs. 61,500/ in 1994 rupees) to a woman who had been working in the Middle East. Please see note 5 and appendix B for more information on monetary values and inflation.

mother, who paid off loans and took care of household expenses. When Ranjani returned to Sri Lanka in 1991, only a minimal sum of Rs. 6,000 / (Rs. 8,100/ in 1994 rupees) remained in the bank.[5] Ranjani worked another two years in Abu Dhabi, UAE, with a similar lack of lasting material benefit. In 1994 Ranjani got a job in Jordan, from which she vowed she would not return until she had saved enough money to buy some land and build a good house. In 1997 her brother-in-law reported that she had worked for three years abroad, bought a small plot of land in a village ten miles distant, and started to put up a house with the help of her grown son. She had remitted a total of Rs. 190,000/ (Rs. 137,500/ in 1994 rupees, or U.S.$2,750) with which her brother-in-law had paid the moneylenders and negotiated the land purchase.

After their separation, Ranjani met her husband once at a fair; she told me with pride that she hit him in the face with her umbrella. Denigrating Sarath with a common trope villagers use to define a wasteful husband, Ranjani said, "He just sat at home eating what I sent." This implication of idle consumption seems to misrepresent Sarath's actions. Ranjani's natal family, not her husband, were the ones who spent her earnings for daily consumption. Jealously defending his wife's remittances from other family members, Sarath successfully invested her money in a large cement house. Once their marriage fell apart, however, he sold the house and appropriated the profits of Ranjani's migration for himself. Despite urging from her family and friends, perhaps fearing that she did not have enough funds to win a legal case, Ranjani refused to go to the courts to claim her half of the money her husband made from selling their house and land.

A group of Kurundugoda women that gathered during one of my several interviews with Ranjani discussed strategies for retaining access to and control over money earned abroad. Many women said that they insisted on opening bank accounts and buying land in their own names, despite inconveniences to people at home. All said that they counseled future migrants to keep their money with them, only sending home occasional gifts for holidays. They recognized that remitted

---

[5] In this chapter monetary values are not uniformly standardized; instead, both nominal values (rupee values informants report paying) and real values (equivalents in 1994 rupees, adjusted for inflation) are given. This shows how dramatically inflation has affected the value of the rupee over the years. In 1994 Rs. 50/ = U.S.$1. To avoid encumbering the text, only U.S. dollar equivalents for particularly salient figures are noted. For more information on inflation, exchange rates, and consumer prices, see appendix B.

money often vanished before the migrant returned home. The group's agreement on ways to manage financial responsibilities indicated a growing awareness of power issues central to the control of remittances. Even these knowledgeable women, however, did not always follow their own advice and remitted money to family members. Thus, whether women prospered from their work abroad depended more on the people handling their remittances than on their own hard labor.

Success and Suicide: Kamala

Five years after Ranjani's dramatic domestic tragedy, a young village migrant named Kamala quarreled with her husband, Pradeep, over control of three-and-one-half years' worth of remittances. Infidelity, ties with the extended family, a house, and land figured in this case, as well.

When I first spoke with Kamala's mother, Caroline, in May 1993, Kamala had been in the UAE for nearly three years. Caroline, a plump and cheerful mother of ten grown children, looked after her daughter Kamala's two sons during the day, and their father Pradeep took them in the evenings. Kamala usually sent all of her money to her husband. Caroline and Pradeep had quarreled fiercely when Kamala sent some money directly to her mother. Resenting both his stinginess and his control over her daughter, Caroline said that although she looked after and fed his children, Pradeep only occasionally gave her money or food items. In January 1994, my research associate Sita and I talked with Caroline again; when we mentioned the Middle East, Caroline started to cry, saying that Kamala, who had returned from Dubai the previous October, had been very rude and unappreciative lately. Although Caroline had looked after her daughter's children for three years, Kamala had given her no money and no thanks. Even when Caroline was in the hospital, Kamala had not come to visit. Crying harder, Caroline pointed toward her daughter's house and said that mothers love daughters more than sons; the sons wander away, but the daughters should stay loving. Kamala's behavior hurt her badly. Several days after Sita and I talked with Caroline, Kamala attempted suicide by drinking a poisonous weed killer. Deep matters clearly distressed both mother and daughter.

Sita and I talked with Kamala about a month after her suicide attempt. In her narrative about life in UAE, Kamala painted herself as practical, self-reliant, thrifty, and strong. She looked after nine children, cleaned, cooked, fed the livestock, and did the laundry. Kamala related how she handled several crises arising during her stay in the Middle East, portraying herself as decisive and assertive. Stressing the importance of self-confidence, Kamala claimed that each time that she stood up for her rights abroad, her situation improved. In contrast, Kamala's life in Sri Lanka seemed beyond her own control. Saying that she went abroad "to improve the family," she mentioned a desire to buy the house her family had rented for six years or to buy land and build another. When Kamala returned to Naeaegama, her husband had not only failed to buy land, but he also denied her access to the money she had earned. He specifically forbade her to give money or presents to her natal kin, a slight they took very personally. Rumor suggested that Pradeep had lent much of Kamala's money to a Berava caste neighbor woman, and some villagers hinted at Pradeep's sexual liaisons with this and another woman. When Kamala suggested that she should return to the Middle East, Pradeep refused. Eyes downcast, Kamala said, "He won't let me go anywhere." Pradeep not only controlled Kamala's past wages, damaged her relationship with her parents, and cheated on her, but he also forbade her to return to her job abroad.

In Sri Lanka, threats of suicide are common and attempts frequent; globally, Sri Lanka ranks second only to Hungary for suicides per unit of population (Marecek 1998), with both men and women attempting and committing suicide in roughly equal numbers. Writing of suicide as an aggressive act aimed at expressing frustration and at causing mental pain, Jonathan Spencer notes its prevalence in relationships where "the overt expression of anger is quite simply unthinkable" (1990, 186). In Sri Lanka, wives and children cannot freely express anger or frustration against husbands and parents. Seen in relation to her self-portrayal as decisive, independent, and courageous abroad, Kamala's suicide attempt represents not only the psychological despair of alienated labor but also the forceful expression of extreme dissatisfaction. Bringing her grievances dramatically into the public eye, Kamala's action seriously challenged Pradeep's authority over her money, social relations, and travel plans. The extreme nature of her protest suggested the ineffectiveness of less drastic measures in her struggle for a modicum of independence. Gender relations entrenched in the household still remained extremely powerful; despite Kamala's self-destructive initiative, she never obtained clear control of her money during my stay in the village.

Piecing together information collected in 1994, I began to understand what Pradeep had done with Kamala's money. Although local gossip implied that he had wasted much of what she remitted, a closer look revealed considerable thrift and business acumen. Caroline and Kamala independently confirmed that one year of Kamala's salary went to pay back the loan taken to finance her job. Caroline noted that Pradeep had purchased a small cinnamon garden for about Rs. 25,000/ (Rs. 30,300/ in 1994 rupees). With two months' salary Kamala purchased a sophisticated cassette player which she sent to Pradeep in Sri Lanka. Perhaps the greatest source of tension was Pradeep's loan: Pradeep (Halaagama) had lent Rs. 65,000/ (Rs. 78,650/ in 1994 rupees) to a neighbor woman of the Berava caste, who promised to pay it back but in early 1994 showed no signs of doing so. While indiscriminate gifts of money hardly counted as a wise investment, lending money for interest or acquiring property in lieu of unpaid loans could benefit the family in the long run. In 1994, village opinions about whether Kamala's and Pradeep's family had improved through migration varied, though many people felt that it had not.

When I returned to Naeaegama in 1997, Kamala again held a job abroad. My research associates Siri and Sita and I spent a long morning speaking with Pradeep. In the three years since 1994, the family's financial situation had greatly improved. Pradeep told us his version of his Berava neighbor's debt. In 1992, with his sister's approval, he lent his neighbor Rs. 25,000/ (Rs. 30,300/ in 1994 rupees), less than half the amount I was told in 1994, taking a copy of her father's land deed as collateral. She promised to pay back double the principal within two years. Unbeknownst to him, she had pawned the original deed to another person; feeling neighborly, Pradeep had not paid close attention to legalities. When Kamala returned to the village in 1994, she challenged Pradeep to show her what he had done with her money. Pradeep asked their neighbor repeatedly to give him the Rs. 50,000/ (U.S.$1,000) she owed. The neighbor said, "Tomorrow, tomorrow," until Pradeep knew that he "had to do something strict." After a heated conversation, the neighbor asked Pradeep to give her another year on the loan, and she would pay him Rs. 100,000/. He asked the neighbor to come to the house of a lawyer at the junction, and they would write an official contract including a lien on the property. The lawyer refused to draw up the document without the original deed. Pradeep threatened his neighbor with a knife, and she went home in tears. Her elderly and well-respected father then came to Pradeep's house. He said that the whole transaction had taken place without his knowledge, but he promised to take care of the problem. The family took a loan to pay their other creditor and then made a contract to pay Pradeep Rs. 75,000/ (U.S.$1,500) within two years, or Pradeep would own the property. Several days before the end of their grace period in 1996, they borrowed Rs. 100,000/ (Rs. 80,100/ in 1994 rupees) from a village moneylender (probably promising to repay twice that sum) and paid Pradeep Rs. 75,000/ (Rs. 60,000/ in 1994 rupees). If Pradeep's statement about the initial value of the loan was correct, then his investment had roughly doubled.

Pradeep said that he had used the money retrieved from the neighbor, and money from Kamala's salary, to buy the house and land that they had rented for the previous nine years. He spent Rs. 125,000/ (Rs. 91,250/ in 1994 rupees). Now he said that he felt happy and freed from worry. He was thinking about building a better house, worth Rs. 400,000/ (Rs. 292,000/ in 1994 rupees) on the property. If his wife worked abroad for four or five more years, they could do it. He also hoped to open a fish shop in the front of the house so the family would have a business that Kamala could run when she returned. His detailed discussion of bureaucratic licensing paperwork convinced Siri, Sita, and me of his seriousness. With land, a house, and a business, Pradeep's family would certainly count as prosperous.

Sita, Siri, and I asked Pradeep about his fight with his in-laws. Pradeep felt that his wife's family, by asking money from him and his wife, kept trying to "pull him down" when he was trying "to raise his head." He claimed that during Kamala's first stint abroad, her family took things from his house in his absence, including a gold necklace. When his mother-in-law took care of the children, she kept asking for Rs. 300/ and Rs. 500/ for this and that. He felt that he had already provided adequately for the children's care and found the requests exorbitant. (His description of the sorts and amounts of goods he gave his mother-in-law varied substantially from her account.) Unbeknownst to him, his mother-in-law asked for Rs. 7,000/ from Kamala, which Kamala sent. When he found out, Pradeep quarreled with his mother-in-law, telling her that since he and Kamala had registered their marriage before two witnesses, he had the *ayitaya* [ownership] of Kamala, and they had no business asking money from her in secret. (During our post-interview discussion, Siri and Sita, sensing my outrage, assured me that "ownership" went both ways, and that the wife also "owned" the husband.) Pradeep felt that both his wife and his in-laws should have asked him openly. In a letter to his wife, he criticized her for sending money to her mother. Sita and Siri later said they had the impression Pradeep felt his mother-in-law was asking for something extra, some payment in exchange for looking after her grandchildren, which he felt violated proper parental etiquette.[6]

Not only had his in-laws asked for too much money, Pradeep also said that they sent letters to his wife, telling her false stories about his behavior in her absence, and asking her to divorce him and go live with them. Replying to her questions by letter, he wrote that if she wanted to divorce him, she should feel free, but if she did, he would commit suicide and kill their two children as well. He related with drama her return to the village in 1993 after "three years, three months, and two days" abroad, saying that he demanded—before she brought her baggage into the house—that she choose either her parents or himself. He portrayed Kamala as saying that her parents were "wrong," that she had been wrong to send them money, and that she had never doubted him. She came into the house to live with him.

Pradeep said that Kamala stayed in the village for three years, and everything was fine. "Oh, well, not quite," he qualified; after six months at home, Kamala drank poison. Pradeep then told his version of his wife's suicide attempt. He claimed that contrary to village rumor, Kamala had not drunk poison because of a love affair he had had with another woman. His in-laws had helped spread the false rumor that nearly killed his wife. Instead, she had drunk poison because of a fight he had had with his father-in-law about an old bicycle frame. (Siri and Sita later found this a very weak point in Pradeep's account. "Why would a grown woman commit suicide over a bicycle?" Sita asked. "Maybe a man might," Siri thought, but never a woman.) At Kamala's bedside in the hospital, Pradeep asked her why she had drunk the poison. She said it was "the anger of the moment." Pradeep told her that if she wanted to commit suicide, he would bring her a good poison, and she could "finish the job." Then he would go "see to her father and brothers" [hurt or kill them]. Pradeep reported that Kamala said, "I was foolish and I am sorry." After Kamala's suicide attempt, he found it difficult to live in the village because everyone believed the story about the love affair, and everyone stopped him in the street to ask about it.

During Kamala's three years at home, they had another son. Two weeks before she delivered, Kamala fought with her parents. Pradeep portrayed Kamala as accusing her parents of "eating" Pradeep (taking all his surplus, and more) while she was out of the country and con-

---

[6] For Caroline's side of this story, see chapter 8.

tinuing to try to do so at that time as well; he depicted her as siding with him against her natal family. Since that time, Pradeep said that he had had no contact with his in-laws and had forbidden his children from visiting their maternal grandparents. Kamala and Pradeep worked closely with Pradeep's parents instead.

Pradeep said that he had originally forbidden Kamala to go abroad again because she had broken their first agreement (that she would work abroad for five years straight) when she came home because of her parents' letters. Financial pressures forced him to reconsider, and since Kamala got a job in the same house where Pradeep's younger sister worked, he had no objections to her going abroad. At the time of our interview she had been abroad for nine months and five days; Pradeep kept count. He sent letters weekly, including notes from the children and his own advice to her on how to conduct herself in her job. He assured us that although Kamala had studied for more years than he had, he surpassed her in writing and math. In control of his wife's remittances, rid of her clinging relatives, and convinced (at least in his narrative) of his intellectual and moral superiority, Pradeep said that he had exclusive control of his family; life was "90 percent okay" and he was happy.

Using purely material criteria, Pradeep's successful venture in moneylending and his purchase of land and a house qualified his family as one that improved through migration. Pradeep continued to work in the village while his wife worked abroad. He seldom turned to drink, and his demeanor in no way suggested that his masculinity suffered from his wife's migration. Instead, Pradeep's control over Kamala's remittances bolstered his social standing in the village. Kamala's estrangement from her natal family and her suicide attempt, however, revealed tensions over the use and distribution of the money Kamala remitted. Although their nuclear family ranked as prosperous and stood to improve further in the future, the internal struggle for control over Kamala's money nearly tore her body and her family apart.

Kamala's situation echoed that of Ranjani, the woman in this chapter's first case study. Both women's husbands saved their salaries carefully and invested in property. Both sought to limit contact between their wives and their natal families, feeling that too much money seeped away in the interactions. Both women resisted their husbands' restrictions vigorously. Both husbands engaged in alleged extramarital affairs in their wives' absence. Separated from her husband, Ranjani returned to her natal family; separated from *her* natal family, Kamala associated exclusively with her husband's relatives. In her separation, Ranjani lost heavily; by remaining with her husband, Kamala maintained her access to the land and property her earnings had purchased, but at a steep price. Well-educated, young, independent, and spirited, Kamala still faced nearly insurmountable resistance to her efforts to control her own money. Kamala's suicide attempt, though very effective in making public her displeasure with Pradeep, did not seem to change the situation she had found intolerable. Indeed, Pradeep's narrative showed his controlling and domineering nature clearly. Perhaps the rising expectations of young village women led them to chafe more at the gendered restrictions imposed by their families. Kamala's case, in particular, gives one pause to consider whether the changes in the village have necessarily benefited the women.

Accountability in the Other Direction: Simon and Chandrika

Having presented two cases in which female migrants struggled with their spouses over control of the money they remitted, I now turn to a case in which a male migrant sent his earnings home to his wife. During her husband Simon's absence, Chandrika controlled both her own salary and the money he sent her every month. Upon his return, Simon held Chandrika accountable for her use of his money in a way that neither Ranjani nor Kamala could hold their husbands.

One of only six village men to work in the Middle East, Simon spent eight years as an exterminator in Saudi Arabia. Simon remitted much of his considerable salary of Rs. 11,000/ a month to his wife Chandrika. Among the best educated in the village, Simon had completed his A-levels (the Sri Lankan equivalent of high school) while his wife Chandrika held a bachelor's degree from a private university in Colombo. Leaving their young son with Simon's sister during the weekdays, Chandrika commuted to work at an import-export firm in Colombo, supervising the construction of their new house in her free time.

With Simon living abroad, Chandrika held considerable power and authority in the village. Able to trace her line of descent back to the Halaagama woman who had founded Naeaegama nine generations earlier, Chandrika inherited land in the oldest and wealthiest village neighborhood, near the temple. Simon's family, also Halaagama, held land in the area as well.[7] Chandrika gave generously and often to reli-

---

[7] The land holdings of Simon's father, Podi Appuhami, are discussed at length in chapter 6.

gious and secular festivals. Upon his return from Saudi Arabia, Simon stepped into a leadership role befitting one of his caste and wealth; until then, Chandrika, acting as his proxy, not only headed her own household but also influenced village decisions in his stead. Chandrika lost much of her authority when her husband returned.

Sita and I spent a leisurely afternoon in April 1993 talking with Chandrika as she supervised bricklaying at her new house.[8] Started in 1991, the large structure occupied land given to Chandrika by her mother. Various items of furniture and household appliances such as a refrigerator, a television set, and a pump for filling an overhead tank to supply running water were stored with Simon's family. Chandrika thought that when fully constructed, her house would be worth about Rs. 300,000/ (U.S.$6,000), not including furniture.

Ebullient over plans to purchase a bus with his savings, Simon returned from Saudi Arabia in July 1993. Disappointed with the slow progress on the house, he began to question his wife concerning her use of the money he had remitted. Things came to a head between Simon and Chandrika in October 1993, with a loud and violent fight. Sita, who lived across the road and heard the argument, told me some of the details. Saying that he had remitted Rs. 250,000/ (U.S.$5,000) to Sri Lanka since he started working in the Middle East, Simon demanded to know what Chandrika had done with the money, and why she had failed to finish their house. He also wanted to know what had become of three gold chains and a pair of gold ear studs, altogether worth another Rs. 50,000/. Chandrika's response, that Simon should not ask about "past things," prompted his reply, "Without asking about past things, I have nothing to say in the present. Now, what have you done with the money and the jewelry?" Simon showed his sister his accounts, lamenting that he could find no trace of the money he had sent home and that his wife not only refused to talk about the money but also refused to cook his meals. Sita said Simon then "got damned wild with Chandrika," and hit her. Crying and screaming, Chandrika shouted that she did not want him as a husband anymore and threatened to jump into the well. Simon's sister restrained her from this suicide attempt.

Drawn by the noise, several neighbors gathered in the road. Approaching the arguing couple, Sita told Simon and Chandrika that it

---

[8] In Sri Lanka, custom dictates that a family member must supervise all hired workers to ensure diligence and prevent theft.

was not educated to shout at each other in public. Chandrika said Simon had struck her. Sita replied that all husbands were like that and recommended that Chandrika tell Simon what she had done with the money. Chandrika again attempted to run away, saying that she would kill herself. Stopped by her sister-in-law, she amended her statement, saying she would first kill Simon and then kill herself. Sita stooped to comfort Chandrika's wailing six-year-old son.

Later I asked Sita what she thought had become of the money. Chandrika, who continued with her own job when Simon went abroad, had told Sita that she saved all the money Simon remitted in a bank account, using her own salary to maintain her family. In retrospect, Sita suspected that Chandrika had been lying. Chandrika had lent a great deal of money to various people, many of whom had not paid her back. In particular, Sita thought Chandrika had covered a debt of about Rs. 50,000/ for a sister, lending even more to a jobless brother.

Chandrika's decision to give her brother some of her husband's money reflected deeply held patterns of family and caste association. In a close-knit kin community, relatives claimed mutual access to assets, and family obligations operated to level out differences in material and economic well-being. Those who accumulated significant assets without redistributing their wealth to poorer relatives made choices about which of their kin ties to sustain on their way up the ladder and which to abandon. Sustaining and severing kin ties had a direct impact on caste and sub-caste relations. The highest grade in the Halaagama caste retained only those who maintained social standing and wealth; poorer relatives and families who lost respectability through "incorrect" marriages dropped to a lower grade or out of the caste altogether. All villagers strove to maintain "far" kin links with rich and respectable relatives while distancing themselves from associations with poorer but "closer" relations. Chandrika's brother amassed considerable debts to a Para caste moneylender. The moneylender offered to forgive the debts if Chandrika's brother married the moneylender's sister. Despite Chandrika's gifts of money, her brother accepted the arranged marriage, thus threatening his own caste status, tainting his family's, and irrevocably demoting his children's. Chandrika's devotion to family and caste accounted for at least some of her husband's missing money.[9]

---

[9] For more on the topic of caste grades, see G. Gamburd (1972, 308ff.). Also see chapter 6 for a more extensive discussion of kinship and caste relations in the Naeaegama area.

In Sita's opinion, Chandrika stood answerable for her use of Simon's money. Although just, such accountability has rarely been applied equally to men and women; in the numerous case studies with which I am familiar, I never found an instance of a husband beaten by his returnee wife when she found that he had wasted her money. By contrast, Sita (and many other village women) found Simon's violent assault well within the range of acceptable masculine behavior; local gender roles legitimated his physical aggression. As Chandrika's and Kamala's stories illustrate, both the accused and the accusing women threatened or attempted suicide to express their emotional displeasure and distress. Kamala swallowed poison in her frustration and rage; panicked and guilty, Chandrika threatened to jump in the well. In both cases, village cultural habits channeled women's violent emotions inward against their own bodies, instead of outward against their husbands (see Waters 1999).

In a society dependent on the extended kinship system, numerous people have claims on the money that migrants earn. Although many couples have allocated the fruits of labor abroad without dramatic, public disputes, the issues over which Ranjani, Kamala, and Chandrika fought with their husbands have prevailed in many households. In their cases, the men sought to consolidate remittances by investing in a house. The violence Sarath and Pradeep deployed to try to separate their wives from their families, and Simon's rage over Chandrika's gifts to her siblings, could be read in two ways: first, as characteristic of abusive and controlling husbands, and second, as a result of wariness of becoming too firmly enmeshed in a large and impoverished extended family, on either the wife's or the husband's side. In all three cases tensions between nuclear family and extended family ran high, precisely because people valued remittances so greatly.

Control of Remittances: Unmarried Migrants

"Not even five cents' worth": Premasiri's Daughters

Similar tensions over accountability, cooperation, and access to money have affected the families of unmarried migrants. Claiming that parents often wasted less money than husbands, Byron, the local subagent introduced in chapter 2, thought that unmarried women often fared better than married ones when they migrated. Considered by many villagers as a family much improved through migration to the

Middle East, three of Premasiri's five daughters had worked abroad, with two leaving before they married and all three remitting their money to their parents.

Siri and I found Premasiri sitting in the dappled morning shade on the cement border that surrounded his spacious five-room tile-roofed house in Gurupitiya, peeling cinnamon for a local landholder. He and his eighteen-year-old youngest son, who scraped the hard green outer layer off the sticks before his father stripped them of their rich, red, inner bark, welcomed our interview wholeheartedly as a chance to chat while working. A tall, lean, graying man in his fifties, Premasiri said that he took good care of the money his daughters sent from the Middle East, declaring, "I didn't waste even five cents' worth."[10]

Premasiri's family (Halaagama) bought their land from a Berava family in the early 1960s. Until 1988 they lived in a small house, which they later enlarged and improved. In 1988 they paid to bring an electricity line down the road to their house, a luxury few except the wealthiest in Naeaegama could afford. In 1992 they added several rooms and replaced the roof, and in 1993 they constructed a carpentry workshop at the back of the property for their son-in-law.

One of the first in the village to go to the Middle East, Lalita, Premasiri's third child, spent nearly six years abroad. Paying an agency only Rs. 675/ (Rs. 4,500/ in 1994 rupees) in 1978 for a job in the UAE, she earned Rs. 3,200/ (Rs. 21,500/ in 1994 rupees [U.S.$430]) a month for the three and a half years she worked abroad. In 1981 she went abroad again and spent two years in Jordan, receiving a free ticket from a sister also working abroad. There she made Rs. 3,000/ (Rs. 12,000/ in 1994 rupees [U.S.$245]) per month. Altogether she earned about U.S.$24,000. With the money Lalita remitted to a bank account in her mother's name, her family bought two acres of cinnamon land. Well tended, the land lucratively supported a family. By peeling their own cinnamon, Premasiri and his son earned even more per acre than other landed proprietors, who had to share their profits with their peelers. Premasiri's cinnamon estate adjoined and rivaled those of several wealthy Halaagama landlords.

Anticipating Lalita's return, Premasiri and his wife arranged a marriage for her. They chose a hardworking young man who had done some carpentry for the family. The boy's mother was from the Para caste, his father Halaagama. The Para shadow on his social standing

---

[10] "*sata pahakvat naesti kalee naeae.*"

matched the loss of respectability associated with Lalita's long absence from parental supervision. At the same time, his industry and work ethic recommended him, just as the dowry Lalita's parents offered recommended her. Despite their daughter's wealth, Premasiri and his wife chose a hardworking son-in-law of mixed caste, rather than making a higher-status match. Their choice indicated that they valued employment and future financial security over caste status.

For her wedding in 1983, Lalita received Rs. 40,000/ (Rs. 130,000 in 1994 rupees) in cash and Rs. 20,000/ (Rs. 65,000/ in 1994 rupees) worth of jewelry and furniture as a dowry from her parents. Premasiri reminisced about the wedding ceremony, which went on for five days and cost nearly Rs. 75,000/ (Rs. 241,500/ in 1994 rupees). Both the size of the dowry and the magnificence of the ceremony and following celebrations enhanced the status of the new couple and their families. I did not ask about ownership of the two acres of cinnamon bought with Lalita's wages from her first job abroad, but I assume that Premasiri held it in his name. Whatever the arrangement, it seemed to please all parties, judging from the high degree of cooperation in the family. Money and goods seemed to flow in abundance among family members, without an exact tally of worth and debt. Premasiri kept close tabs on his daughters' money, however. When another of Premasiri's sons-in-law (also from an arranged marriage) took to wasting money and selling liquor while his wife was abroad, Premasiri said that he and his sons "chased off that useless dog," supporting and protecting the divorcée in a village that stigmatized such women. Premasiri's investments ensured enough wealth for all those in his extended circle, also making him a patron to some of his poorer relatives.

Mahinda's Elopement

Whereas women with good relationships with their families have often profited by allowing their parents to arrange a marriage for them, women who chafed against their parents' authority have found freedom through choosing their own mates. Unmarried migrants at odds with their parents or not receptive to arranged marriages have either eloped with men of their own choice or renounced matrimony entirely. Their financial independence has given them more authority in making such decisions.

In mid-January 1993 Mahinda, the eldest son of a poor Halaagama family in Naeaegama, sneaked off in secret with a neighbor's niece.

Her father (hoping for a better match for his daughter, who had just re-turned from the Middle East) chased the couple, trying to catch them before they had "lived as husband and wife" and to separate them by force. Having hoped to arrange a marriage for Mahinda, his family also disapproved of the love match.

Several days after the elopement, Siri met Mahinda at the junction. Offering him a cigarette and calling him a bridegroom, Siri asked what business brought Mahinda to the market street that evening. Sitting on his bicycle and checking frequently over his shoulder, Mahinda replied that he had sent a message to his mother and feared that his father might intercept it and come in her stead. Legally married, the new hus-band and wife had accepted an invitation to dinner at Mahinda's father-in-law's house. To keep their self-respect, they felt they needed to ar-rive at the house by car, but after a small wedding party and registration fees, they had exhausted all of their money. To hire a car, Mahinda had asked his mother for money in secret. Later that evening Siri saw mother and son talking, and money changed hands. Siri noted that Mahinda had no steady job and that neither bride nor groom owned property. Observing the couple's youth, Siri predicted a dearth of long-term planning and asked, "What do they know about the world?"

When I interviewed Mahinda a month later, his wife had found an-other job abroad. Borrowing Rs. 13,000/ to pay the job agent, she left to work for two years as a housemaid in Kuwait. Mahinda claimed that his wife's parents had used all of the money she earned abroad, wast-ing much of it. "She had nothing left when I got her," he said, except for Rs. 3,000/ that they spent on the wedding. Before they married, she had told Mahinda she planned to go back to the Middle East. Mahinda's bride found herself in the unenviable position of starting afresh, tak-ing loans to finance her third job abroad rather than using savings to pay the agency.

During the year following her departure, Mahinda lived with his par-ents. He held no steady job but spent his time with another young mi-grant's husband, telling jokes and smoking cigarettes at the junction. Neither man's wife sent money during that time, though both hus-bands accrued considerable debts that they promised their wives would repay. Mahinda's wife escaped what she must have seen as the trap of her parents' control by marrying, thus ensuring that she could manage her own finances. At the same time, future relations with her husband, especially those pertaining to administering her money, re-mained open to negotiation.

While Mahinda's wife chafed at parental control, Premasiri's daughters did very well by letting their father control their remittances. Mahinda's wife married a penniless, jobless young man without her parents' permission, with only Rs. 3,000/ in hand. In contrast, Premasiri and his wife arranged good marriages and hefty dowries for their daughters, trying to ensure that their husbands had good jobs and stable characters. While Mahinda's wife had no assets to her name when she went abroad for her third job, Premasiri's daughters had all acquired houses and land. In the case of one of Premasiri's daughters, where an arranged marriage failed, her father continued to look after his daughter's finances, children, and house. By marrying for love, Mahinda's wife renounced her claims to all such help from both her parents and his; parents felt less responsibility toward couples who eloped than toward those whose marriages they arranged. In these cases as in others, prosperity depended not only on the industry of the migrant but also on the wise investments of the people at home receiving and managing the migrant's remittances. Whereas a family working in harmony could perform miracles with the incoming money, migrants from families at odds with each other found it difficult to control their money and improve.

Other Motives and Meanings for Migration

Although most Naeaegama women said that financial necessity impelled their migration, other more troubling and less socially acceptable motivations often emerged under the surface. Speaking of Filipina migrants who worked as domestic servants in Hong Kong, Nicole Constable (1999) argues that economic explanations of migration sometimes supersede other motivations (such as wishing to escape bad marriages, or enjoying life abroad) in women's stories. Naeaegana women often said that they went abroad because they wanted to help their families, but sometimes they also went abroad to get *away* from their families, particularly in the case of physical abuse or unfaithful husbands. Constable notes that if migrant women admitted that they enjoyed their work abroad, then their "exile" would lose its selflessness, and their loyalty to home would come into question. Sometimes women enjoyed their time in Hong Kong, especially the independence and the new sense of self they gained. After spending long periods of time abroad, some no longer felt entirely at home in the Philippines.

Similarly, although many Naeaegama migrants worked abroad purely for the money, others left the village because of the "push" of their social situations at home or the "pull" of new destinations. The following two cases demonstrate alternative motivations for migration above and beyond the wish to improve.

Dreaming of Travel: Shriyani

Of all the village women with whom I spoke, Shriyani was the only one to say that she had gone abroad primarily in order to see new places, meet new people, and learn new languages. Ever since she was fifteen, it had been her dream to travel. An unmarried middle daughter in a family of seven children, Shriyani worked as a housemaid in Pakistan for four years. She then went to Jordan, where she worked for a year and a half. In February 1993 she left Jordan to go to Vienna, Austria, to work first as a housemaid and later as an assistant in a nursing home. I met her in April 1994 when she visited Gurupitiya for the Sinhala New Year holiday. In 1996 she married a man from Austria, and in 1997 she brought her husband and their new baby to see her family in Sri Lanka.

Shriyani came the closest of any village woman with whom I talked to voicing what might be called explicitly feminist ideas. During our midmorning interview at her parents' house, Shriyani dressed in white cotton pajamas and a bathrobe and spoke in German-accented English. Describing herself as "a lot like a man," Shriyani said that she did the adventurous, away-from-home things that men often did, that she cut her hair short, and that she preferred to wear trousers. Because people in Sri Lanka "had different ideas," she tried to tell them what life in Austria was like. For instance, her mother often told Shriyani not to walk alone in the village. Shriyani said that even before she went abroad she thought such rules were "nonsense," and she often fought with her parents about them. Elaborating on her "masculine" skills, Shriyani mentioned that in high school she captained the debate team and that as a child, she used to ride a bicycle (an activity reserved largely for men). I asked if she could swim, and she replied, "Yeah, sure." Most village women (and even some men) could not. "That's why people hate me," she said. In Austria, despite hard work and racism, she found a freedom and acceptance unattainable in the village.

Before her marriage, Shriyani remitted most of her surplus salary to her parents in the village, who had clearly prospered through her work abroad. She portrayed herself as a loving and selfless daughter. Nevertheless, she had no intention of returning permanently to the village. Looking over her shoulder and remarking that it was good her parents spoke no English, Shriyani told us that she had overheard her parents planning to arrange a marriage for her. They were anxious because she was nearly twenty-eight years old. Shriyani felt that she could not consider marrying a Sri Lankan man. Her experiences in Vienna made her sure that she would prefer to live there than in the land of her birth. Despite her love for her family, the values of female independence that attracted Shriyani to Europe in the first place left her few viable options in the village.

Burnt and Beaten: Winitha's Escape

Hunger, grinding poverty, and domestic violence have motivated a number of village women to seek employment in the Middle East. In some cases where unions disintegrated, migrant women have found the end of their marriages a relief, not a tragedy. Despite the difficulties of living alone, they have preferred their new independence. Official pronouncements and national news items that lament the adverse effect of migration on matrimony rarely take into account the premigration quality of many of the failed relationships in question.

One day in late December 1992, when Siri, his wife Telsie, and I were walking along a back road near Siri's cinnamon garden, a woman with a small child in her arms approached us tentatively and asked Siri if he would read and translate the English on a postcard she had just received from a Colombo job agency. The card informed Winitha that she had been selected as a housemaid and that she should come to the agency immediately. Winitha had four children, the youngest just over a year old. She had been in Kuwait when the Gulf War broke out, and although she had managed to pay off her loan, she returned with absolutely nothing else, "not even a dress or a biscuit for my children." As she told us this story, she started to cry.

On our walk home, Siri told me that Winitha's husband, Sunil, could peel cinnamon very efficiently but instead worked with the local illicit liquor producer and spent a great deal on alcohol while his children went hungry.[11] Siri and Telsie speculated on two motivations for Winitha's migration: to alleviate the family's poverty, and to escape a

---

[11] For more on alcohol production and masculinity, see chapter 7.

husband who drank and beat her. Telsie, who taught Winitha's eldest daughter at the local school, claimed to have seen burn marks on Winitha's arms where her husband had hit her with the firewood from the cooking hearth. Siri said that some nights the children stayed at the house next door for fear of their father, and Winitha stayed with her sister in a nearby village. With no money for herself, no food for her children, and problems from her husband, migration to the Middle East represented Winitha's best option.

Several days after meeting her on the road, Siri and I went to Winitha's house to interview her about her upcoming job as a housemaid in UAE. One of the numerous little girls in the area ran to tell her that we were there, and she came quickly from bathing, wearing a wet sarong. Siri and I took shelter from a light rain under the narrow porch of the house next door. After changing, Winitha joined us there, wearing a dress with a large rip in the shoulder. Several times during the interview she made some polite but urgent gestures for us to please speak softly or change the subject; she worried that Sunil, drunk on the bed in the front room of their hut, could overhear our conversation.

Winitha planned to stay abroad for three or four years, hoping to pay back her loan and then earn enough money to build a new house. She said that the packed-earth floor of her damp clay house got muddy when the land flooded during the monsoon season. Keeping most of her wages in the bank, Winitha expected to send some money to her husband's mother, who would look after her four children while Winitha worked abroad. Asked what her husband Sunil thought of her new job, Winitha replied quietly that, although he anticipated money with pleasure, two days earlier he had gotten very drunk and broken all the clay cooking pots in the house.

Women migrated to the Middle East with a variety of different motivations. In Winitha's case, the need to leave merged with the goal of earning money for land and a house. In the Middle East, women were sometimes confronted with grueling labor, beatings, burns, even rape. But many found work abroad safer than life in the village, where they might face similar or worse treatment. Paradoxically, the Middle East provided them a refuge from the home. Although some felt Winitha had abandoned her children to a fearful and hungry existence, she had succeeded in saving herself temporarily from the same. In 1997 Winitha's family lived in one tiny room of a partially completed cement house, while she again worked abroad. Regardless of whether the money she remitted eventually completed the house as she hoped, Winitha had successfully accomplished several of her main objectives merely by leaving the country. Unable to reform her husband, she nevertheless curtailed his power over her by leaving, and by sending back money that she hoped would, at least in part, benefit her children.

Remittances and Social Change

R. B. M. Korale and Malsiri Dias, two Sri Lankan social scientists whose views are summarized at the beginning of the chapter, suggested respectively that wage-earning from migration would revolutionize women's social standing, on the one hand, and that returned migrants passively reassumed their roles as housewives on the other. Gender roles that emerged from the flux of individual lives in Naeaegama revealed a reality somewhere between these two extremes. Women constantly negotiated their relationships with their parents, their husbands, and their extended families, with no guarantees that change would be for the better. Sri Lanka's "army of housemaids" abroad and the reserve troops back at home fought innumerable individual battles within the enmeshing power structures of their own families.

Few would dispute that images of women have changed, literally and figuratively, through labor migration. In the middle of our interview, Premasiri sent his son to fetch a large, framed picture of one of his daughters, taken in a Jordanian studio, posed against a backdrop of Grecian columns. Before the burgeoning of migration of labor to the Middle East, nearly all of the large studio photographs found in village houses depicted couples on their wedding day, with smaller snapshots capturing the wedding ceremony and celebrations. In 1994 most migrants' houses contained photo albums filled with scenes from abroad: housemaids in veils and long dresses, smiling Arabic children, foreign houses, and exotic landscapes. Sent from abroad to make the strange familiar, these pictures occupied the same physical space as marriage photos in village houses. The photographs from the Middle East, however, emphasized a woman's work instead of her marriage, picturing her as an individual in service, not as half of a couple.

Questions of women's empowerment did not rest with the individual woman alone. Just as a photographic portrait always hung in the context of the living room it graced, so migrant women always functioned in the context of their families. Rarely did women explicitly voice expectations of increased individual power and authority as motivations for their migration. Benefits of migration for a woman depended more on the budgeting and planning of the person controlling her remittances than on the skills of the particular migrant. Migrants and the other individual members of their families often held different priorities, and various parties exerted different forces to further their own goals and objectives. In relating case studies of struggle between parents and children, husbands and wives, spouses and in-laws, I by no means wish to suggest that family tensions arose exclusively due to the migration of labor to the Middle East. Such disputes occurred regularly in the village, even in families with no one overseas. In the face of limited resources, decisions over the allocation of money inevitably aroused tension and dissent. Remitted money merely raised the stakes and clarified the contestants.

These five case studies of married and unmarried migrants illustrate the obstacles women and men have encountered in their efforts to retain control of money they sent back to Sri Lanka. Ranjani, whose husband sold their house and land, felt powerless to seek redress for the theft; her family also seemed unable to reclaim the loss. Kamala's dramatic suicide attempt drew widespread village scrutiny of her husband's extramarital affair, but it did not shake his control over her finances. In 1997 it remained unclear whether she found Pradeep's acquisition of a house and land adequate compensation for her alienation from her natal family. Simon, in his public verbal and physical assault on his wife Chandrika, held her accountable for having distributed his money to her family members instead of using it to build a house. While Mahinda's wife chafed against the tyranny of her parents and sought independence through her elopement, Premasiri's thrift, forethought, and business acumen allowed him to give lavishly to poor relatives and arrange desirable marriages for his daughters. Struggles over control of remittances often revealed tensions between the desire to redistribute wealth earned abroad along the network of extended family and the equally strong desire to accumulate wealth in the form of real estate and housing. How much of the extended family unit shared in a migrant's prosperity depended on the political maneuvering, economic savvy, and luck of the people handling remittances.

Holding a series of priorities in mind, female migrants have set forth not only to improve by earning money for a house and land but also to feed their families, earn dowries, see the world, and sometimes to escape abusive husbands and dominating parents. A lack of visible material affluence does not always count as failure to prosper. While a family might not immediately buy land or construct a house, migration has enabled people to pay back old debts and live more comfortably. Social scientists analyzing the success and failure of migrants' endeavors need to consider both the goals with which people went abroad and the initial conditions under which they labored. I found that many individuals and families whom villagers had counted as "not improving" in 1994 had "improved" markedly by 1997; for example, a number of houses only half-constructed in 1994 had roofs, doors, and furniture in 1997. Large, poor families burdened with debt required a number of years with a steady salary before showing signs of material prosperity such as buying land, building a house, and starting a business. Similarly, women laboring under older gender hierarchies might need years of economic independence before they can overthrow cultural prejudices and sexist restrictions.

Villagers negotiate not only their standing in a prestige system but also which system of prestige to join among the many operating simultaneously in the village. Individuals and families have positioned themselves with respect to multiple intersecting identities and forms of oppression, searching to find and to legitimate the system offering them the most upward (or the least downward) mobility. Favoring an individualistic, capitalistic direction, Premasiri married his daughter Lalita to a mixed-caste man of industrious character; by spending lavishly on her arranged marriage, he increased the family status with a traditional ceremony. Despite their family disputes and seeming lack of money, Chandrika and Simon retained considerable authority in the village, a residue of former wealth and continuing prestige. One could read Chandrika's attempt to use Simon's money to prevent her brother's mixed-caste marriage as an effort to preserve her family's high-caste position. Using multiple hierarchies and multiple methods to evaluate standing, villagers joust for status in many different arenas simultaneously. Women's struggles for gender equity are enmeshed in equally compelling social contests within systems of kinship, caste, and class.

6 Caste Relations: Social Mobility and Land Reform

Female labor migration has sent ripples through various local social structures in Naeaegama, including the institution of caste. The lived experience of caste in the Naeaegama area centers on social norms regulating marriage, sexual relations, and commensality (who can eat together). Families use money from the Middle East to improve their caste status in many different ways. A long history of caste antagonism and land disputes, including gradual changes in the institution of caste over the past several hundred years, sets the context for changing landholding patterns. Funds earned abroad have played an important role in facilitating the displacement of Berava caste by Halaagama caste residents in a land reform project in Polwatta, a village in the Naeaegama administrative area. Delving into the intricate interactions among religious practice, political affiliation, and caste identity, this chapter will not only analyze caste in relation to other categories of social stratification but also question which characteristics mark which hierarchies, and how the hierarchies themselves are changing.

Caste

Literature on caste ranges from predicting the imminent decline and fall of an outmoded social structure to analyzing the features of its

adaptive resilience. Castes are endogamous kinship groups often correlated with traditional occupations, ranked in a hierarchical system
of purity and pollution.[1] Some theorists view caste as an extreme form
of occupational and economic stratification (Berreman 1981); some see
it as constituted by transactions and flows of substances (Marriott
1990); others see caste as the manifestation of hierarchy, founded on
the fundamental distinctions between pure and impure, sacred and
secular, society and individual (Dumont [1970] 1980). Theorists have
examined caste in historical and political context as well, exploring
the formation of caste identities in the colonial and post-colonial
world (Dirks 1989, 1990, 1992; Raheja 1988, 1990).

Arjun Appadurai criticizes the "preoccupation with caste that has
bedeviled South Asian anthropology" (1986, 757), finding two main
faults with the theoretical approaches that dominated the field through
the 1970s: first, they treated caste as the master trope with which to
explain society, and second, they conceptualized one overarching caste
system with which to explain caste throughout the region. Newer approaches to caste celebrate the complexity and diversity of regional
variants of the caste system and examine how caste interacts with
other systems of power, hierarchy, and identity (McGilvray 1982;
Quigley 1993). In recent years Sri Lankanists have focused their attention on ethnic identity and the civil war. Nevertheless, caste remains an important aspect of social hierarchy.

The Halaagama and Berava Castes

In Naeaegama, Halaagama and Berava caste identities reflect and shape
etiquette for marrying, having sex, eating, and socializing in the village
area. The norms and standards governing inter-caste interactions create
and maintain boundaries between the groups. Although relatively arbitrary, these habits mark well-known, intensely meaningful, compulsory
aspects of everyday behavior internalized by members of the society.

As mentioned in the introduction, the Sinhala-speaking Buddhists
and the Tamil-speaking Hindus in Sri Lanka have separate caste hierarchies. The Sinhala caste hierarchy consists of over twenty castes
whose relative rankings differ in areas around the country. Although
the Halaagama caste makes up only a small fraction of the total Sinhala population, it ranks third in the local caste hierarchy in the

---

[1] Endogamy refers to the practice of marrying within particular social boundaries.

coastal district around Naeaegama where most of its members reside. The Berava, a caste group distributed throughout the Sinhala areas of Sri Lanka, falls in the lower ranks of the local caste hierarchy, well below the Halaagama. In 1994 Halaagama villagers made up nearly 80 percent of the Naeaegama-area population and owned most of the land. The Berava accounted for 15 percent of the area population, with the remaining 5 percent made up of other castes.

The Halaagama dominate local politics and economics in several districts on the Southwest coast and act as the dominant caste in Naeaegama. M. N. Srinivas writes, "A caste may be said to be 'dominant' when it preponderates numerically over the other castes, and when it also wields preponderant economic and political power. A large and powerful caste group can more easily be dominant if its position in the local caste hierarchy is not too low" (1955, 18). In Naeaegama, a few Halaagama families have monopolized positions of authority in the village for at least the past fifty years, controlling the temple and the *Graama Seevaka* [village administrator] position and owning the bulk of the land.

The Halaagama caste traditionally works with the cultivation, preparation, and distribution of cinnamon. Cinnamon peelers tend cinnamon gardens, carefully pruning cinnamon bushes and stripping the red inner bark from six- to ten-foot shoots harvested every four to six months. Garden owners sell their harvest to dealers, paying peelers between a third and a half of the profit. In the 1990s 15–20 percent of the Halaagama men worked in the caste occupation, peeling cinnamon both locally and in the extensive cinnamon estates fifty miles to the south, near the town of Matara. Many families also made brooms and rope from coconut fiber, and a number of men worked in the armed services and in private security firms. Most of the Naeaegama-area cinnamon garden owners were of the Halaagama caste, and these same wealthy villagers also held nearly all of the local leadership positions.

In 1997 members of roughly one third of the Berava households in the village area practiced their traditional occupations of drumming (*bera gahanavaa*), astrological consultation (*shaastra kiyenavaa*), and magical "charming" (*maetiriima*, or spell-casting through the repetition of secret mantras). Only a few of the older generation still performed the healing rituals known as "devil dancing" or exorcism (*yaktovil*).[2] The financially secure had family members employed in the

---

[2] For more information on ritual healing practices, see Bruce Kapferer 1983, 1997 and David Scott 1994.

Middle East, in the armed forces, or in tourism. Members of the less secure households held jobs as laborers, occasionally supplementing their income through carpentry, masonry, and drumming.

Due to ritual status, village settlement patterns were segregated by caste. Halaagama people lived mostly in Naeaegama and Kurundugoda. A number of Naeaegama families could trace their ancestry to the Halaagama woman who founded the village circa 1735 (G. Gamburd 1972). In the late 1960s, Gurupitiya and Polwatta were inhabited mostly by members of the Berava caste, but by 1994 Halaagama families made up the majority in both villages. Although Halaagama families eagerly bought up land in Polwatta and Gurupitiya, many Halaagama residents gave their postal addresses using names of neighboring higher-caste villages, such as Naeaegama and Kurundugoda, because the Berava village names still conveyed a stigma of inferiority.

Caste as Lived Experience

Opinions differ on the extent to which caste has affected the ordinary lives of Sinhala villagers. In 1953 Bryce Ryan called caste in Sri Lanka "unobtrusive" and noted that it "has seldom the obvious inhumanities and degradations commonly associated with such a system of human relations" (21). He observed that "most villagers meet and pass on equal terms today, with no sign of aggressiveness in the lower castes' emancipation and no resentment by the high" (1953, 207). Caste in Sri Lanka takes a milder form than caste in India; however, in Naeaegama in 1997, child-sized "half-chairs" once reserved for those of lower status still graced the back porches of many richer Halaagama houses, and one elderly Halaagama woman remembered when Berava neighbors greeted Halaagama ladies by the respectful term "*hamu*," while receiving inferior and impolite forms of address themselves. While some villagers cited the example of boys of different castes playing cricket together and calling each other by their first names as a sign of upcoming equality, older high-caste men remembered the camaraderie of the games of their own youth ending abruptly when they assumed positions of authority in the village. In Naeaegama, Halaagama informants suggested that caste prerogatives were on the decline, but many Berava insisted that the discrimination continued, though less openly.

Cultural norms and standards surrounding marriage, sexual relations, and food all serve as indexes of caste hierarchy. Upholding caste endogamy, families have rarely arranged marriages for their children with individuals from other castes, although such marriages have occurred, both through arrangement and elopement (see also Yalman 1969). In arranged marriages, the size of a woman's dowry offers a measure of her family's social and economic status, and a higher dowry facilitates a higher-status match. Other considerations, such as the compatibility of the couple and the bride's and groom's education, occupations, horoscopes, and personal characteristics also figure in arranging a match.

The Para caste (lowest caste, Untouchable) moneylender Elsie, introduced in chapter 3, and her husband arranged an inter-caste marriage for their daughter. Elsie's wealthy father was of the Halaagama caste, and her mother and husband were of the Para caste. My research associates Sita and Siri thought Elsie's son-in-law, a hardworking construction contractor, was of the Karava [fisher] caste, which comes second on the island-wide ranking of castes, just above the Halaagama (Ryan 1953, 94). Elsie and her husband provided their daughter with a good dowry consisting of land, jewelry, wooden wardrobe, sewing machine, and cash. While this marriage represented an increase in caste status for Elsie's family, it probably represented a step down in caste terms for her son-in-law's family.

In her analysis of norms and fears surrounding interracial sexuality during the age of empire, Ann Stoler (1989) suggests that restrictions on social interactions, especially sexual access across racial or ethnic lines, defined differences and maintained hierarchy between the colonizers and the colonized. Mixed race children violated cultural categories and challenged the assumption that differences between colonizers and colonized were clear-cut and self-evident. Despite prohibitions, sexual relations between members of different groups did occur and often carried political implications. Similar power dynamics surrounded cross-caste marriages in Naeaegama. Unlike Elsie's daughter and son-in-law, who continued to live in the village, many mixed-caste couples—especially those who eloped for love without their families' approval—left the area, seeking the relative anonymity of the city, where people knew and cared less about caste status. The out-migration of mixed-caste couples has preserved caste hierarchy and the impression of caste endogamy in the village.

Caste endogamy forms only one part of the whole story about cross-caste sexual relationships and caste hierarchy. Srinivas notes that dominant castes in Indian villages often exercise force against others and that they express their dominance in part through forced sexual access to the women of non-dominant castes. He writes, "Statements are often made by members of minority castes that they have no protection against bullying and exploitation on the part of men of the dominant caste. The members of the non-dominant castes may be abused, beaten, grossly underpaid for work done, or their women required to gratify the sexual desires of the powerful men in the dominant caste" (1987, 102). Feminist anthropologists analyze rape not as an aspect of "desire" but as an aspect of violence and control (Zimmer-Tamakoshi 1997). Discussing race relations in the American South in the 1890s, for example, Hazel Carby (1985) notes a prevalent fear that black men would rape white women. Miscegenation laws granted white men the power to terrorize black men (especially those who gained any economic or political power), portraying them as potential threats to the virtue of white women. Images of lusty black men also gave white men the duty to control the movement of white women under the guise of "protection." In the meantime, white men regularly raped black women with impunity, an act that asserted white racial dominance. Cross-culturally, then, groups often express dominance through forced intercourse (Etherington 1988; J. Hall 1983; Inglis 1975; Knapman 1986; Stoler 1991, 1992), a dynamic also found in caste identity in Sri Lanka.

In Sri Lanka, communities have often dealt with cross-caste sexual relations (either consensual or forced) between high-caste women and low-caste men much more strictly than those between high-caste men and low-caste women (see also Gough 1969, 37; Ryan 1953, 76, 156). In Naeaegama, if a Halaagama man had a serious affair with a Berava woman, the man's family found it embarrassing; the woman's family and their neighbors worried that people would consider their daughters whores and use the affair as an excuse to assault or rape other Berava women in the area. In contrast, people rarely discussed relations between Berava men and Halaagama women; the only innuendo I heard involved a powerful Berava exorcist (*aeduraa*) of the previous generation called in to cure married Halaagama women's infertility— "And we all know what sort of charming that requires!" Siri remarked. Since most Berava men in the current generation have not cultivated the skills of their predecessors, that avenue of access has narrowed. While villagers frown on all cross-caste relations, the double standard that has given men of the dominant caste semisanctioned access, even violent access, to minority-caste women has formed a major aspect both of caste and of gender identity.

In some ways sexual access to the women of a caste correlates with physical access to the more intimate areas of a family's house. Just as minority-caste men have not been allowed access to dominant-caste women, so minority-caste and lower-status individuals of either sex have not been allowed access to the inner recesses of dominant-caste homes. Progressively more intimate approaches to yard and house cross the boundaries of the outer fence (often protected by canine teeth and vocal cords), the garden, and the veranda, with only honored guests, close family, and the painter invited through the front door into the living room and the bedrooms. Berava individuals closely associated with a Halaagama family might be offered half-chairs, or sit on the steps on the back porch. Though dominant-caste people do not visit lower-caste families often, when they do, they are treated with the greatest respect and allowed much further inside, being ushered immediately to the living room (in poor houses often the only room in the house).

Lower-caste homes maintain indirect but effective barriers against intruders, however. On one occasion Siri and I visited a wealthy Berava family, where our hosts graciously guided us to cushioned chairs infested with voracious insects. We did not linger long. These creatures, bedbugs and chair-bugs (*makunoo*), live in the cane seats of wooden chairs and thrive in mattresses, cushions, and pillows. Their bites raise large but not lasting welts on portions of one's anatomy best not scratched in public. Siri remarked later that most wealthy families exterminated such pests and speculated that our hosts might reserve those chairs for particularly "honored" guests. In many ways, villagers re-created in access to space the same caste hierarchy created through access to women's bodies.[3] This metaphorical parallel between houses and bodies does not, however, fully capture the violent violation of rape, or allow for the possibility of nonviolent high-caste guests.

Many of the same rules governing inter-caste sexual relations reappear in discussions of commensality. High-caste individuals consider eating food handled or cooked by lower-caste individuals polluting; sexual contact with people of lower castes similarly diminishes purity. E. R. Leach writes of Sri Lanka that "the sharing of food is taken

---

[3] See also Ryan 1953 (164) on space relations and access to houses.

as symbolic of sexual intercourse" (1961, 89–90), and Nur Yalman notes that men involved in consensual and forced relationships with lower-caste women thought that "interdining with 'low' women was worse than sleeping (and having children) with them" (1969, 97).

Although Siri felt that prohibitions against inter-dining had much less force in the 1990s than they had had during his childhood in the 1950s and 1960s, gossip and rumor suggested both the currency of commensal taboos and the ambivalence with which they were regarded. During my stay in Naeaegama, a story circulated about two individuals in the group of elderly women who regularly attended the monthly meditation class at the temple. Siri jokingly referred to these lessons as "karate classes," a phrase that aptly summed up the martial nature of many of these prominent women's social interactions. An older, respected Berava woman had offered tea to a Halaagama woman, who refused the offer and drank from her own thermos bottle instead. The storytellers disapproved of the Halaagama woman's actions, particularly because they took place on temple grounds, which are traditionally viewed as an area set apart from caste concerns. The covert and overt violence of asymmetrical standards governing marriage, sexual relations, dining, and socializing reflected the continued currency of, and the ongoing negotiation surrounding, the caste hierarchy.

Raaj*a*kaariy*a* and the Valavv*a*

Caste relations in Naeaegama show signs of both continuity and change. While some theorists root justifications of the South Asian caste system in Hindu religious doctrine, Sri Lanka specialists usually discuss caste in Buddhist villages in relation to land tenure and the political system, both of which have changed dramatically over time.[4]

Historically, caste in Sri Lanka stems from the tradition of *raajakaariya* variously translated as work for the king, caste service, or duty to the lord (Kirk 1992, 406). Kings turned land over to the authority of followers, who in turn distributed it to clients of their own, receiving goods and services in exchange, often those of the caste occupation (also called *raajakaariya*). After the colonization of Sri

---

[4] For more on caste in India and Sri Lanka, see Beteille (1969, 1974); Daniel (1984); Dumont ([1970] 1980); Gough (1969); Leach (1969); Mandelbaum (1970); McGilvray (1982); Ryan (1953); and Yalman (1967, 1969).

Lanka's coastal areas by the Portuguese in the early sixteenth century, trade in cinnamon took on an enhanced importance. During the seventeenth and eighteenth centuries, the Halaagama, originally weavers (Ryan 1953, 107), managed cinnamon production on land granted them by the king. The status and authority of the caste increased as their occupation grew in importance. Major landholders received land grants from the Sinhala kings and Portuguese colonists and distributed land to client members of the potter, drummer, washer, and goldsmith castes, who set up hamlets around the manor houses or "palatial residences" (*valavvas*) of their patrons.

Although other *valavvas* continued as centers of power and influence, family members from the *valavva* nearest Naeaegama had abandoned their large house on the hill. Control of land and other wealth, access to government jobs, political connections, and high standards of education provided many opportunities for members of this elite group, the wealthiest and most talented of whom had moved permanently to the capital city of Colombo (and even out of the country). Except in fictional representations and nostalgic gestures, the patrons, leaders, and recipients of *raajakaariya* were conspicuous in their absence. In the early 1990s "The Doctor," a native son who practiced medicine in England, sent back several hundred dollars to a poor relative to replace the collapsing roof of the manor house. A film crew for a local teledrama whitewashed the front of the building and shot several scenes depicting a historical narrative. Descendants of the family had sold their land bit by bit until, in 1997, only the two acres surrounding the house remained. In recent years these and other rich elite remaining in the area turned their attention outward, mingled less often with other villagers, and contributed less frequently to local political discussions and religious and civil ceremonies. Wage labor and contractual relations superseded older patron-client relations. Villagers of different castes, formerly gathered to perform services for the *valavva*, moved in new ways through a changing economic and political environment.

Several state initiatives hastened the decline of the *valavvas*, and these changes in political organization altered local power structures. In 1965 the state replaced local village headmen (proxies of the *valavva* in times past) with government-appointed village administrators (*Graama Seevakas*). The *Graama Seevaka* took over many of the headman's duties but did not inherit a similar patron-client structure. Local patron-client relationships instead came to revolve around those who had political connections to Members of Parliament, the police, and other influential individuals in the government structure. *Raa-jakaariya* came to refer not to caste service but to work done for wages by government employees or work done for free by villagers on local-level government projects.

The new breed of patrons, such as local political party organizers, often controlled access to government goods and services, including rice ration booklets; access to piped water, paved roads, and electricity; and government-sector (and even some private-sector) jobs. All goods and services clients received came as a reward for political loyalty and carried an implicit obligation to continue to vote for the party of the provider. Caste groups acquired political influence as organized voting blocs. But dissatisfaction leading to the violent Janatha Vimukthi Peramuna (JVP) insurgencies in 1970–71 and 1988–90 rested in large part on youthful anger at unequal access to opportunities, an inequality arising from nepotism and political favoritism among the dominant castes in various village areas. Party factions divided the village in new ways, often cross-cutting older caste hierarchies and reorganizing community solidarity.

In the 1980s and 1990s a new group of influential villagers moved into the vacuum left by urbanizing and outward-looking elites. These wealthy and well-educated leaders depended on politics, trade, tourism, and jobs abroad, rather than on land, as their main sources of income. On occasion these newcomers, and members of the old elite who had diversified their economic activitices, found themselves in conflict with poorer relatives of the vanished old guard; these poor relations called on tradition, kinship, custom, and caste to enforce their claims to authority. Abandoned by their rich relatives, despised by equally poor neighbors for their perceived arrogance and snobbery, and challenged by the newly influential leaders, poor men and women with important caste and kinship ties struggled constantly to bolster their eroding status and authority. These two groups, new leaders and poor members of the dominant caste, struggled over which systems of power and influence—either wealth and political connections or kinship and caste—should prevail. As the social systems organizing labor and political allegiance changed, so did the meanings and practices surrounding caste.

Two Paths to Prestige and Prosperity

During the time of my visits, many interrelated systems of social stratification operated simultaneously in Naeaegama. Individuals and groups sought to rise in the particular status hierarchies they favored, improve the ranking of their chosen hierarchy over other competing hierarchies, and change the very nature of those hierarchies. Introduced into this chaotic, fluid realm of social rivalry, money earned in the Middle East provided the economic means for those who wanted to improve their family and caste status. This section compares two Berava families' use of money earned from migration and tourism. One family chose to better their personal and caste status by contributing lavishly to the local temple (a theoretically caste-free setting but a traditional Halaagama stronghold); the other family planned to leave the village to live and work in the relatively caste-free context of a nearby city. Caste alone did not determine the course of events. In both cases, many overlapping and conflicting identities, grudges, and friendships affected the decisions made and the strategies adopted.

The Buddhist Temple

The local Buddhist temple provides a space for community activities in Naeaegama.[5] It offers a social setting open equally to members of all families and castes but at the same time mirrors hierarchical competition in the village. Buddhist doctrine suggests that ethical behavior matters in the search for Nirvana, but caste status, wealth, and political influence do not. Men who enter the *sangha* [order of monks] renounce their family, caste, and village affiliations when they take the robe. They vow to be chaste and to eat food offered to them by any villager, even one of the lowest caste. Ideally equal in worship, laypeople hypothetically find in the temple a caste-free setting open to the whole community.

Despite Buddhism's theoretical openness to people of all castes, the Halaagama have had a special interest in the local temple. Denied ordination in existing orders of monks, in the early 1800s influential members of the Halaagama caste arranged to start a Buddhist sect in Sri Lanka by bringing over monks from Burma to ordain a new line of Sri Lankan monks (Ryan 1953, 39). This sect, the Amarapura Nikaya—unlike the older and more widespread Siam Nikaya—allowed the ordination of men of lower caste, not only men of the highest Goyigama

---

5 A rich literature describes similar dynamics surrounding temple donations and caste status in South India (Appadurai 1978, 1981; Appadurai and Breckenridge 1976; Bayly 1999; Rudner 1994; Washbrook 1976). For a discussion of religion and politics in Nepal and Sri Lanka, see Sherry Ortner (1989) and Mark P. Whitaker (1999).

status. In the 1990s most of the temples in the Naeaegama area belonged to the Amarapura Nikaya, serviced Halaagama populations, and were run by incumbents "formerly" of the Halaagama caste. Although initiates to the robe formally renounced individual, family, and caste identity, in practice, many of these allegiances remained active.

Although Buddhist doctrine in no way supports caste ideology, historically, temples have mirrored and maintained many aspects of hierarchical caste relations. Regarding a village in the upcountry where the temple stepped into the former role of the king, Andrew Kendrick writes, "The *raison d'être* for caste is thus placed in the past, in the time of the Sinhalese kings, but the relationship between caste and *rajakariya [sic]* is reproduced and re-enacted in the performance of temple ritual" (1992, 192). Kendrick argues that upcountry villagers performed their traditional caste occupations for the temple, thus reinforcing doctrines of caste. In Naeaegama some older ritual traditions continued in the 1990s. For example, village families took turns supplying meals for the monks at the temple. At the same time, monks and devotees often conducted temple business for wages and payment, rather than as *raajakaariya*. The temple served as an all-inclusive symbolic center, but its economic integration into local society (as only one of several wealthy institutions) rested more on wage labor than on traditional caste duties.

Temple grounds and religious ceremonies, despite their integrative functions, also provide ample opportunity for the display of hierarchical village relations. In 1980 Dineris *Gurunnaasee*,[6] a prosperous Berava charmer, began the construction of a new temple "Image House" (*vihaara gee*), a hall to shelter religious statues, using money that four of his children made in the Middle East. Although the temple complex had needed a new Image House for years, no Halaagama families had taken the initiative to build one. Dineris's wife Wijitha said that Rs. 200,000/ (the equivalent of Rs. 550,000/ in 1994 rupees, or U.S.$11,000) had been spent on the project. Siri, who on several occasions went out of his way to show me the stone plaque in the wall that commemorated the building's donor, noted how unusual (and, in many ways, upsetting) the donation was in the predominantly Halaagama temple and village. Dineris's financial contribution also earned him the informal post of a temple donor or "trustee" (*daayaka*), which entailed the coveted right to contribute to decisions about temple affairs.

---

[6] *Gurunnaansee* is a respectful title given to specialists in exorcism and charming.

Dineris passed away before the official opening of the building, when the eyes of the three statues in the Image House were ceremonially painted, ritually sanctifying the statues (*neetra pinkama*). Wijitha said that he died of psychic poison (*aes vaha* [the evil eye] and *kaTa vaha* [poison from the envious tongue]) because the Halaagama people were jealous of his accomplishment. She claimed that Halaagama neighbors denigrated her family's contribution by spreading ugly rumors about how the money they used for construction had been earned. Although she did not elaborate, I assumed that she referred obliquely here to the accusation that their daughters were involved in prostitution in the Middle East—an accusation commonly made against financially successful female migrants. Jealous neighbors, especially of the Halaagama caste, countered Dineris's family's rise in ritual status and religious prestige with degrading gossip about the chastity of female family members.

The monthly meditation lessons attended by elderly women at the Naeaegama temple provided another story concerning inter-caste relations. The story, which illustrated the aptness of Siri's "karate class" analogy, contradicted the restful image of benign, white-clad grandmothers engaged in peaceful contemplation. During a meditation class, a Halaagama woman allegedly refused to meditate in the Image House, saying, "We don't worship the Berava Buddha."[7] I have heard derogatory things said about the Image House only once on account of the caste of its donor, but the vigor of the rumor indicated the volatility of the subject and the combative nature of the monthly meditation lessons.

Funded by money from the Middle East, Dineris *Gurunnaansee*'s large, visible, and lasting gift to the temple pushed a Berava presence to the fore in what had been for several centuries a stronghold of Halaagama influence. Openly challenging the ability of local Halaagama to provide adequately for the temple, he expressed his family's financial well-being through a gift no one could reject in the supposedly caste-free arena of the Buddhist faith. A landmark in local caste relations, this unusual gesture initiated the possibility of Berava caste people as major lay supporters of the temple. David G. Mandelbaum urges ethnographers to note such cases "not only because such abnormal instances help define the norm but also because the irregular, untypical, and contrasystemic cases may portend important social

---

7 "*berava budu haamuduuruvanTa api wandinne naeae.*"

change" (1970, 219). Continued Berava financial success and a sustained Berava presence at the temple would indicate an increase in Berava caste status in the Naeaegama area. Not all successful Berava families, however, chose to demonstrate their prosperity in the same way, as the next case study illustrates.

Deepak's Story: "Those who leave, prosper"

While Dineris used the wealth his children earned in the Middle East to improve their family and caste standing through a major donation to the Buddhist temple, other families chose other, less traditional arenas for advancement. Deepak, a Berava man in his mid-thirties, came from a relatively privileged background. His maternal grandfather, an influential Berava charmer, performed complex and expensive exorcism ceremonies. In the 1950s and 1960s the family was far richer than the poor Halaagama in Polwatta and nearly as rich as the higher-status Halaagama in Naeaegama. In 1994 Deepak held a good job, and both of his sisters worked abroad, thus ensuring the family's continued financial prosperity.

Since 1985 Deepak had worked at a nearby five-star tourist hotel. He started as a casual laborer in the kitchen, washing dishes, cleaning, and helping the cooks. Deepak's good friend and drinking buddy, a Halaagama man, showed him an article from *Reader's Digest* about how to get ahead in a corporation by arriving a bit early, working hard, and staying a bit late at the end of the day. Following these rules and learning to cook, Deepak advanced to the position of a senior chef. Deepak's security in the village came from his family's reputation, from his (and his sisters') money, and from friendships with several influential Halaagama men, friendships that had stood the tests of time, family disapproval, and caste tensions. Despite his stable position, however, Deepak hoped to move out of the area. He had purchased a small piece of land in Kalutara, a large town about twenty miles north of Polwatta, and planned to move there in several years. Kalutara offered better educational opportunities for Deepak's children and enough anonymity that a lower-caste man could consider starting a business catering food for strangers.

Deepak said that all the "thinking people" who want to give "a bit more" to their children left the village to work in cities like Kalutara or Colombo. He noted that those who left "prospered" and that those who "prospered" left. In his terms, only those who "thought only for the moment" remained in Polwatta. Lower-caste individuals, as well as those in mixed-caste marriages, found opportunity and haven in the urban setting, where people could disguise, lie about, or minimize caste identities (see also Yalman 1969, 100). In the city, improvements measured in terms of wealth, education, and business acumen predominated over more traditional, group-oriented caste identities and systems of prestige.

Deepak chose a strategy for social advancement diametrically opposed to that of Dineris *Gurunnaansee,* the wealthy Berava man who donated the new Image House to the temple. Both men chose situations nominally free from caste discrimination but intrinsically steeped in caste privilege and hierarchy. The latter chose symbolic assertion in the Halaagama-dominated temple; the former focused on the more modern arenas of education and business to display his standing. Dineris worked for visible and collective caste-group advancement, whereas Deepak opted for caste anonymity and focused on his own individual "class" status. Dineris's statement had the most impact in the village center of Halaagama power; Deepak's chosen strategy for improvement worked best in the setting of the city, where his low caste would not hamper him in his chosen profession, despite traditional taboos against high-caste people eating food prepared by those lower than themselves in rank. Their decisions and strategies showed that individually, as families, and as caste members, they sought to improve their social status. Perhaps due to their age, or to a generational shift in perspective, each favored a different avenue for advancement, implicitly validating that hierarchy over other competing hierarchies. In the process of competing, however, each changed the very nature of the hierarchies in question.

Land Reform in Polwatta

Anthropologists have often noted that the spatial distribution of houses, neighborhoods, and villages reflects social segregation, hierarchy, and ranking (Gough 1969, 18–19; Ryan 1953, 165). This section investigates changing forms of land ownership as they related to a case of land reform in Polwatta. As property changed hands, patterns of caste residence shifted, influenced both by the availability of money earned in the Middle East and by political affiliation.

Land use and land tenure follow complex rules. In this area of Sri Lanka, both male and female children have rights to family property.

A share, however small, in a property ensures one's right to live on that land. After many generations of intermarriage and bilateral inheritance of land, individuals often hold small shares in many properties and thus have rights to multiple residences (G. Gamburd 1972, 180, 187). A person's claim to use the land does not entirely disappear even if he or she pawns land shares to a richer relative or patron.

Data gathered in 1968–69 provide longitudinal information on land ownership (G. Gamburd 1972). In Polwatta, generations of inheritance had fragmented land holdings. In 1968 roughly twenty households inhabited Polwatta, 85 percent of them from the Berava caste. The richer Berava households owned shares of the land they lived on, whereas the poorer families rented or borrowed land from Halaagama landlords, the government, or the Buddhist temple. Some tenants had lived on the land for generations, acting as "watchers" for an absentee landlord's coconut garden (*pol vatta*). When Siri and I visited the local Land Registry, we found numerous written records that indicated share transfers of 1/24, 1/63, 1/108, and even 1/135 of properties already too small for meaningful subdivision. Oral histories confirmed the multiplicity of shareholders, suggesting the complexity of land ownership and use patterns.

Changes in landholding patterns brought about by a government land reform project have affected interpersonal relationships of caste and kinship. By nationalizing and redistributing property in Polwatta, the government erased former claims to residence and usufruct, assigning residence rights instead according to political and caste affiliation. Whereas the older system of fragmented shares emphasized familial co-ownership of property, the government land distribution simplified, clarified, and rigidified ownership, emphasizing the individual with a deed over the family with a share. In several generations land fragmentation will again bring back older residence patterns, but for the moment the new landholding pattern sets the stage for relatively straightforward exchanges of property for cash—cash infused into the system by the migration of labor to the Middle East.

The idea to nationalize and redistribute the land in Polwatta first cropped up around 1954, when the government distributed lands in a nearby village to the Badahaela (potter) caste residents.[8] The idea resurfaced in 1957 due to a quarrel among four Halaagama shareholders in

[8] Ryan (1953) lists the potters near the bottom of the caste hierarchy, only slightly higher than the drummers.

a large section of the property in question, and, in a political climate of socialist reform, the shareholders agreed to give their land to the government. The rest of the land involved in the Polwatta land reform belonged to Berava and Halaagama residents, the Buddhist temple, and the government. Not until 1980, however, did the project come to fruition.

A case study of this small size must of necessity touch on personal ambitions. In many of my interviews with Berava people, the family of Podi Appuhami was mentioned as driving Berava families from their land and "hungrily" taking it over for themselves. As a Halaagama man of few means when he came to the village in the 1930s, Podi Appuhami had only a small share of land in his wife's family garden. With what little money he had, Podi Appuhami bought other small shares of land, or fabricated false deeds, and then filed court cases that his poorer adversaries, both Berava and Halaagama, could not afford to contest. He also lent money to those in need and then forced them to sign over their land deeds to him at greatly reduced prices if they could not repay the loans. Legal and financial pressures were also combined with more blatant intimidation; local oral history portrays Podi Appuhami's brother-in-law as fond of drinking and womanizing and not averse to using rape, drunken threats, and intimidation to force Berava families off their land. Through these diverse methods, Podi Appuhami acquired a significant amount of land in and around the Polwatta area, in the process earning the enmity of a large portion of the village. People referred to Podi Appuhami as a "land-worm" and called him "Podi Oppu-hami" ["Little Deeds-Sir"] in a pun on his name.

Podi Appuhami and another landholder delayed the redistribution of Polwatta land for twenty-three years, from 1957 until 1980. Oral histories suggested that Podi Appuhami bribed various officials, first to hold up the land reform and then to stop the distribution of the land on which he lived. One informant suggested that Podi Appuhami gave delicacies like buffalo-milk curd and fresh tuna fish to the private secretary of a certain government official. Even after the ruling political party changed in 1977, and the idea to nationalize the land resurfaced, some of Podi Appuhami's machinations held firm.

The process of land distribution reveals politics and power structures in the Naeaegama administrative area, which includes the village of Polwatta. In an arc around the Naeaegama temple live the most respected families in the area. All related by marriages reaching back as far as nine generations, these rich Halaagama families have dominated local political and religious functions for over 180 years. Chief priests, usually sons of these families, have passed control of the temple's rich lands and ideological platform to their nephews or other close kinsmen in the robe. As dedicated United National Party (UNP) supporters, these men have lent unofficial administrative and religious assistance to the party cause whenever possible.

Soon after the UNP government came to power to 1977, the authorities took positive action on the land reform initiative.[9] Working with the Assistant Government Agent of the district, a local committee selected a list of potential land recipients. The committee included the local government administrator (*Graama Seevaka*) who was a staunch UNP supporter, a retired school principal (the local UNP party organizer), the local UNP Member of Parliament, and the incumbent monk (a relative of the *Graama Seevaka*). These men regularly made most of the political decisions for the entire village. All staunch supporters of the UNP, they drew up a "Temporary Choosing List" of eligible villagers and posted the list for public scrutiny and petition. The land reform divided the seven acres of land that became the village of Polwatta into fifty-three twenty-perch (one-eighth acre) housing blocks, which provided room for a house, several coconut trees, and a small garden. Although Berava households accounted for 85 percent of the original inhabitants of the area, Berava families—mostly those already living in the area—made up only 41 percent of the suggested recipients. Nearly all nonresident land recipients were Halaagama families associated with the ruling political party. Clearly, caste and party affiliation played a strong role in the selection of land recipients.

Podi Appuhami's manipulations and skulduggery continued to affect the land distribution. Of the 54 people listed as eligible for 53 land plots, only 45 ultimately received property. Of the land pieces distributed in 1980, 11 went to Podi Appuhami's family. In the land distribution Podi Appuhami's family received all of the land that once belonged to Deepak's father's family, some land nationalized from Dineris *Gurunnaansee*'s family (for which they received compensation), and a portion of temple land formerly occupied by several poor

---

[9] This land reform was not connected with the Paddy Lands Act of 1953 or with the land ceiling act (Land Reform Law) of 1972. For more information on agricultural reform and paddy lands, see Ronald J. Herring (1983) and James Brow and Joe Weeramunda (1992).

Berava families. All together, Podi Appuhami and his family received about an acre and a half of land reform land, or about 20 percent of the total. In addition, the family obtained exclusive use of one acre of adjoining paddy land, which Dineris *Gurunnaansee*'s family claimed they had once farmed.

Perhaps more superstitious than he would care to admit, Siri inadvertently revealed an arena of Berava resistance. One day during the rainy season, the roof of a house belonging to one of Podi Appuhami's sons collapsed. Walking past the ruins, Siri attributed this bad luck to magical curses cast by the Berava. He then listed more of the family's troubles. Notwithstanding the lush vegetation in the fields and the evidence of new construction, Siri insisted that Podi Appuhami's family "would never prosper" because the villagers hated them so much; powerful Berava charmers expert in mantras and magical spells had laid subtle curses on the family and the land, blighting both. Sinhala villagers believed that any envy and anger could bring bad luck to its object, but Berava expertise in exorcism and charming made them particularly potent enemies. Any ill fortune befalling Podi Appuhami's family stirred up old stories and village resentments.

The government land redistribution in 1980 brought an end to the richly textured system of land use and land ownership by reversing many years of land fragmentation, making claims clear and the sale of property relatively straightforward. Although illegal, the transfer of land reform plots took place frequently in the Polwatta area. In theory, households replacing those that had vacated land plots should have been drawn from eligible families on the official waiting list, but in practice no one ever enforced this procedure. Instead, those buying the land counted on a government law that gave them property rights after occupying the land for five years.

Even the most cursory survey of changing landholding patterns in the village revealed a direct correlation between transfer of ownership and money earned through female migration to the Middle East. In the fourteen years between 1980 and 1994, 30 percent of the land plots changed hands, sometimes more than once. Sixteen Halaagama purchasers acquired land from eight Berava and eight Halaagama sellers; money from the Middle East figured in thirteen of these transfers.

While Middle East money has not created the push and pull factors encouraging an out-migration of Berava families, it has facilitated and sped the transfer of property. Both Berava and Halaagama women have worked abroad, but Berava families have chosen houses and property

away from Polwatta when they invested in real estate; Halaagama
families have bought property in Polwatta so as to live near their relatives. Berava families leaving Polwatta have often moved to villages
with higher concentrations of their own kin and caste group.[10] Open
to poor women of all castes, jobs in the Middle East have helped level
the former distribution of wealth in the village. Money earned abroad
has increased mobility and, by facilitating movement toward single-
caste villages, also served to accentuate caste differences.

Sexual threats and assaults have formed an integral element of inter-
caste relations and influenced the transfer of property in Polwatta.
Physical violence has occurred only rarely in the village, but violence
and the threat of violence have been active and necessary elements in
maintaining caste and gender hierarchies. Lower-caste women struggle
constantly against derogatory images portraying them as prostitutes,
an accusation leveled against many, regardless of their actual behavior. Generic bad reputations have "justified" or even "invited" hu-
miliating comments and insulting actions, even leading up to assaults
that could drive an entire family from the village. Halaagama men's
reputation for impatience and hot tempers has exaggerated their monopoly on the use of unjust force. High-caste men assert their dominance over the lives, bodies, and lands of lower-caste neighbors by
beating the men, raping the women, and throwing stones at the
houses. These elements of violence, then, form a vital dimension of
status and power within caste and gender relations.

The following incident reveals the interrelation between caste identity, threats of sexual assault, and control over land. In early 1992 a Berava family sold half of their land plot to their Halaagama neighbor. A
few days later the neighbor, Abeyesiri, took over the rest of the land,
and the Berava family moved to a nearby Berava village. Rumor suggested that either Abeyesiri or one of his sons attempted to sexually
assault a young woman in the Berava family, and because of that incident, the Berava household left the area, abandoning the rest of their
land or selling it at a much reduced price to Abeyesiri. Three doors

[10] As I did no fieldwork in the villages to which Berava families moved, I cannot
say what effect this redistribution of households had on caste relations in other areas.
From the eagerness of Polwatta Berava families to join these communities, I infer that
they suffered less caste discrimination in villages where they formed the majority
population. With the influx of Halaagama in Polwatta and Gurupitiya, the Berava no
longer dominated in those villages.

down and a year earlier, a Halaagama man attempted to rape a Berava mother and daughter but was chased off by a Halaagama neighbor. That Berava family did not move, but the rumor of assault spread fear and doubt among lower-caste men and women. Such violence formed an effective technique of domination. Access to the bodies, or at least the reputations, of minority-caste women by dominant-caste men has shaped the power dynamics of land transfer in the village.

The government-initiated land reform project in the mixed-caste area of Polwatta illustrates changing patterns of land use and ownership between 1968 (when 85 percent of the households in Polwatta were of the Berava caste) and 1994. Figures show a steady displacement of Berava by Halaagama households. In 1980, when government officials and local notables divided and distributed seven acres of land in Polwatta, they gave only 36 percent of the plots to Berava families. The land reform erased land fragmentation in the area, clarifying titles and making it easier to buy and sell property. The Berava made up only 21 percent of the resident households in Polwatta in 1994, with the Halaagama holding 79 percent of the land plots. The slow but steady displacement of Berava by Halaagama households involved caste identity, government land reform policies, party politics, intimidation, and money from the Middle East.

Conclusion

On first questioning, many Halaagama villagers suggested that in the 1990s caste in Sri Lanka pertained only to marriage restrictions. Interviews with Berava villagers and field research performed in 1968–69, 1992–94, and 1997, however, suggested a darker underside of current and historical caste antagonism. Food taboos created and maintained subtle but powerful barriers between caste groups. Prohibitions on intermarriage maintained kinship boundaries between castes, and mixed-caste couples who eloped found life easier if they moved out of the village, thus preserving the appearances of endogamous caste groups. Inter-caste sexual relations, either forced or consensual, paradoxically both violated and reinforced caste hierarchy. Part of the subordinate position of Berava families stemmed from the ever-present fear that higher-caste men might rape Berava women and girls or assault Berava men. Berava resistance took subtle but effective forms, such as biting insects in sofa cushions, ostentatious gifts to the local temple, magical curses, and changes in residence. While villagers experienced long periods of relative peace and cooperation, conflict and violence remained vital to the overall structure of caste authority. Physical and psychological threats and intimidation maintained and extended the hierarchical relations between castes.

Historically, caste stems from the *raajakaariya* system, in which caste members received land in exchange for performing their caste occupation for influential landholders. Gradually, newer political and economic alliances based on political parties, employment, and wealth have altered the patron-client networks of the caste system. As these new organizations replace the *raajakaariya* system, caste has changed and adapted but has continued to operate as a strong basis for individual and group identity.

Middle East migration has affected caste struggles in two ways. First, money remitted by migrants has given village families the financial wherewithal to try to improve their social status. The examples of Dineris *Gurunnaansee* and Deepak, two Berava men, reveal the different arenas and the contrasting strategies each used to improve his individual, family, and caste standing. Second, migration has affected caste residence patterns associated with the government land distribution. Population growth over time put pressure on members of both castes in the village to secure land for family use. By erasing land fragmentation and simplifying ownership, the 1980 land reform drastically changed landholding patterns in Polwatta. Remittances from the Middle East aided transfers of property for families of both castes with Berava families leaving the Polwatta area and Halaagama families moving in. A steady displacement of Berava by Halaagama has formed an unofficial subtext of the land reform project. Influential village leaders have also rewarded political allegiance to the ruling party by granting land to clients. Political favoritism, caste discrimination, and violence against lower-caste women have all played a part in the complex dynamics of land reform and caste residence.

Changing material circumstances brought about by the influx of money from remittances and by government land reform initiatives have affected caste hierarchies in the village but not in a straightforward, uncomplicated fashion. Preexistent social structures of gender, wealth, politics, and religion have shaped and directed the changes, undergoing gradual shifts themselves in the process.

7   Breadwinners No More: Masculinity in Flux

The migration of labor from Sri Lanka to the Middle East has brought about many changes in local gender roles in the village of Naeaegama. Theorists often distinguish between *sex*, a biological category, and *gender*, cultural knowledge about sexual difference. Sex is, with rare hermaphroditic exceptions, a human universal. In the abstract, gender distinctions are also human universals; every society constructs ideal behaviors for men and women. Despite this abstract universality, the specific content of gender roles varies cross-culturally, and within any community the roles shift and change over time. Characteristics deemed masculine and feminine depend on each other for shape and definition. Although based loosely on reproductive capacities, gender roles are, like any cultural construct, learned, relatively arbitrary, and subject to disagreement. As a major aspect of lived identity, they are also intensely meaningful, deeply ingrained, tenaciously maintained, and central to a sense of self.

Feminist anthropologists examine patterns of power and inequality in human societies. We look at cultural categories implicit in gender symbolism, explore how gender intersects with other patterns of dominance and subordination, and analyze how these overlapping cultural constructs affect political relations among people. We investigate how individuals and groups re-create and challenge the hierarchies implicit in everyday institutions and social structures.

Early feminist anthropologists sought to explain universal male domination with respect to a number of gendered dichotomies. They proposed a cross-cultural sexual division of labor, with women taking care of domestic duties such as housekeeping, cooking, and child care and men spending more of their time in the public sphere, earning a living for their families and making important political decisions (Rosaldo 1974). Related dichotomies divided labor between female reproductive activities, which centered on kinship, and male productive activities, which centered on economics (Sanday 1974), and associated women with nature and men with culture (Ortner 1974).

Later feminist anthropologists have challenged these gendered distinctions on a number of fronts. First, theorists suggest that the domestic/public, reproduction/production, and nature/culture dichotomies exist not in the social constructs of the people in question but rather in the minds of Western, middle-class anthropologists, who learn these historically shaped categories as children, find them particularly familiar and compelling, and read them into other ethnographic contexts (Collier and Yanagisako 1987a). Jane Collier and Sylvia Yanagisako suggest that instead of thinking in terms of static, universalistic, unchanging, so-called traditional categories, scholars should approach gender in terms of the symbols and behaviors meaningful to the people in question, asking how individuals learn and absorb the gendered structures of their world and how these relatively arbitrary structures come to seem natural, authoritative, and fixed (1987a, 1987b).

Second, even in situations where indigenous cultural categories (or categories imposed through colonization) *do* reflect distinctions between private and public, kinship and economics, theorists question whether women participate solely in the domestic and reproductive spheres. Numerous authors examine the nature and extent of women's public, economic, and political authority, finding significant female influence even in societies where at first glance one might expect women to be most confined to the home (Abu-Lughod 1986; Nelson 1997; Lamphere 1997). Trying to see beyond our taken-for-granted Western folk concepts of gender, many anthropologists now agree that gender analysis should not attempt the impossible separation of the domestic and the public, kinship and economics.

Women's work in domestic service blurs the distinction between the domestic and public spheres. While scholars have often failed to count female-gendered tasks as "work," or to count unpaid housework as employment, the sale of domestic services on the global market forces both rural villagers and social scientists to recognize that the tasks housewives usually perform for free in fact make significant contributions to household finances (Sacks 1989). Many feminist anthropologists argue that the myth of the housewife's economic inactivity supports cultural ideologies that devalue women's labor (Collier and Yanagisako 1987a; Joan Scott 1988). One might hypothesize that the widespread recognition of women's economic contributions will strengthen and enhance their gendered positions, both in the home and in the public sphere.

In Naeaegama, local, national, and international forces have challenged and changed gendered images and roles for both men and women. High local unemployment for men and women in Sri Lanka presents a push factor for migration; the demand for female domestic servants in the Middle East presents a complementary pull factor. Village women leave their families to work abroad while men remain at home, often unemployed and subsisting on the money their wives remit. As more and more married women have gone abroad, common images of mothers have shifted to include long absences from home. At the same time, many men feel a loss of self-respect and dignity when their wives take over the breadwinner role. Strongly felt gender roles central to male and female identity dictate that many men only reluctantly take over the "women's work" of child care and cooking; if possible, they arrange to have female relatives do the work instead. Freely circulating images of uneducated, slothful husbands suggest that men waste the money their wives earn abroad and turn to alcohol (an exclusively masculine beverage) to drown their sorrows. Representations of delinquent, emasculated men appear in tandem with images of promiscuous, selfish, pleasure-seeking women who neglect their husbands and children.

Transformations in images of men and women reflect changing activities and newly emerging meanings surrounding female labor migration. As social and economic realities force villagers to violate boundaries of older gender norms, people generate new ideals to correspond with new behaviors. In many instances change affects the gut-level, commonsense conceptions of how the world should work that Raymond Williams refers to as "structures of feeling" (1977, 132).

In the following three chapters, I examine changes in gender roles and images of ideal men and women, addressing changes in images of masculinity in this chapter, shifts in the concept of motherhood in chapter 8, and the politics behind local, national, and international representations of Sri Lankan women and their Arabic employers in chapter 9. The following case studies explore male identity in the village of Naeaegama, focusing on employment, wealth, political authority, marriage, and alcohol consumption as indicators of masculinity.

"Sri Lankan men must be donkeys"

In Sri Lanka, many people believe that women should stay at home and tend their families while men earn a living and provide for their wives and children. The realities of local poverty and lack of job opportunities for men, however, mean that often women go abroad to work. In the Naeaegama area in 1997, 90 percent of the migrants were women. Of the women, 30 percent were single, and 70 percent were married, separated, or divorced. Most of the latter group had at least one child. Of the married, separated, or divorced women, approximately half had husbands who contributed regularly to the household income; the other half had husbands who were generally under- or unemployed. Despite the relatively high proportion of employed husbands, many villagers lumped all the husbands of Middle Eastern migrants together under the category of "lazy spendthrifts."

Commonly circulating images associated with female migration challenge Sri Lankan husbands' competence as breadwinners and lovers. In Naeaegama a number of housemaids told me that "Arabic people say that Sri Lankan men must be 'donkeys' because they send their wives abroad." The phrase carries two sets of implications. First, it emphasizes Sri Lankan men's inability to provide for their families; they have proved incapable of fulfilling their role as breadwinners. Second, the phrase also carries an overtone of sexual impotence. It implies that Sri Lankan women are not satisfied with their husbands; if they were, they would not travel to the Middle East (and sleep with Arabic men). The themes of financial and sexual dissatisfaction infuse another stereotypical phrase about migrant women: "If they can't eat grapes and apples, they go abroad; if they can't eat cheese and butter, they go abroad."[1] Grapes and apples, luxury fruits imported from

---

[1] "*grapes, apples kanne naetnung, raTa yanavaa; cheese, butter kanne naetnung, raTa yanavaa.*"

abroad, signify a life of leisure and affluence. Cheese and butter, also luxury products, signify a rich and satisfying sexual life. This phrase suggests that migrant women, dissatisfied with their lives (and husbands) in Sri Lanka, travel abroad in search of more gratifying economic and sexual situations.

When Siri, Sita, and I repeated the phrase about "men must be donkeys" to people we interviewed, it often sparked a lively conversation. Many men and women, after a moment's contemplation, replied by describing their financial situation. Some slightly shame-facedly, some matter-of-factly, cited poverty as the reason women went abroad. Families, they explained, could not make ends meet on a man's wages as a casual laborer. Migrant women were not searching for anything as fancy as "grapes and apples"; they were merely hoping to support their families above the poverty line. Fewer of the people we interviewed addressed the implicit suggestion of sexual impotence in the phrase about "the donkeys." Pradeep, the articulate young man introduced in chapter 5, bounced his two-year-old son on his knee as he said that he knew and trusted his wife. Despite his own hard work, his family could not afford to buy land, build a house, and start a business on his salary alone. If he could save the money his wife sent from abroad and build a house, and if she came home without being unchaste, then it would prove that he was not a donkey.

Despite the pragmatic discussions of local poverty and international economic opportunities offered by families of migrants, negative stereotypes of local men unable to live up to older gender ideals have continued to circulate. Female migration symbolizes a man's failure to provide adequate financial support for his family, and a woman's absence deprives her husband of his legitimate sexual partner. Both the stereotype of the Sri Lankan man as a "donkey" and the pragmatic discussions of poverty reflect the slow, difficult, and often painful negotiations of changing gender roles and family structures.

Alcohol: Group Bonding and Masculinity

Alcohol forms a rich and polysemic point of reference in the village; it is a business, a medicine, a pleasure, a need, and a mark of masculinity. Drinking, an exclusively male activity and a sign of wealth (if only temporary in certain cases), preoccupies many of the under- and unemployed village men. Men and women talking about families that do not prosper from female migration to the Middle East often put the blame on husbands who quit work and take up drinking in the absence of their wives. At once scorning and tolerating such husbands, villagers include drink in the phrase "He sits idly, drinks, and wastes,"[2] commonly used to describe migrants' husbands. When I inquired into the motives for such behavior, several people suggested that the drinking men emulated richer land owners of the previous generation. One village notable explained to me, "It is good to be rich and look idle; in the absence of riches, looking idle will suffice." Hard work, particularly physical labor, carries significant stigma in the village; light skin, clean white clothing, and a sweatless brow indicate leisure, high status, or at the very least a respectable office job out of the burning sun.

Alcohol has been the despair of many a wife and a basis of community between drinking buddies. When a migrant woman comes home, her husband often makes claims on her money, mainly using it to drink and improve his status by buying "rounds" for poorer male friends and relatives. Recognizing these needs, some Naeaegama area women have brought home high-prestige foreign liquor purchased at duty-free shops. Complicit in their husbands' drinking, these women have nevertheless sought to limit alcohol intake. Blame for bad male behavior—such as gambling, smoking, drinking, and womanizing—often falls on the absent wife, without whose control a husband, considered constitutionally incapable of controlling his baser urges, drifts helplessly into bad habits and bad company. Many people also note, however, that characteristic patterns of drinking and wasteful spending, as well as failure to prosper economically, predate, and often prompt, female migration. While women bear the responsibility for disciplining the family and regulating household finances, people have increasingly pointed out that these same women hold little authority with which to enforce their will, especially during the periods when they work abroad.

Norms for drinking alcohol in the village do not resemble the Western idea of social drinking or having a beer or a few cocktails before dinner. At weddings, funerals, and other mixed-sex social get-togethers, the host often "runs a bottle" of hard liquor out of a back room visited surreptitiously by most of the male guests, who become progressively drunker as the event proceeds. While drinking, men do not eat because food reduces the "current" or high. This style of drinking

---

[2] *"nikan innavaa, bonavaa, naasti karanavaa."*

spans social classes. I once attended a university dinner party where I learned (a little too late) that respectable unmarried women rarely lingered at such functions past seven or eight in the evening. While their wives (and two uncomfortable, female, Western academics) huddled together in one room, married and unmarried men drank bottle after bottle in another until, nearing ten or eleven in the evening, the host decided to serve dinner. Immediately after eating, the visitors departed, most in cars driven by drunken guests. Men strove to get as drunk as possible as quickly as possible; drinking to excess was the norm, not the exception to the rule.

The production, distribution, and consumption of alcohol form a large subsection of the village economy. Extremely expensive in the village, a bottle of the legal hard liquor, arrack, costs roughly what a manual laborer might earn in a day; in 1994 a bottle of the officially distilled arrack cost Rs. 118/ (U.S.$2.36) while a laborer's daily wage was between Rs. 100/ and Rs. 125/ (U.S.$2.00–2.50). Women, who rarely if ever touch liquor, constantly pressure their husbands to spend money for family consumption instead of alcohol. To save money, most local men drink *kasippu*, the local moonshine, engaging in recurrent games of hide-and-seek with the police (as well as with their wives). A bottle of *kasippu*, a fruit-, yeast-, and sugar-based fractionally distilled moonshine, cost about Rs. 60/ (U.S.$1.20) in 1994. Despite debts and hunger in the family, many men spend a great deal on alcohol, and some work for local *kasippu* manufacturers who run their stills at night in remote, wooded places. In 1994 offering wages of Rs. 150/ (U.S.$3) a night, with free food and drink, one village outfit went into production twice a week, running three stills all night, with each still requiring six people's constant attention. Including production crews, complicit landowners and law enforcement officers, and distribution networks, the business (one of several in the area) directly involved over fifty individuals.

Alcohol proves important not only economically but also socially in the village. Drinking groups, often centered around a particular *kasippu* producer, form strong factions of loyalty and identity. Heavy drinkers adopt the values and norms of their group, which tolerates, even encourages, such activities as gambling, stealing, rape, and assault. Jonathan Spencer glosses *lajja* as shame, shyness, and social restraint, all essential ingredients of good public behavior. He glosses *lajja-baya* as "shame-fear," particularly the fear of ridicule and public humiliation (1990, 169–72). Those who drink are thought not to know *lajja* or *baya,* and Spencer notes, "It is assumed that people who drink alcohol will no longer be in control of their actions and easily aroused to anger which would be likely to spill out in physical violence, given the opportunity" (1990, 183). Shifting groups of local men, usually of similar age and status, gather together regularly to drink, surreptitiously visiting a distribution center several times or purchasing a bottle and taking it to a private location. Often those with money spot drinks for those without, receiving the favor in return at a later date. Providing drinks free to others and working with the manufacturer ensure ready access to liquor in one's own less affluent times.

Although rarely acknowledged by the more respectable leaders in the village, drinking groups form an influential axis of political power. Outsiders occasionally employ such groups to assault opponents (within and outside the village) and burn their houses and property (Ratnapala 1985). Other villagers fear these individuals, especially those with histories of thuggery and intimidation. At the same time, drinking men remain integrated into the structure of village kinship and friendship networks, and producers provide generous financial and other support and protection to individuals and to village institutions such as schools and temples. *Kasippu* production groups maintain guardedly friendly ties with some law enforcement officers and often contribute financially to individuals with political power. For reasons ranging from loyalty to fear, villagers rarely challenge drinking groups or report their misdeeds to higher authorities (some of whom are already complicit in the network).

Alcohol consumption provides relief from personal responsibility for men who fail to earn as much as their wives or who fail to apply their wives' salaries toward prospering. An extenuating condition that can be entered whenever needed (Ratnapala 1985, 26; Fekjaer 1993), drunkenness provides the perfect alibi for poor judgment and socially unacceptable actions. Responsibility falls on the alcohol for any foolish actions and on the absent wife for the drinking itself. With prosperity in the village resting primarily on female migration to the Middle East, some men look to their male peer group to reassert their self-worth in the face of the loss of male power and respect inherent in their wives' new economic roles. Involvement with *kasippu* production and distribution provides poor men with alcohol, money, community, political power, and a mode of rejecting the dominant idiom of improvement. Drinkers thus paradoxically emulate the idle rich of prior generations while rejecting the work ethic of the newer breed of wealthy villager. Migration and alcohol consumption inextricably intertwine in the construction of new identities for village men and women.

Meaning in the Making:
An Interview with Rukmini and Ramesh

Although many families hope to save a female migrant's earnings for large purchases, such as buying land and building a house, in many cases supporting the family in Sri Lanka on the husband's wages proves difficult. Presented with the choice between sporadic, grueling physical labor for very low wages and the opportunity to dip into their wives' remittances, many men in the Naeaegama area come to rely on the money women earn abroad to finance their daily needs. The following case study represents a fairly typical example of voluntary male underemployment and the concomitant use of a migrant woman's wages for family consumption. In a series of interviews, family members struggled to explain to me and to themselves their lack of improvement despite seven years of work abroad. In the process they negotiated the meaning of their continued poverty and its effect on individual and family identity.

Siri and I interviewed Hema, an elderly Berava caste woman, and her son Ramesh, asking about Ramesh's wife Rukmini, who was then working as a housemaid. Rukmini, about thirty years old, had spent most of the previous seven years abroad. During the four years Rukmini worked in Jordan, she sent her money to her own mother. Having no stable home, Rukmini's mother went to live with each of Rukmini's siblings, staying roughly six weeks with each, spending lavishly from the checks Rukmini sent under the pretext of looking after Rukmini's daughter. The next time Rukmini went abroad, she left her daughter with her mother-in-law Hema instead. While Siri, Hema, Ramesh, and I sat in the shade of Hema's unfinished cement house, Siri explained to me in Sinhala that Rukmini did not send money to her husband Ramesh, an infamous drinker and gambler. With the ice broken by Siri's accurate but joking assessment of the situation, Ramesh's mother Hema took over the story, saying that she had told Rukmini not to send money but to keep it herself. Feeling that Ramesh's betting on races and drinking left no balance money even to support himself and his daughter, Hema said Ramesh had taken credit with many local stores and owed interest-bearing debts to several moneylenders.

Hema suggested that if Ramesh could earn money for himself and his daughter, his wife could save all of her salary, and they could buy land and build a house, the original goals of her migration. Sober and embarrassed, Ramesh said nothing to contradict his mother. I asked Ramesh about his work. He said he made about Rs. 125 / (U.S.$2.50, a good salary) a day doing labor work and more than that when he drummed. Silently contradicting the impression that all of his wife's earnings had evaporated into thin air, Ramesh took us into the small two-room clay house where he, his mother, father, daughter, and several brothers all lived, and he showed us a crowded collection of furniture (table, chairs, bed, and a cabinet with broken glass) bought with Rukmini's savings from her work in Jordan.

Soon after her return to the village for the New Year holiday in mid-April 1994, I asked Rukmini to come to Siri's house to talk with me and Sita. Usually I spoke with people at their own houses, but at the time of the interview, Rukmini and Ramesh were living in a tiny six-foot-by-twelve-foot lean-to built against the new cement wall of Hema's unfinished house. Unexpectedly, Ramesh came along; moreover, he was drunk. Uncertain about how to handle the situation, Sita and I began the interview with the couple. With Ramesh on the porch, Sita and I found that Rukmini could barely finish a sentence. Quickly sizing up the situation, Siri, who had planned to work on kinship charts in the other room during the afternoon, came to the rescue, politely and repeatedly coaxing Ramesh off the porch so that Sita and I could talk with Rukmini.

Palpable tension between Rukmini and Ramesh pervaded the interview. When I asked Rukmini about the gifts she had brought back from the Middle East, Ramesh, who had rejoined us on the porch despite Siri's efforts, said that Rukmini had given him a shirt but that he had gotten his sarong for himself. She replied that she had given him a shirt, shoes, and cigarettes. She left her comment at that; it was only later that Siri, who had gotten the full story from Ramesh, explained the implicit barb. Rukmini had given Ramesh a new pair of sandals, a pack of prestigious foreign cigarettes, and a new shirt. The police had raided the illegal toddy (coconut beer) brewery where Ramesh had gone to drink, and he had run through a drainage canal toward the ocean. Ramesh escaped arrest, but the canal muck claimed his brand new sandals, and the salt water ruined the pack of cigarettes in his shirt pocket.

Siri said that Rukmini had also brought back twelve beers and two whiskey bottles, all already consumed. Ramesh replied to Rukmini (in what seemed to us at the time a non sequitur) that even if he drank, he still saved her clothing. Sita, Siri, and I later realized that he must have been comparing himself favorably with the husband of another village migrant, who had sold his wife's dresses during her absence. Siri then persuaded Ramesh to go and inspect a rare plant in the garden.

With Ramesh gone, I asked Rukmini if she planned to go back to the Middle East. Saying she intended to go back "no matter what," Rukmini explained animatedly that she had gotten fed up with her husband's habits. Speaking very quickly, she lamented that there was no use earning money when he was drinking. Some of the money Rukmini had just brought home had gone to settle Ramesh's debts and to finance his New Year drinking and gambling binges. Although she liked to come home and see her daughter, problems with her husband "unsettled her mind." Complaining that her husband never listened to her, Rukmini said, "He breaks things and wastes and drinks."[3] Rukmini's variation on the common trope, "He sits idly, drinks, and wastes," showed that she felt Ramesh's destructive behavior to be worse than the indolence and dissipation embedded in the more common rhetorical phrase.

Ramesh returned to the porch. Hoping for a neutral topic, but inadvertently stumbling into a minefield, I asked Rukmini what had been the worst time in her life. She said the hardest part of her life started after getting married. Ramesh exclaimed, "Really?" They talked heatedly about a fight several years earlier that had ended with both of them filing separate complaints at the police station at the junction, a common conclusion to serious village disputes. Protesting loudly, Ramesh drunkenly accused his wife of abandoning their daughter and neglecting her wifely duties. Silenced, Rukmini picked up Sita's umbrella from the table, examining it with great care. Center stage and unchecked, Ramesh went on talking about himself and how hard he had been working for the family's sake. Ramesh's monologue continued for several minutes, without Rukmini's interaction, Sita's or Siri's translation assistance, or my note-taking. In the uncomfortably confrontational atmosphere, Rukmini slouched low in her cane armchair, turned slightly away from her husband. I caught her eye and winked at her. Suddenly sitting up straighter and relaxing physically, Rukmini told Ramesh to go home and she would answer my questions.

3 "*poDi karanavaa, naasti karanavaa, bonavaa.*"

I am not well versed in the cross-cultural connotations of winking, and this was my only use of the wink as an interview technique. I can only guess at how Rukmini might have interpreted my gesture. I think that she might have worried that I would accept at face value everything I heard about how she had neglected her family and how hard Ramesh had worked to make up her shortfall; my wink positioned me with many local women, who often listened to men talk without interrupting or contradicting them but also without believing all that they heard. Realizing Ramesh's impaired state but also recognizing his prerogative as a male to dominate the conversation, no one on the porch that afternoon directly challenged his assertions beyond Rukmini's initial spirited protest that her married life had been hard. Perhaps Rukmini, caught between the wish to defend herself and the embarrassment of arguing with a drunken husband in front of a foreigner and two higher-caste villagers, chose silence as her best defense until my unvoiced support assured her that none of us took Ramesh's drunken ramblings seriously. That leverage allowed her not to confront his representations directly but to ask him to leave. (In situations where empowered people dominated conversations, I often found that others approached me later in private with contradictory information they had not wanted to voice in public.) While for the most part accepting men's right to dominate the public transcript (James Scott 1990), women made ample use of other opportunities to communicate their own opinions.

That afternoon on the porch, Rukmini and Ramesh negotiated interpretations of their continued poverty and their failure in the community mind to prosper. Each attempted to control the narrative, influence judgments, and shape appraisals. I look at the husband-wife dynamics in this interview as a struggle over meaning in the making, as each attempted to define his or her own agency, identity, and self-worth with respect to the story. By including himself in my invitation to talk, and by excluding Rukmini from conversation when he could, Ramesh sought to prevent his wife (and me) from portraying Rukmini as the decision-maker and breadwinner. Ramesh wanted to be thought of as part of a team, even as a leader, instead of as a deadweight or someone who "sits at home idle, eating while his wife works." His monologues sought to retell the story of what happened to all the money Rukmini had sent home, simultaneously reworking his own image in his and my eyes.

Three years later, in 1997, Sita and I crowded into a trishaw (a covered, three-wheeled motorcycle) with Hema and her nephew so that Hema could show us the way to Rukmini's new house in a Berava village ten miles from Polwatta. Some months after the interview related above, Rukmini had gone to work abroad again, this time to Jordan, where she stayed about one year. When she returned, she and Ramesh bought land and built half of a house. Deciding that they would rather live elsewhere, they sold one property and bought another. Their second house, much smaller than the one they first started to construct, had two tiny rooms and a tin-sheet roof. Rukmini had spent Rs. 5,000/ to add a toilet to their tiny, five-perch (1/16 acre) land plot. Bouncing her one-year-old daughter on her lap, Rukmini said that she would like to go abroad again, but neither her mother nor her mother-in-law would look after the girls because their father would "come fighting" to the house, causing trouble for them as he currently did for his wife. Rukmini had asked a doctor for medicine to stop Ramesh's drinking, but the doctor would only write a prescription to Ramesh himself. Hema suggested asking the alcohol distributors not to sell Ramesh any liquor. Although Rukmini still had some money in the bank (and she and her baby both wore gold necklaces), she said that the family had trouble making ends meet on Ramesh's earnings. She did not want to dip into her savings for daily expenses because she wanted to have a large coming-of-age ceremony for her elder daughter. Fanning herself and her baby under the hot tin roof, Rukmini said that sometimes she thought she would have been better off not going abroad at all; if her husband "had a brain" she could have "brought the family up," but Rukmini wondered if her small land and house were worth eight years of hard work abroad.

When I asked during the 1994 interview how Rukmini envisioned her life in another ten years, she said that she would like her whole family to live in a nice house of their own. After Ramesh and Rukmini left our porch that afternoon, Siri, Sita, and I discussed their situation. Voicing what he claimed was a unanimous village assessment, Siri commented, "It's a real shame that she/they are living like that having just come from the Middle East."[4] In 1994, seeing Rukmini as pressured from all sides for money, Sita portrayed not only Ramesh but many members of Rukmini's extended family as judging their relationships with her by the sort of present she gave them.[5] Despite Ruk-

---

[4] "*hari pavu, araabiyee indala aevit ohee innavaa.*"

[5] On a similar topic, T. Mook notes, "The hopeful visits of neighbors and distant relatives to return migrants are not always appreciated as expressed in the remark 'the bats only come to the trees with fruit' made by one husband" (1992, 124).

mini's generosity, many were disappointed, and Sita doubted whether enough money remained for land and a house as Rukmini had asserted. In 1997 villagers voiced different opinions. Despite adversity and a wasteful husband, Rukmini did indeed live in her own home. Although small, the land and house counted as improvement in the eyes of the Polwatta villagers and demonstrated that despite his heavy drinking, Ramesh had not wasted all of the money his wife earned abroad.

Women's Work

Negotiations over new images of men's and women's work have included not only whether a woman could respectably work abroad but also who would take care of a woman's duties and responsibilities in the home she left behind in Sri Lanka. As migrant women left their families, their absence created a vacuum to be filled by others. Despite the number of under- and unemployed husbands in the village, only four or five families of the ninety or so I interviewed admitted openly that men had taken over more than the bare minimum of housework. In all but one of these cases, the men in question held other jobs as well and had not taken sole responsibility for the domestic duties. While migrants struggled with their new identities as domestic workers and breadwinners, those who filled their shoes at home also faced complex transformations.

The gendered division of labor in the village has clearly marked child care and cooking as female. Most men's sense of masculinity would be threatened by doing household chores and caring for young children. Carla Risseeuw writes of a rural Sri Lankan village near Naeaegama:

> Men cannot "stoop down" in the widest sense, without experiencing severe emotional stress.... The principle that he is "higher" than a woman, and more specifically his wife, permeates the actions, thoughts and emotions of both men and women.... Handling dirt, faeces, cleaning toilets, being impure, doing repetitive, relatively less prestigious work, which often lacks the status of work as such or "prestige" of the proximity of danger, is the female expression of the principle of gender hierarchy. (1991, 271)

To a large extent both men and women in Naeaegama accept this division as just and judge themselves and others according to it.

Most migrants said that they left their children in the care of their mothers or mothers-in-law, but in my daily interactions in the village, I noted more male participation in child care than people generally reported. Priyanthi, the Polwatta migrant introduced at the beginning of the introduction, left her four sons in the care of her husband and his father while she was abroad. In such cases, men and their families often glossed over men's housework to preserve the man's masculine image. Since Priyanthi's husband Ariyapala held a well-paying job at the hospital, he was in part sheltered from village ridicule for taking on his wife's work. When questioned, Ariyapala somewhat defensively explained his domestic duties as a pragmatic solution to Priyanthi's absence. Ariyapala's heavy drinking also reaffirmed his gender identity. As a few men gradually took over what were generally considered women's chores in the place of their migrant wives, they both challenged and reaffirmed older concepts of gender roles and family responsibilities.

Joker, Simpleton, Freethinker: Lal

The following case study explores how two other men dealt with the presence of a female breadwinner in their household. Tagged as one of the most successful village families involved with the migration of labor to the Middle East, Indrani (introduced in chapter 4) and her husband Chandradasa represent a new elite in the Naeaegama area. Indrani had worked for the same family in Doha, Qatar, for twelve years and earned a very generous salary. Chandradasa worked as a security officer at a hotel near Colombo, returning home for the weekend twice a month. Siri said that they had used their money "in a perfectly correct way," saving and spending both spouses' salaries wisely. In Indrani's and Chandradasa's absence, Chandradasa's mother and brother took care of their five children and supervised the construction of their new house. Although Indrani named her mother-in-law as the primary caregiver, the older woman's arthritis severely restricted her movements, and the children's uncle Lal, a colorful village character, did the lion's share of the cooking and housekeeping.

Living across the road from Siri's house, Lal drew drinking water from the well in Siri's garden. Members of our household replied to the greetings Lal called out every time he entered the compound with teasing comments and questions. About the state of the meal Lal was preparing, Siri invariably asked, "Is the (cooking) course over?"[6] For a man to study cooking in school would be just slightly more astounding than to find him cooking at all. In a world of simple structural reversals, when the houseworker leaves to earn a living, one might expect the former breadwinner to do the housework. In Naeaegama, however, in most cases other women, not men, took over "feminine" chores, with grandmothers and aunts looking after the children left at home. Lal, a man who for the past twelve years had cooked, kept house, fetched water, done laundry and shopping, and taken care of children, was a figure of some astonishment and amusement in the village.

Many villagers associate full male adulthood with having a wife and a stable job. Lal had neither. At his mother's insistence, Lal had reluctantly married some years before I met him. His beautiful wife asked him to move to her relatives' home in the capital; when he refused, she found work in the Middle East and never returned to the village. Although fairly sure that she had come home safely, Lal had no desire to visit her relatives in the city or to see her again. Lal had worked as a laborer and as an "office peon," but he had not held a job since he was hit by a van while walking on the side of the road a number of years before.[7] Lal said that he had no wish to return to work and no ambitions to set up a business. His mother, who had persuaded him to marry in the first place, thought that he should do so again. Quoting a proverb, Lal said, "The man who is hit with the firebrand from the fire is afraid even of the firefly" (the local equivalent of "Once bitten, twice shy").[8] After his mother's death, when all of his family duties were fulfilled, Lal said that he would like to become a priest. In the meantime, when his sister-in-law Indrani left for Qatar, Lal and his mother moved in with Chandradasa to look after Indrani and Chandradasa's children. Lal's single status, his lack of a salaried job, and his attention to chores often thought of as women's work caused a number of chuckles in the village.

Curious about Lal's sexuality, two village notables arranged to question him informally. One afternoon the nearly-illiterate Lal asked Siri's

---

[6] "*koos-eka ivara da?*"

[7] In Sri Lankan English, "peon" carries much less of the derogatory tone it has in American English. An office peon runs errands, makes tea, sorts mail, and performs other menial tasks.

[8] "*gini penellin baeta kaapu miniha kanamaediriyaTat bayayi.*"

father (the local Justice of the Peace) to write a letter to the *Graama Seevaka* [local government administrator] asking to be put on a list to receive aid from a local non-governmental organization (NGO). The JP deliberately and in jest wrote a completely unsuitable letter telling the *Grama Seevaka* the stark truth, that Lal lived in a good cement house with electricity and a television set. (Lal's official residence, a collapsing clay hut, formed the basis of a subsequent successful application.) The innocent Lal took the letter to the *Graama Seevaka* who laughed and said, "This won't do at all," and suggested that he and Lal both go talk to the JP. Siri, curious but sensing himself not welcome in the discussion, took a long bath at the well adjacent to his father's porch and overheard the gist of the conversation. The JP and the *Graama Seevaka* teasingly but somewhat cruelly peppered Lal with questions about his long-absent wife, asking if he had sent cards and sweets to her in the Middle East. They also asked about Lal's private sexual life. In a village where everyone knew all the gossip about everyone else, there was not even the hint of a rumor suggesting that Lal might be actively homosexual; several other men were known to be so. The JP and the *Graama Seevaka* merely determined that Lal did not know "which end was up," which Siri thought might account for Lal's wife's desertion. Having satisfied their curiosity, the JP wrote a suitable letter for the *Graama Seevaka* and gave it to Lal, who went home to start the evening meal.

Lal's usual calm, slow, joking style made him a hard target to tease. Of the recipients of government aid, he was the only man who waited in line with the women to collect food at the local cooperative store. Lal regaled those pointing out his feminine behavior with humorous stories of his finicky taste in groceries; attempting to laugh at him, people found themselves instead laughing with him about the dead gecko in the rice bag and the dried fish so smelly it must have been fertilizer. He met comments on his domesticity with exaggerated stories of the latest crises in the kitchen, the rough quality of a new soap, and the price of beans. Lal's complaints were uniformly within his domestic role, not about it. He created an ambiguous self-image, somewhere between a simpleton with no understanding of his failure to fulfill a man's proper role and a freethinker impervious to criticism who held a singularly different set of values. With his deliberate opacity and his nonstop wit, Lal carved out a unique space for himself as man doing no job but women's work. The good-humored probing of the *Graama Seevaka* and the JP indexed at once the community's awareness of Lal's unusual behavior and their baffled and amused acceptance.

Lal himself seemed to have ambivalent feelings about his role. When I spoke with him in 1997, at one point he said that he needed to be "bailed out of jail" and set free from the kitchen. A little after that, he noted with pride that his family preferred his cooking. When Indrani cooked, Chandradasa and the children could tell. "*Bappa* [uncle] didn't cook this," the children would say, with head gestures indicating that they did not like the food. Lal said that his sister-in-law made coconut milk by machine; he himself scraped coconuts the old-fashioned way, generating a richer milk. Her curries had a foreign taste; his had a better flavor. Lal said that neighbors had asked him why he was still cooking while Indrani was home for a visit. He said that he would like to find a job, but Indrani and his mother had asked him not to leave. If he no longer took care of the family, Indrani would have to give up her job and look after her mother-in-law, a possibility neither of the strong-willed women viewed with pleasure. I asked if Lal were ashamed or shy (*lajja*) about the work he did. Suddenly completely serious, he held his head up very straight and said one should never be ashamed of the work one does to eat and drink. He took care of his mother, the house, and the children, and he did not try to hide what he did. He said he was ready to do any job that came his way, either men's work or women's work. He was not ashamed.

While Indrani's migration changed household gender roles for both Lal and Chandradasa, only Lal's behavior drew extensive village comments. Although Chandradasa took over some of the household chores during his infrequent visits, for the most part his job as a security guard kept him out of the domestic sphere, at the same time reaffirming his breadwinner role. In contrast, Lal's daily routine included many activities commonly thought of as women's work; he lacked any other form of regular employment that reaffirmed his masculinity; he had no wife and family of his own; and he did not drink alcohol. When a local committee arranged to resurface the paved road that led into the village, Lal, who had worked on road construction in the past, eagerly volunteered for the overtly masculine job. I believe he sought both the modest paycheck and the highly visible change of gender role.

Lal's ambiguous gender position complemented the new status and prestige that his sister-in-law Indrani's accumulated wealth gave her in the village. Participation in local events has often indexed changes in social and economic rank (G. Gamburd 1972, 354). Indrani and

Chandradasa contributed yearly to a large ceremony at a popular local shrine, spending over 5,000 / (U.S.$100) on food and decorations. Contributing lavishly to community projects correlated with a rise in prestige and social standing and entitled Indrani and Chandradasa to positions of authority in community politics and temple decision-making formerly monopolized by wealthy, high-caste, elite families. Several days after her return from the Middle East in 1993, Indrani received an invitation from three village youths to "open" a community food distribution event. Indrani accepted the offer and also made a generous contribution. Indrani's financial capital metamorphosed into prestige: symbolic capital, respect, and renown (Bourdieu 1977). Watching each other cynically for signs of returning poverty, villagers have recognized the difficulty of maintaining wealth. Patrons who have sustained their positions for a significant length of time, as Indrani and Chandradasa have, achieve recognition in the village as people who have truly prospered.

How Lal and Indrani would negotiate the transformation of their roles when Indrani returned permanently to the village remained to be seen. In 1997, returning home for a vacation after four years without visiting, Indrani showed no desire to relieve Lal of the household chores. Having spent lavishly for her daughter's coming-of-age ceremony, Indrani insisted (against her husband's will) that she should again return overseas to continue earning money for the family. Many villagers felt that she should have stayed home to look after her daughter instead. Indrani rebutted her critics, saying that she had spent all of her money on improving her house and holding a grand ceremony for her daughter. Now that they were older, her children needed money for their schooling. Indrani said that she had promised to fund the construction of the new cement house where Lal and his mother hoped to move when Indrani returned from abroad for good. The family also needed money for further improvements on their own house and might also need capital to start a business, perhaps a small shop. For all of these reasons, Indrani felt that she needed to return to her job in Qatar.

Indrani's prolonged absence had changed not only Lal's social position but also her own; like many other migrant women, she no longer fit into village society in the same way she had before she left. Though her primary motivations for migration remained economic, issues of identity, independence, and a dual sense of loyalty also impinged on her decision (Constable 1999). Like Lal, Indrani seemed ambivalent about assuming the housewife's role in her home in Sri Lanka.

Conclusion

Female migration to the Middle East changes gender roles and power relations in the village. The preceding case studies present both the taken-for-granted world and instances where contention questioned and challenged sedimented behavioral patterns in the village. Ramesh, Lal, and Chandradasa, three village men associated with female migrants, all asserted their masculinity differently: Ramesh through idleness and alcohol, Chandradasa through work and wealth, and Lal through a humorous, playful self-parodying exaggeration of the feminizing nature of his housekeeping role.

Ramesh's drinking, his excessive braggadocio, and his deliberate cultivation of the idle life challenged Rukmini to prosper despite, not with the aid of, her husband. Membership in the drinking group affirmed Ramesh's masculinity, assuaged his shame or guilt (*lajja*) for not improving, and provided the economic and social community he may have missed in his wife's absence. Chandradasa, by comparison, found his identity in hard work away from home. The cooperative and trusting relationship he shared with his wife gave him control not only of his own salary but also of the money she earned abroad. Willingly remitted for the construction of their house, her pay enhanced both spouses' standard of living and prestigious standing in the village. Lal, who took on all of the domestic chores in Indrani's absence, encountered daily joking comments about his cooking and household work with unfailing good humor. With his lack of other employment, Lal brought villagers face-to-face with the possibility of men taking over not just individual chores but entire social roles left by migrant women. Lal's behavior created a crisis in gender categories, generating a mixture of laughter and unease when he assumed a traditionally domestic role as his sister-in-law moved out into the public sphere of the international labor market.

8 Migrant Mothering: On Love and Money

Current economic hardship and a dearth of employment opportunities in Sri Lanka have driven women overseas to earn money as live-in domestic servants in the Middle East. With one in eight adult women in Naeaegama employed abroad, and with 65 percent of these migrants leaving behind small children, migration inevitably and significantly affects family roles. Since female migration began in the early 1980s, local images of ideal mothers, wives, and families have undergone subtle yet wide-ranging changes. As migrant women take on the formerly masculine role of breadwinner, they fragment the bundle of family responsibilities previously thought of as "mothering," redistributing parts of the role among a number of different people, both male and female. As the ways women love and care for their husbands and children change, so do social opinions about the worth and meaning of each option. Emerging behaviors in Naeaegama reaffirm and conflict with existing values, ideals, and practices of mothering, both reproducing and transforming more established ways of thinking about gender hierarchies, personal identity, financial responsibility, and women's work.

Motherhood and Women's Work in South Asia

South Asian women are often defined through their family roles as wives and mothers. Sri Lankan and Indian history, mythology, and literature contain multiple examples of submissive, self-sacrificing, modest women and benevolent goddesses bringing honor to their families and harmony to the cosmos. Similarly, examples abound of evil women and malevolent goddesses who challenge the authority of their fathers and husbands, aggressively asserting their sexuality and openly wielding power, thus bringing disaster to their families and chaos to the cosmos. Authoritative images portray the "good" woman as sexually restrained, submitting her will to the "civilizing" will of her father, husband, or son (Jacobson and Wadley 1995; Lynch 1999). Traditional images provide few examples of how women can hold legitimate power outside the family and home.

In Naeaegama, men and women alike often consider the standard actions associated with motherhood and family work as straightforward expressions of women's intrinsic nature. Culturally constructed gender roles are naturalized and legitimized as biological necessities (Jordanova 1980). The anthropological literature characterizes South Asian villagers as eager to have children because offspring, especially sons, act as social insurance for a couple's old age (Schrijvers 1985). A woman's power increases with the birth of her children, reaching its peak when her own sons bring wives into the household. Women's fulfillment of their "natural roles" in home activities—birth, child care, housework, and food preparation—leave paid labor as a secondary activity (Jacobson 1995, 60). Sirima Kiribamune argues that because people think of unmarried women as inauspicious, most Sri Lankan families do not approve of women who want a career instead of a family (1992, xli). Whatever the more nuanced realities in particular families, these images still act as an ideal in Naeaegama.

My research on women's work not only reveals the idealized images of wives and mothers, it also reveals how important these images are to the socialization and identity of those who hold them. I found in Naeaegama that parents taught girls to do housework and stay close to home, while boys played and roamed freely. Kiribamune argues that "upward social mobility [is] associated with the confinement of women to the household and the economic dependence on a male bread-winner" (1992, xxxi). By leaving her home to work abroad, a migrant woman violates the ideal role for a wife and mother and indicates that her husband cannot earn enough to support their family. Many poor, working women who cannot afford to stay at home travel widely and socialize freely. However, they too prize the same ideal that respectable women should not (by definition) venture too often into the public sphere.

Local gender ideologies shape how men and women think and speak about women's work. In Naeaegama, many villagers, even my perceptive research associates Siri and Sita, have discounted housework as a category of "work" and felt that housewives "did nothing" for a living. For instance, Elsie, the wealthy and influential moneylender who ran a flourishing trade in coconut fiber products (introduced in chap. 3), insisted modestly during an interview that her husband, also present at the time, supported their family while she stayed at home and "had no job." Though villagers clearly recognize women's work and value it highly, the dominant ideology brands a family where women work outside the home as low-status, which contributes to the masking of women's work *as* work.[1]

Official Sri Lankan statistics, which often ignore or erase the economic contributions of housewives or unpaid family workers, reflect these same gender assumptions (see Kiribamune 1992, xxvi). Many surveys disregard women's efforts in the informal economy, contract work, and casual labor. Such surveys call a large category of economically active women, who opportunistically perform a wide variety of different tasks, "unemployed" (Marecek 1992, 207). Similarly, surveys on migration (e.g., Korale 1989) struggle to decide if a woman who leaves the work force in Saudi Arabia to return home to her duties as a housewife in Sri Lanka should be called "unemployed" merely because she looks after her own family for free instead of someone else's for a salary.

In their stories, migrant mothers try both to conform to older ideals and to challenge the validity of these restrictive images. Migrant domestic labor highlights the conceptual dissonance in the taken-for-granted categories of work and home, contesting the "naturalness" of mothering and the power structures that surround it. Women offer to strangers, in exchange for wages, the same housework once universally accepted as a biological destiny and "sacred calling" performed for family. New consciousness of women's roles and personal identities make women more critically aware of the gender hierarchies, class differences, and international relations of power with which they live. At the same time, women remain at least partially rooted in older thought patterns and gender discourses that shape their sense of self and their

---

[1] Teaching, a high-status job acceptable for women, has proved a notable exception to the rule that women should not work outside the home.

concepts of ideal behavior. Anna Tsing identifies a "magic that allows groups defined by externally imposed categories of cultural difference simultaneously to resent and to embrace those categories" (1994, 280). In many of the cases discussed in this chapter, women's own political interests conflict with their internalized sense of cultural order. As women struggle to make sense of their roles in the face of the new economic and social realities associated with migration, they both re-create and challenge older structures of power and inequality.

The Fragmentation of Motherhood

Several Naeaegama migrants interviewed mentioned that the Madams of their Arabic families worked outside the home. By helping another woman manage the overlap between office and home, or by giving an affluent woman in the Middle East more leisure time, the domestic servant takes over many aspects of the Madam's role as wife and mother. As housemaids live and work in West Asia, ties of affection begin to bind them to their employers and especially to the children of their employers, for whom they often "care" in more than one sense of the word (see also Colen 1990). Neither family nor strangers, the housemaids gradually become familiar with new customs, foods, places, languages, and people. As they integrate into the households of their employers, those left in the village develop new habits and patterns to compensate for their absence. As the years pass, their children miss them less and less, growing fonder of their more immediate caregivers, the men and women who look after them on a daily basis. Just as housemaids grow emotionally attached to their charges abroad, their own children back in Sri Lanka come to love the caregivers at home (M. Gamburd 2000). Between the employer's family, the migrant's family, and the families who step in to care for the migrant's household, there is a continual redistribution of jobs, roles, labor, love, and money in the reproduction of children, families, and laborers. The dynamics of social change envelope not only economics but also, and perhaps more significantly, local and international patterns of love and affection.

Mommy's Booby: Mothering Children Abroad

Housemaids' duties vary from family to family, often including housecleaning, laundry, ironing, shopping, cooking, car washing, light

Fig. 5. A boy and his grandmother, Polwatta. The woman looks after her grandson while his mother works abroad. (Courtesy of the author.)

gardening, and child care. Of all of these intimate functions, child care proves the hardest to classify purely as work. Although migrant women set out to nurture their charges (for money) while providing material benefits to their own offspring (for love), the bounds of duty and affection are quickly blurred (see also Colen 1990, 101).

Lakshmi, the moneylender introduced in chapters 3 and 4, worked for British expatriates in Bahrain. Pregnant, Lakshmi's Madam returned to England to have her child. When she came back to Bahrain, the Madam handed Lakshmi the new infant, saying, "This isn't my baby but yours." Lakshmi expressed a real and lasting love for the baby boy. She was the one to bathe and nurture him, and she said, "It was my heart that was sad if the baby cried." Although his mother told her not to spoil the youngest baby by coming every time he cried, or he would never give her any time to work, Lakshmi found it very hard to obey this order. Since both the Madam and the Boss were very busy, Lakshmi did everything for the child, even remembering which medicines needed to be given and when. She said that she was more of a mother to the boy than his own mother; he did not call her by her name but called her "Mommy" instead.

Lakshmi recalled that during the time when the baby's mother was breast-feeding him, the baby would occasionally reach down Lakshmi's shirt, touch her side (she was fat then, she said, and her flesh hung out of her short blouses), and say, "Mommy's booby." The love and desire in the gesture emphasize the physical connection between the housemaid and her charge. Lakshmi said that she felt quite embarrassed when this happened in front of the Boss. Although the housemaid in many ways acted as the children's mother, she did not act as the Boss's sexual partner. Not yet familiar with hierarchy and difference, the baby by word and gesture assumed the woman he loved to be a part of his family in every way.

Long-Distance Mothering

Interpersonal dynamics just as complex as those arising in the Middle East between nannies and their charges surround the absence of mothers from their Sri Lankan homes. Critics of migration often extol "the mother," in the process nostalgically idealizing a traditional family of yesteryear. Many critics feel that the migration of mothers has bad effects on their children, leaving them malnourished, neglected, unruly, and truant from school. With a large portion of the adult women absent from the village, migration affects not only the migrants' children but also the children of local women assuming extra child care duties. Critics note the possibility of eldest daughters leaving school early to take care of the family, with early pregnancies and marriages resulting. They predict a higher divorce rate among couples and a rise in extramarital affairs, misuse of money, drug addiction, gambling, and other social ills due to the absence of one spouse (Gunatilleke 1992; Gunatilleke and Perera 1987; Korale 1983; Schampers and Eelens 1986; Rodrigo 1998). But while some scholars blame migration for the breakdown of family life, often the troubles that have made marriages in Naeaegama break down (e.g., economic hardship, wife-beating, alcoholism, sexual coercion and abuse, infidelity, and desertion, to name but a few) form part of the reason the migrants choose to leave the country in the first place. Understanding how migration has changed women's roles and personal identities requires both an accurate understanding of ideals and stereotypes, as well as a realistic vision of village family life.

In 1987 Gameela Samarasinghe, a Sri Lankan psychologist, looked at the social and psychological costs of female migration, noting that

Sri Lankan mothers rarely left extremely young children, especially those under one year of age (1989). Yet she found that mothers of forty thousand children under the age of five were working in the Middle East (1989, 15). The primary caregivers with whom the migrants left their children unanimously felt that they were fulfilling all the functions that a mother would perform, and the majority of them claimed they were more loved by the children than were the biological mothers (1989, 34). Samarasinghe found children's health and emotional well-being not noticeably harmed, especially after they adjusted to the situation, but she did note a possible neglect of children's schooling (1989, 39). In another longer-term study, Dias and Weerakoon-Gunawardene (1991) found that the longer the migrant mother stayed away from home, the more difficult the situation became for the children and the greater the rates of child neglect and delinquency.

Some neighbors, newspaper reporters, and scholars feel that migrant mothers heartlessly abandon their children in pursuit of money, but migrants say that they work abroad to be able to support their children. They do not divide working for wages from looking after children and family. Kiribamune writes that "when women work solely to support their families, it is extremely difficult to differentiate the roles of mother, home-maker and income-earner. For them earning an income is the means to keep the home fires burning, to make the children a little more comfortable and to give them the material needs or that little extra for which the husband's income alone is not sufficient" (1992, xliii). In poor families where husbands, when present, often lack full-time employment and work only occasionally as casual laborers, migrant women go abroad not only to supplement their husbands' salaries but also as the sole breadwinners providing for their families.

Nancy Scheper-Hughes argues that many of our commonsense conceptions of "mother love" are culturally learned instead of biologically given (1992, 15). Many Naeaegama mothers who have left their children to earn money abroad feel a sense of pride in accomplishment, and frustration in failure, stemming from their new financial obligations to their families. The emotions attached to this new facet of female identity complement and compete with the satisfactions and guilt associated with older images of the South Asian mother as the source of all nurturing and the absolute center of family life. As they struggle to come to terms with the psychological effects of their migration, village women broaden the spectrum of acceptable ways for women to "love" their children and "care" for their families. Shifting roles and identities highlight the constructed and contextual nature of motherhood and mother love in Sri Lanka.

"But look at what's happened to the boys!": On the "Neglect" of Priyanthi's Children

Some villagers occasionally have wondered if the considerable material wealth accumulated by migrants justified mothers in "abandoning" their children to work abroad. Others, both migrants and caregivers, have felt that the arrangements made for the children, which often involved extended kinship networks, proved satisfactory and minimized disruption. Although migrants did worry about leaving their children behind, they argued that they went abroad primarily to benefit those very children by providing them with money for food, clothing, and school fees; a new and better house; and better prospects for the future. Priyanthi, the Polwatta migrant introduced in the introduction, had substantially improved her family's material well-being with her earnings abroad, but she encountered mixed reactions to her decision to spend ten years away from her family. While many admired her industry, some people also judged her an inadequate mother.

Before Priyanthi returned from her fifth two-year trip to the Middle East, I interviewed her husband, Ariyapala. His four sons were all at school, and he had just woken up after working the night shift at the hospital where he had been an attendant for fifteen years. Ariyapala said that in 1982, although he held a good job by village standards, he and his wife had agreed that they needed extra income to make ends meet.[2] They decided to send Priyanthi to the Middle East to work. Their youngest son, a year and a half old when she left, cried when she departed and did not recognize her when she came home two years later. While Priyanthi was away, Ariyapala continued to work, and he and his father took care of household chores, but life had been difficult without his wife's presence.

Later that day, talking in the kitchen at Siri's house, Siri remarked that Ariyapala and Priyanthi might be able to start a business with the money she brought back from abroad. Siri's wife Telsie overheard this and commented, "Priyanthi's good at making money, but look at

---

[2] Over the course of one month, Ariyapala usually worked fifty-two hours overtime, for which he received Rs. 430/ extra a month. With that bonus, he earned Rs. 3,700/ each month (U.S.$75)—roughly what a schoolteacher or security guard would earn.

what's happened to the boys!" Village gossip, perhaps fueled by jealousy over Priyanthi's material prosperity, condemned Priyanthi for "abandoning" her sons, saying that they had all "run wild" in her absence. Although some people found Priyanthi's sons undisciplined, even the older two boys, whom neighbors judged the most reckless, had studied well beyond the neighborhood average, and their "disreputable" interests in fashion and foreign tourists were not unusual among their peers. Priyanthi's youngest son, whom I knew the best, seemed a cheerful, intelligent, levelheaded fourteen-year-old. Nevertheless, Telsie remarked disapprovingly that the sons did not always eat their meals at their own house, especially when their father was drunk, but wandered widely. In the local idiom, eating from tea shops and spending time away from home indicated a lack of coherence in family life—a clear condemnation of their absent mother, who was faulted for valuing money too much and her family too little.

I spoke with Priyanthi several months later, four days after she returned from her fifth trip abroad. Confronted with the accusation that she had abandoned her sons, Priyanthi made it very clear that she had gone abroad to earn money not for herself but for her children, to improve their lot in life. Priyanthi emphasized how difficult her work had been, stating, "It is better to *beg* in Sri Lanka than to work abroad!" Priyanthi sent little home for daily consumption because her husband was earning money for the family. Instead, she saved her salary for large endeavors. Upon returning home in 1983 after her first trip abroad, Priyanthi bought a house and land from a Berava caste family. The house, a large tile-roofed building with seven rooms, was one of the most impressive structures in Polwatta. After subsequent trips, she purchased furniture, constructed a well and a toilet, wired the house for electricity, and replaced the clay floor with cement. These accomplishments were concrete and lasting symbols of what she had done for the sake of her family.

In her narrative, Priyanthi portrayed herself as a hardworking, self-sacrificing mover and shaker who took responsibility for the family's material well-being. She did not dwell on the emotional issues of her sons' development, saying merely that their father earned enough to feed them and that their father and grandfather should certainly have been able to look after them adequately. She felt that her shift toward material mothering should have been accompanied by a corresponding shift toward competent psychological fathering and grandfathering. Priyanthi stated that her first priority was to provide material necessities for her children, and she firmly refused responsibility for any domestic problems that occurred during her migration.

Money Matters

As women come to express their love for their children in terms of the money and material benefits they bring home from the Middle East, they also come to have an added stake in controlling their remittances while they are working abroad and in maintaining an adequate level of material prosperity after they return to Sri Lanka. Having irrevocably missed some or all of their children's childhood, mothers struggle to preserve the financial well-being for which they worked. Shifts in the meaning of mothering brought about by migration add new significance to daily village conflicts over household finances.

Older gendered patterns of money management in the village have often pitted husbands and wives against each other in a struggle over limited resources. If a man provides the bulk of the household income, most village couples assume that ideally the husband would bring about two-thirds of his wages to his wife, who manages the household accounts with that money. The remainder of his salary he would keep for his own social needs, such as cigarettes and alcohol. However, the housewives with working husbands I spoke to often lamented that the men gave them too little and still left them with the responsibility of putting food on the table. Women could try to get more money from men by concealing any money they did have, ridiculing their husbands in public for being poor providers, or refusing to cook for, speak with, or have sex with their husbands (see also Risseeuw 1991). Even if a woman has contributed to the family income or become the family's sole breadwinner, her husband remains, at least in people's perception (including his own and his wife's), the main decision-maker and the head of the family. Women's wages usually go directly for family use, and women who spend even small sums of money (much less than the one-third allowed working men) for their own individual pleasure confront public condemnation of their "selfishness." Unemployed husbands, however, feel it within their rights to demand money from their wives for their social activities. Returned migrants regularly confront complex negotiations over the distribution and use of their savings and often fight an uphill battle to maintain their standard of living without fresh remittances from abroad.

"Take him by the ear"

The long-term success or failure of a migrant's bid to improve her family's financial and material well-being has often depended on the thrift and planning of her relatives, particularly her husband. "A good husband" does not drink, waste money, or beat his wife. Young women learn not only these criteria but also that they should never appear to object to a husband lacking these good qualities (see also Risseeuw 1991). Women have often hesitated to challenge the gender hierarchy directly, fearing what others might say about their breach of tradition (see Kiribamune 1992, xix). Instead of openly voicing their feelings or publicly rebelling against unjust treatment, many women instead have learned how to manage their husbands through endurance, manipulation, and deception. Even in cases of alcoholism and abuse, women rarely leave their husbands because they see no viable alternatives to married life. In contrast to these existing patterns, returned migrants, more vocal than many other women, have occasionally criticized their husbands openly, blaming them for the irresponsible behavior that drains away the household's wealth—wealth the women see as a concrete manifestation of their love and work for their family.

Priyanthi's husband Ariyapala drank heavily throughout my stay in the village. Siri confidently expected Priyanthi to "take Ariyapala by the ear" when she returned from the Middle East, collecting his monthly salary and putting it toward household expenses instead of toward liquor. In village opinion, the wife should control household spending, and Priyanthi's absence was held partially responsible for Ariyapala's behavior. When I interviewed Priyanthi shortly after her return from the Middle East, she gave unusually open vocal expression to her displeasure with her husband, humorously indicating her disapproval of the state of their household as she had found it on her return. Dreaming aloud, Priyanthi said that she could have had a special "American" (luxurious) house and a car if she had found generous places to work in the Middle East, and if she had had a good husband. Priyanthi accepted the responsibility of running the household budget, a responsibility that came with both older and newer images of "motherhood." Her role in earning much of the wealth in question gave her a greater stake, more leverage, and increased assertiveness in her task. With these attitudes, Priyanthi challenged some of the existing gender roles, while accepting and reinforcing others.

On Money and Love

Migrant women often find themselves negotiating the complex con-
version between love and money. Lakshmi, the moneylender introduced earlier, related two stories that explicitly tied her sense of self
as mother and daughter to her power to earn money. Lakshmi's personal narratives often contained detailed descriptions of financial
transactions. Like many Middle East migrants, Lakshmi on occasion
faced charges of valuing money more than people. But Lakshmi portrayed herself as someone for whom money took a back seat to personal relationships; paradoxically, she illustrated great emotional
value in terms of being willing to pay "any amount" of money to accomplish a task.

The first story concerned her daughter's coming-of-age ceremony.
In the Naeaegama area, many families celebrate a girl's puberty with
a bathing ceremony followed by gifts for the girl and a large party for
friends and family. Second only to a marriage in its size and extrava-
gance, a coming-of-age ceremony holds special significance in the village. In 1990, while Lakshmi was working abroad, her eldest daughter
came of age. By the time Lakshmi's family succeeded in contacting her
by telephone, only a week remained before the auspicious time to begin the ceremonies. Lakshmi said that she got upset and cried when
she heard the news. "Where is the time to prepare?" she asked. With
the family for whom she worked away on holiday and their house open
for repairs, Lakshmi could not leave Bahrain to go to Sri Lanka. She
felt that she had to send something to her daughter, but since her Boss
was out of the country, she had no money on hand.

In turmoil, Lakshmi called on the help of Sri Lankan friends whose
husbands worked in Bahrain. Since Lakshmi had no ready cash, her
friends took up a collection, gathering together 150 dinar (U.S.$400 at
1990 exchange rates), which Lakshmi sent to her family. She also
wanted to send a suitcase full of dresses to her daughter. Lakshmi ran
into a friend who was returning to Sri Lanka, and the friend agreed to
deliver the suitcase to Lakshmi's family. Recalling herself crying with
happiness, Lakshmi rejoiced that everything had been provided for her
daughter. Lakshmi concluded the story by stating that in addition to
the U.S.$400 and the parcel she had sent from Bahrain, her daughter re-
ceived Rs. 10,000/ (worth the equivalent of Rs. 15,000/ in 1994 rupees)
from a paternal aunt and Rs. 3,000/ (worth the equivalent of Rs. 4,500/

in 1994 rupees) from her maternal uncles.[3] Few other Naeaegama residents would have felt comfortable putting exact figures on such gifts, but for Lakshmi, revealing the large sums of money that she and others sent served to index the strength of the personal ties.

The other story Lakshmi related emphasized human relationships over and above those based on money. Lakshmi's mother passed away in December 1995, three years after Lakshmi returned from working abroad. In 1997 Lakshmi told Sita and me an elaborate narrative of her mother's death. Ill with gastritis, the older woman's health declined rapidly, first at home and then in a local hospital. Lakshmi's story, laden with details of conversations and financial dealings, climaxed with a moving description of how she pleaded in the middle of the night with a sleepy van driver to take her mother to a Colombo hospital. Promises of money did not move the man, but an explanation of the dire circumstances did. Lakshmi's story highlighted the idea that money cannot bring the dead back to life; at the same time, she quantified her care for her mother by telling us the prices she paid for the services she requested that her mother receive. Her story emphasized her ties with village people, detailing her own involvement in local life-crisis rituals from five days before her mother's death to seven days after it. She described attending a coming-of-age ceremony for a friend's daughter, a wedding reception, and a neighborhood funeral; she also described the ceremonies surrounding her own mother's funeral and the villagers' support and attendance. Lakshmi emphasized human compassion, community solidarity, and grief in her story but quantified them with descriptions of financial considerations. Usually calm and in control, in her narrative Lakshmi presented herself as overcome with emotion for her family and (to a lesser extent) for her village friends, with intense emotion expressed explicitly as superseding concern for haggling and cutting costs.

Lakshmi's narratives highlighted both her interest in money and her regard for personal relationships. Although in most of her Middle East stories Lakshmi portrayed herself as a calm, thrifty, and hardworking individual, in the coming-of-age story she characterized herself as a

[3] In the Sri Lankan kinship system, as in other Dravidian systems, the terms for maternal uncle and paternal aunt are the same as those for father-in-law and mother-in-law. In a system with preferential cross-cousin marriage, the participation of these relatives in a coming-of-age ceremony foreshadows their ideal participation in the girl's marriage to her cross-cousin.

mother in emotional turmoil, frantic to send gifts to her daughter, and careless of expense. Similarly, the story of her mother's death emphasized the value of human life as greater than any sum of money. If the purpose of Lakshmi's migration was to provide a better life for herself, her mother, and her daughters while she was abroad and after she returned to Sri Lanka, then her daughter's coming-of-age ceremony and her mother's illness represented major instances when the fruits of Lakshmi's labor had to be extremely evident. In these cases Lakshmi said that she valued love more than money, using money itself as the measure of her love.

Grandmother's Nursery: Caroline

Tensions have often filled the relationships between migrant mothers and their children's caregivers, revealing strains brought about by the fragmentation of motherhood and the difficulties created by the commodification of nurturing. Kamala, a migrant introduced in chapter 5, relied on her mother, Caroline, to look after her two children when she first went abroad. Herself a mother of ten children, some of whom still lived at home, Caroline looked after a house full of grandchildren while her daughters and daughters-in-law worked in the Middle East. Caroline's crippled sister and her mother also lived with the family, helping Caroline with coconut-fiber rope-making and child care. Her husband, who worked in another part of the country, returned home twice a month for the weekend. Caroline said that she prayed continually for good health so that she could continue to look after her many grandchildren.

While their mother was working in the UAE, Caroline looked after Kamala's two boys, sending them back to their father in the evenings after dinner. One could describe relations between Caroline and her son-in-law as "strained" at best. Caroline mentioned that although she fed her grandsons while Kamala was away, their father rarely reimbursed her for the cost of their food. (The boys' father, Pradeep, told a different story, which is related in chapter 5.) Once, when Kamala sent Caroline some money from the Middle East, Pradeep got violently angry, and the quarrel ended at the police station. Kamala sent neither money nor letters to her parents after that time. With tears in her eyes, Caroline said that Kamala had behaved very ungratefully. Although Caroline had looked after Kamala's sons for three years, Kamala had sent no money, given her no thanks, and had not even come to visit Caroline in the hospital when she was recovering from an operation. Hurt by Kamala's behavior, Caroline and her husband had not visited Kamala when she was hospitalized after attempting suicide (see chapter 5).

Caroline's reaction to her daughter's "ingratitude" showed a budding awareness of the changing value of women's work. Although migration brought about some professionalization of mothering as women worked abroad for wages, the general image that women took care of children, naturally and gladly, remained. But while Caroline loved her grandchildren, she also said that child care was costly and time-consuming labor. Aware of her pivotal role in facilitating the migrations of her daughters and daughters-in-law, Caroline articulated her sense of hurt and injustice, saying that her labor should be reciprocated with both love and money.

Conclusion

Migration fragments the duties of the mother both at home and abroad, with three sets of women providing very different types of care to three sets of children. Women sell their nurturing skills abroad, leaving their own children in the care of others. In the Middle East the efforts of the foreign maid free the biological mother from child care for leisure or for waged work. Nannies such as Lakshmi often express the impression that they are more "mothering" than the biological mother of the children for whom they care while abroad. In Sri Lanka, mothers leave husbands and children (to whom they should ideally dedicate their lives) and move into the public sphere, selling their labor as a commodity on the international market and earning valuable foreign exchange for their country. Migrant mothers such as Priyanthi and Lakshmi negotiate new roles and identities that incorporate their work abroad. Having become breadwinners to secure a good life for their offspring, migrant mothers try pragmatically to dismiss charges of greed and heartlessness for failing to fulfill a more traditionally nurturing role. Instead, they often index their love in monetary terms. Women who remain in Naeaegama and look after the children migrants leave behind show their love in well-worn ways, but their perceptions of love, work, and motherhood have also changed. Many, like Caroline, have a growing awareness of the potential monetary value of their work. With few role models and ever-changing personal circumstances, each woman continually negotiates her emergent identity in her family at home and her family abroad. Their new practices widen the range of acceptable ways to "mother."

When village women migrate from Sri Lanka to the Middle East, they challenge and alter the stereotypes for the behavior of good mothers and wives. Changing images of motherhood suggest changes for fathers as well. While ideal roles have lagged behind village practices, more men, especially younger fathers whose wives are in the Middle East, have found themselves at least partially responsible for taking care of their children. Although most of the caregivers have been female relatives, men also contribute to household tasks, further fragmenting the role of the mother.

By redefining a mother's role in terms of money and materials, labor migration has also spurred changing images of family responsibility. While older traditions of female subservience shield male breadwinners from criticism, some migrant women have attempted to hold their husbands responsible for managing the household budget, a traditionally female obligation. Priyanthi outspokenly condemned her husband's lack of financial accountability. Although such complaints are not new, migration makes them more powerful. With migrant women's "mothering" demonstrated most obviously by the material well-being of their families, women have an added stake in maintaining the family's financial prosperity not only during but also after their migration. To hang on to the money they earn and the goods that they purchase for their children, migrant mothers publicly demand radical adjustments in the roles and behaviors of their husbands. Anger, frustration, and pain—as well as joy and satisfaction—clearly accompany these gradual changes, as men's participation in household duties and financial planning accompany migrant women's new roles as working mothers.

9 Immoral Maid
and Abusive Employer:
The Horror Story Genre

Before the dawn of the postmodern era, literary critics often distinguished between the real and the ideal, nature and art, history and fiction. Ethnographers distinguished between what people did and what they said they did, between social standards, norms, and stereotypes on the one hand and everyday behavior on the other. More recently, as part of the post-structuralist turn, scholars have blurred the neat boundaries that used to shape analysis, asking how images and reality—fiction and fact—affect one another.

A few minutes after midnight on 31 August 1997, Diana, Princess of Wales, died in a car crash. She, her companion Dodi Al Fayed, a bodyguard, and a chauffeur drove through downtown Paris at high speeds, pursued by freelance paparazzi, and their journey ended in a heap of mangled metal. Diana, arguably the most photographed woman in the world, had become a household fixture, a storybook princess, a soap-opera character among the *dramatis personae* of the continuing royal saga. To feed an image-hungry world, nine photographers on motorcycles pursued a shot of Lady Di with her lover—a shot of their private life that the couple were reluctant to share. Appearance and reality, fiction and truth, stereotype and everyday behavior: Are they so separate? The tragic death of the Princess of Wales provides a graphic and startling example of the image returning to strike its original—an original, many note, not unskilled at manipulating the press. The story of Diana's life, marketed in tabloids around the world, fueled a media mania that even Diana's own impassioned pleas for privacy could not stem. The story took on a life of its own—and in the process, took the life of the princess.

In this chapter I examine an equally powerful instance of image overwhelming reality. The subjects of my analysis, migrant housemaids, rarely make the front pages of newspapers, and their deaths fail to inspire six days of frenzied global mourning. Their bereaved loved ones rarely get Charles Spencer's chance at fifteen minutes of international television time to set the record straight. But images of housemaids' dreary lives, fictions about their immoral characters, and stereotypes of their sexual vulnerability and promiscuity turn up regularly in the national and international media. These narratives, which I refer to as "horror stories," shadow each and every migrant's experience of her migration, both at home and abroad. Like Diana, housemaids strive to fashion and manipulate their public images, with varying degrees of success. Horror stories affect how a migrant experiences her own migration, how she expresses her experiences to others, and how others in her community—on the family, village, national, and international levels—judge, assess, interpret, regulate, legislate, and make policy about migration.

In speaking of media images and local tales of migrants' woes as horror stories, and in equating them with fiction, I wish in no way to suggest that abominable things do not happen to housemaids abroad. Maids are raped, abandoned, beaten, overworked, underpaid, and subject to a slew of other exploitative, unjust, and illegal abuses at the hands of their recruiting agents and their sponsoring employers on a depressingly regular basis. But the average experience of the average maid (if there ever were such a person) is very different from the common stories we hear about her. Similarly, the woman named Diana Spencer, the Princess of Wales, corresponded in many ways to the image that the media created of her. But what parts of her story remained unpublished? Which images never left the paparazzi's darkrooms? And how did the media image acquire the power to lead indirectly to Diana's death? The same questions can be asked about images of migrant housemaids and their Arabic employers. Who retells tales of migration? What situations send bulbs flashing and what scenes leave the shutter unmoved? What, politically, is at stake in the conscious and unconscious manipulation of these images? And how do these images, having taken on a life of their own, come to govern and shape the lives of the women they claim to represent?

Media Representations

On occasion, when I talk about my work on the migration of labor from Sri Lanka to the Middle East, my acquaintances raise their eyebrows and remark with concern, "Oh, yes, I have heard about that. Those Asian housemaids are dreadfully abused." Now *my* eyebrows rise. I wonder, of all of the myriad aspects of migration, why have they focused on this? As isolated encounters built into a recurrent pattern, it finally dawned on me to ask where this knowledge comes from and why it takes such a predictable shape. Answering these questions has forced me to look at the circulation of images and stories about Asian migrants in a transnational context.

Information on migrant domestic labor available to the news-conscious in the United States often takes a form similar to that in an article by Chris Hedges in the *New York Times:* "Foreign Women Lured into Bondage in Kuwait" (1992). The author explains that employers do not allow their housemaids to leave the house, receive or send letters, or make telephone calls. Housemaids work long hours, with no days off. Often their employers deprive them of food, withhold their salaries, rape them, and otherwise abuse them. Section headers throughout the article read "Beaten and Raped," "Almost Like Slavery," and "Some are Trapped," highlighting the vulnerability of the housemaids.

Similarly, major U.S. newspapers followed the case of Sara Balabagan, a fifteen-year-old Filipina maid, who in July 1994 was raped at knifepoint by her eighty-five-year-old employer in the United Arab Emirates. Balabagan, able to wrest the knife away from her attacker, stabbed him thirty-two times, killing the man. In July 1995 a court awarded her the equivalent of U.S.$27,000 in damages for rape, fined her U.S.$40,500, and sentenced her to a seven-year prison term for manslaughter (Lancaster 1995). During a retrial in September 1995, the court sentenced Balabagan to death amid outraged protest from the Philippines (Ambah 1995). After much negotiation, Balabagan served a year in jail, paid the U.S.$40,500 fine, endured one hundred light lashes, and returned to the Philippines, where she received a considerable sum of money, from a non-governmental group organized in her support, and a scholarship for university study (*Migration News* 1996d).

In critiquing these articles, I in no way intend to minimize the gravity of the cases described in the international press. I wish only to point out that sensational stories involving rape, death, and moral outrage appeal to the appetite of the media consumer. Stories of modest successes of village housewives working abroad, or even stories of lonely boredom and hard work, rarely hit the headlines. But even if the reporting scarcely correlates with the experience of the typical maid, the reporting directly influences that maid's experience of migration. Two articles from Sri Lankan newspapers illustrate how the prevailing image of the housemaid impinges on ordinary women's migration.

The *Sunday Times*, a conservative English-language newspaper, published an article in August 1996 entitled "Abroad, Astray" (Seneviratene 1996). The caption accompanying a photo of eight women with suitcases reads, "Uprooted, isolated and defenceless these women have little support when in trouble." The author quotes Colonel Nissanka Wijeratne, the then-chairman of the Sri Lanka Bureau of Foreign Employment (SLBFE), as saying, "The real problem is that 80 percent of the women in Kuwait must sleep with their masters. They are merely regarded as sex slaves." Later in the article Wijeratne says that the legal status of migrant women is that of private property. The author reports that Wijeratne would like Sri Lanka to "take a stand on the rights of the migrant labourer[. P]erhaps we should follow in the footsteps of India, Bangladesh, Nepal and Pakistan in banning unskilled/semi-skilled women migrants working abroad." The author then briefly notes that women working abroad earn twenty-three billion rupees of foreign exchange annually and that the migrant women themselves wish to continue working abroad despite the dangers involved.

The article "Abroad, Astray," especially the SLBFE chairman's scarcely-veiled assertion that job agencies sold women into prostitution, infuriated members of the Association of Licensed Foreign Employment Agencies (ALFEA) in Colombo. Research staff at the SLBFE, the major government agency regulating migration, remarked to me in 1997 that their past chairman had on occasion been more influenced by imagery than by solid research. The article's author gives little credence to a lower official who, supported by SLBFE statistics, called the number of "cases of sexual harassment of domestic workers ... 'negligible' in labor importing countries." The chairman of an influential government agency—and, to a certain extent, the reporter who inter-viewed him—both seem to have found socially circulating stereotypes of migration more persuasive than sober scholarship. Wijeratne used anecdotal "evidence" to advocate the prohibition of migration—a policy move few if any of the migrant women I knew in the village would support.

Critics of migration have emphasized not only the vulnerability of women working abroad but also a supposed disintegration of family life connected with the migration of female labor to the Middle East. For example, *Daily News* (a daily English-language newspaper con-trolled by the government press) ran an article relating the story of a painter remanded (arrested) for stabbing his wife (Razik 1997). She had recently returned from Saudi Arabia and was making arrangements to return to work against her husband's wishes. The couple were at the police station concerning their domestic problems when the man stabbed his wife with a carpenter's tool. This article, and many more like it in the Sinhala and English press, emphasize the role of migra-tion in causing personal and family disruptions such as suicide and do-mestic violence. Working women take the blame for many social ills; newspaper stories rarely consider that domestic violence and other problems at home could *cause* (instead of result from) migration.

These four stories, two from U.S. newspapers, two from Sri Lankan papers, encapsulate many of the main themes in the horror stories about Middle East migration: tales of abuse, rape, prostitution, dis-solving marriages, and neglected children. Geraldine Heng and Janadas Devan coin the phrase *narrative of crisis* to describe a scenario (often largely fabricated or imagined) used by those in power to justify their use of power, thus reaffirming their qualifications to save the nation and continue to lead the country (1992, 343). Like narratives of crisis, horror stories advocate particular political actions and empower spe-cific actors. Unlike narratives of crisis, though, horror stories do not spring solely from national initiatives but span a larger segment of the population. Above and beyond the all-too-frequent reality of tragic events, I wish to show the pattern and the purpose behind the circu-lation of such horror stories. Reading this genre against the grain, with a critical eye trained on inconsistencies, exaggerations, and politically motivated assertions, reveals their role in local, national, and inter-national relations.

Typical versions of the horror story differ from descriptions of ex-periences I collected from female migrants in Naeaegama. But these discrepancies are not the end of the analysis. More significantly, the stories *create* a reality. The horror stories are important in and of themselves, above and beyond whether they accurately represent the state of affairs in West Asia. Edward Said refers to entrenched stereotypes about Asia as "muscular truths" and "programmatic ignorance" embedded in Western discourse about the East (1986, 219). I find Said's evocative formulation useful for conceptualizing how stereotypes work not only in colonial and post-colonial depictions of East-West relations but also in more general and mundane instances. The migration horror story genre contains the same sorts of fixed patterns of thought, predetermined meanings, and indisputable interpretations that Said identifies. Like any culturally constructed set of stereotypes and categories, the images and representations common in the migration horror story genre embody a socially situated system of knowledge and power (Foucault 1994; 210–13). The genre monopolizes representation not only on the national and international levels but also shapes memory and identity on the village and the individual level.

Pierre Bourdieu argues that "the construction of reality is a major dimension of political power" (1977, 165). Just as Princess Diana cultivated the media, attempting to craft an image that worked to her political advantage, so too do narrators of horror stories strive to manipulate the dominant images from generic tales to further their own specific goals. Through their creative use of common cultural constructs, these storytellers work within, challenge, and reproduce hierarchies of power and inequality (R. Williams 1977). The rest of this chapter will explore patterns in subgenres of horror stories, asking how these stories influence conceptions of migration in the eyes of individual women, their relatives, their fellow villagers, and the national and international media. In the gray area between fiction and fact, in the discrepancies between sensational story and mundane reality, I hope to shed light on the power dynamics shaping the stereotyped characters and plotlines of the genre in question and explore the processes that build group and individual identity through the politics of representation.

A Thrice-Told Tale

Storytelling never takes place in a vacuum; narrator, audience, and context shape the text and its impact (Derrida 1977; Gumperz 1977).

I found in my research that people often preferred to talk about secondhand dramatic disasters rather than their own firsthand stories of
more mundane and benign experiences. During interviews, having
given their own accounts of migration, women often felt it necessary
to relate several instances of generalized adversity to complete my picture of work in the Middle East. Images of "the" Sri Lankan housemaid and "the" Arabic employer had lives of their own, significantly
independent of personal experiences.

While in Naeaegama, I heard many horror stories about experiences in the Middle East. Some narrators related personal experiences
or those of close relatives while others verged on hearsay and rumor.
Often those further from personal experience of the story borrowed
from common tropes in retelling a tale, with generic details supplied
from models prevalent in the growing repertoire of horror stories
about the Middle East. Those closer to the source gave more particulars, supplying idiosyncratic descriptions at variance with the standard scenario.

The following three versions of the same story illustrate the politics
of narrative in Naeaegama. I heard the first version during an interview with a group of Kurundugoda sisters and cousins who had all
worked abroad. In the course of telling me various terrible tales, the
gathered women collectively recalled the case of two Naeaegama sisters working in the same house overseas. In 1986 one sister had stolen
something; her employers killed her and sent the other sister home
with the body. Two months later, their father died from the shock.

I heard a second, slightly different version from a sister-in-law of the
woman who died. This storyteller said that the employers claimed
their children had pushed the maid from the upstairs balcony. She
never mentioned the issue of theft. The employers paid compensation
to the dead woman's father, who used the Rs. 25,000/ (Rs. 63,000/ in
1994 rupees) they sent as a dowry for the other daughter.

I heard a third story from Liila, an older sister of the deceased
woman, Chitra. Showing me a small picture, cut out of her sister's
passport, that rested on her light switch, Liila said that her youngest
sister Chitra was only nineteen when she died. A very "joyful" person, Chitra used to win bicycle and motorbike races along the main
Galle Road. Another of Liila's sisters, Triksi, worked at a house in the
Middle East for three years. In 1986, when Triksi said that there was
too much work for one person, her employers told her to send for
someone to help, and she chose her youngest sister Chitra. The spon-

soring family employed Triksi in their shop while Chitra worked in their house. Liila said that her youngest sister died seven months into her stay in the Middle East. She had been leaning on an unsound balcony railing, which gave way under her weight. She broke her neck in the fall and died. Chitra died on a Thursday at noon, and her employers sent the embalmed body back to Sri Lanka with Triksi on Friday. They also gave Rs. 40,000/ (Rs. 100,800/ in 1994 rupees) for the funeral and sent Rs. 55,000/ (Rs. 138,600/ in 1994 rupees) as compensation. Triksi went back to the same house to work; the employers sent the compensation money with her return ticket.

Moving from outsiders to in-laws to nuclear family, the dramatic story line changes, first from death as punishment for theft to malicious murdering children to pure accident. Outsiders make no mention of compensation; in-laws placed the amount at Rs. 25,000/, while Chitra's sister estimated compensation and funeral expenses at nearly four times that amount. Similarly, the degree of rupture between the surviving housemaid and her employers decreased with the familiarity of the teller. Outsiders implied that the surviving woman was sent home in disgrace with the corpse of her thieving sister; the in-laws displaced the killing from adults to children; and Liila made no references to the villainous nature of Arabs, stressing instead their generosity and claiming that her surviving sister returned to the same house to work. Outsiders linked the death of the father to heartbreak over the murder of his daughter, whereas insiders made no such connection between the tragedies befalling their family.

I doubt that I will ever find out what "really" happened in this case; for my argument, it is the very diversity of stories that proves fruitful. Although the idiosyncratic details and lack of generic tropes argue for the veracity of Liila's version of the story, Liila's story is also a representation coloring listeners' judgments of the people involved. The women least familiar with the family of the deceased seemed to borrow freely from tropes available in the horror story genre, embellishing events by adding theft, crime, and high family melodrama to the story. For reasons that I explore later, the narrators furthest from the source gave the least sympathetic presentation of both the Arabs and the housemaids involved. Generalizing from this one example, one cannot help but wonder how many of the other stories one hears in person and reads in the newspaper have been shaped by similar standardizing processes.

Subgenre #1: Promiscuity and National Pride

For the purposes of this analysis, horror stories about the Middle East are divided into several large and overlapping subcategories. First, many stories circulate about women's sexuality, highlighting both their promiscuity and their vulnerability to sexual abuse. A second category of stories emphasizes the hard work and house arrest that characterize women's domestic service. Third, stories of severe punishment create a daunting image of Arabic discipline. Finally, many narratives portray disasters befalling the family left behind in the mother's absence. Chapter 8 addressed stories of the latter type; the remainder of this chapter will focus on horror stories of the first three subgenres.

This section examines the production, distribution, and consumption of the first subgenre of horror stories: tales about Sri Lankan women's sexuality that emphasize the national importance of female chastity. Many village men and women worried that some Sri Lankan women worked abroad as prostitutes instead of as housemaids and that others suffered from sexual and physical abuse. Locally told tales, as well as stories in the national press, continually reassert these ideas. (Female returnees and their foreign employers also perpetuate stories about promiscuous housemaids, but since the patterns and implications in their narratives differ significantly, their horror stories are analyzed in the following section.)

The steady smattering of sensational news items appearing regularly in the Sri Lankan Sinhala- and English-language press have dealt not only with the possible promiscuity of housemaids abroad but also with their vulnerability to sexual and physical assault. For example, one headline announced, "Lankan Housemaid Dies in Abu Dhabi," and published a picture of the body, hair loose and face lax (*Daily News* 1993b). (Unbound hair often signifies madness, sexual desire, or promiscuity in Sri Lankan aesthetics.) Another reported, "Safe-House Set up for Housemaids in UAE"; P. Navaratnam, the Labour Secretary at the Sri Lankan embassy said that he "received sixty telephone calls and three written complaints a day. They ranged from non-payment of wages to rape" (*The Island* 1992). Government and private agencies strove to provide some minimal security for housemaids while staying on the right side of the Arabic countries' rulers and police.

Another article reported that a woman recently returned from Middle East "died of hemorrhage" in the Kurunegala Hospital, implying that she had suffered a faulty abortion (*The Island* 1993). In another instance, an article headline reported, "Newborn Found in Garbage Cart" at Katunayake airport; simultaneously, a housemaid who had disembarked from a flight was admitted to a nearby hospital with heavy bleeding. "It is suspected that the housemaid had given birth in the aircraft and dumped the child in the toilet of the plane" (*Daily News* 1993a), the article continued. Unwanted pregnancies, secret abortions, and attempted infanticide endangered the health of women and children. Pregnancy or disease of any sexual nature reflected badly on the women in question, whether they were the aggressors or the victims in sexual encounters. Such sensationalized stories emphasized the sexual nature of the women who went to the Middle East and the misdeeds and deceptions they kept hidden.

Men from Naeaegama who had worked abroad most vocally advised against sending women overseas. They unanimously agreed that they would never send their daughters or wives to the Middle East and based their accounts of what happened to migrant women partly in rumor, partly in experience. Those who knew the least had the most extreme opinions about the extent of women's promiscuity.

Elson, a poor but ambitious cinnamon peeler who had worked for fifteen months in Oman, said that he would never send his daughters abroad because he did not like to see them "walking around," a sign of lack of supervision and possible promiscuity in local symbolism. Ideally, Sri Lankan daughters were supervised from the moment they reached puberty until their wedding day. Perhaps in deference to my nationality, he said that he would let his daughters travel to the United States or to Australia but not to the Middle East. He had "seen the trouble there." Although in some houses the people looked after their housemaid "like they would look after their own daughter," he felt such places were rare. Like Elson, many people with conservative opinions counseled against unmarried women working in the Middle East, claiming that a respectable family arranging a marriage for their son would retract a proposal if they discovered that the woman had worked as a housemaid. A number of fathers with adult, unmarried daughters emphatically condemned out of hand all jobs requiring overnight stays away from the family home. More pragmatic villagers noted that a woman returning from abroad with money for a dowry had little difficulty finding eligible suitors, especially as migration grew more common and the stigma attached to it decreased.

Commenting that while men needed skills such as carpentry or driving heavy machinery to go abroad, Elson noted that women only needed to look pretty. "Why would they want a picture for a housemaid's job?" he asked, and speculated about the nature of the work for which beauty was a qualification. "Some families do not let the housemaid outside of the house; is there a secret inside? People do not allow the housemaid to make telephone calls or keep her own passport; it is like prison." He concluded that since women could never know in advance the situations they might find, it was better that they not go abroad at all.

Many of the Sri Lankan women in Oman have sold sex for money, Elson claimed: "In the Middle East, Sri Lankan women are like prostitutes. They get together in the parks after work and on their days off, and then they go off somewhere else. They say that they're going shopping and do this instead." Since none of the women's relatives were present, they could behave any way they pleased. When I pressed for details, Elson said that although he had never seen this in person, he had heard about it from the Pakistani men with whom he worked. The Pakistani men told the Sri Lankan men that they had had sex with Sri Lankan women and that the going price was ten riyals (U.S.$3). All the Sri Lankan men in his group felt ashamed. (Several other reliable sources corroborated Elson's point, noting that men in cars stopped frequently for Asian women walking on the streets and that male guest workers formed a large subset of prostitutes' clientele.) Defensively striking back at his Pakistani coworkers, Elson said that he had seen Pakistani women "getting into cars," a possible though unlikely event, since Pakistan does not officially allow women to work overseas as housemaids. Elson's anger and humiliation on hearing that his coworkers had purchased the sexual services of Sri Lankan women mushroomed into an issue of national pride and a sweeping accusation that *most* women working abroad were promiscuous. When speaking of two close relatives who worked abroad, however, Elson tempered his critique, saying only that they had "gone down in people's estimation."

Elson felt migrants sinned not only on the streets but also in their employers' homes. Suggesting that women lied about the conditions of their work, Elson said that if a maid came home before the end of her contract and said she had gotten a "bad house," she was an honest woman who refused sexual advances. Elson suggested that Muslim people's sons were fond of womanizing, and so the family hired a couple of housemaids so that the sons stayed home instead of going out. The women received free televisions and refrigerators and other gifts, in addition to their salaries, for the "extra work." Elson named several local migrants who talked about "good houses" and came home with more money, jewelry, and gifts than he thought they could have earned honestly. He claimed that these women "of bad character" had agreed to dishonorable sexual arrangements. He insisted that all the men who had been abroad told the same story and that all criticized the women for their behavior.

Simon, a well-educated village man, spent eight years in Saudi Arabia. His more nuanced discussion of prostitution among migrants showed more direct knowledge and less patriotic fury than Elson's. During a long interview soon after he returned from abroad, he suggested that women who worked as prostitutes mainly held jobs in hospitals and factories; they lived in their own quarters and had Fridays off.[1] Housemaids, who had little time or liberty to go out, had to arrange something "private" if they were going to be involved in that business. Simon said that the manager of his company used to "get a girl or two" every Friday; he paid 200 riyals (about U.S.$50) a session. If a woman could go with two men on a Friday, four times a month, she could make 1,600 riyals (U.S.$400), which was probably three or four times as much as her official salary.

Aside from his knowledge about prostitution, Simon's experience also included direct contact with Sri Lankan women who found themselves in trouble. He related a case of two women working at one house, along with a chauffeur from Sri Lanka. The man was caught with a woman from the Arabic family. The two Sri Lankan women had known about the affair but had not told their employers. The man of the house assaulted the chauffeur and the two housemaids, beating them severely. Wearing only very scanty clothing, the women ran to Simon's vehicle. He and two other people got together one hundred riyals to get each woman a long black dress (the head-to-foot variety) and then left them at the police station; he did not know what had happened to them after that point but expected the worst. Simon said that even if Sri Lankan

---

[1] Friday is the weekend holiday in Muslim countries. Caitrin Lynch, who studies factory work in Sri Lanka, suggests that Sri Lankan employers try to supervise factory workers very closely, both during and after their shifts, especially in village factories. She has heard that women working abroad in the apparel industry experience similar surveillance and control (letter to author, 1 July 1999).

women were killed in front of witnesses, cases rarely went to court because the police believed the Saudi employer's word before the foreigner's.

Simon's story of the housemaids beaten merely for their knowledge of an affair between an Arabic woman and a Sri Lankan man raises a question concerning the media's double standard. While coerced and consenting relations between female migrants and Arabic or non-Sri Lankan men have formed a common theme, the press has rarely speculated about the sexual activities of Sri Lankan men. I suggest two reasons for this "programmatic ignorance." First, local gender norms distinguish between the effects of male and female sexual activity. Whereas women are seen as "clay pots," stained by intercourse, men are seen as "metal pots," untarnished by lack of chastity. Since men cannot get pregnant and do not have to be virgins at marriage, their sexual activity does not threaten Sri Lankan national purity and has aroused little media interest in Sri Lanka.

Second, many scholars suggest that men's group identity and pride rest in part on preserving sole access to women of their group (see Carby 1985; Pedersen 1991; Graber 1992). Challenges to exclusivity are met in kind. For example, Elson felt rage and humiliation when his Pakistani coworkers told him of their sessions with Sri Lankan prostitutes, and he retaliated in his narrative by accusing Pakistani women of prostitution. Similarly, stories of Sri Lankan gardeners, handymen, and chauffeurs sleeping with Arab women would position Sri Lankan women as targets of revenge. Image-makers could not without hypocrisy portray Sri Lankan women as innocent victims of unprovoked attacks while also relating stories of the sexual exploits of Sri Lankan men. Considering women's bodies as loci of national identity clarifies the heated rhetoric surrounding female sexuality and the silence surrounding male sexuality.

The local media has also picked up the theme that the Sri Lankan government has a duty to protect migrant women. A letter in *The Island*, a Sri Lankan English-language daily newspaper, details two instances of violence and sexual assault against "hapless victims" in the Middle East and blames the government because these women "had to leave the country in search of jobs abroad to eke out a living, as no such avenues were open to them in our own country." The author concludes, "We must hang our heads in shame to allow such things to happen to our womanhood" (Poopalan 1993).

While concurring with the author's outrage at abuse and rape, it is interesting to note the assumptions fueling the author's passion. The letter portrays women as victims, men as their protectors. "Allowing" another country's men to rape "our" women threatens Sri Lankan men's power and authority; men, and the government, should keep women at home or protect them better abroad. The author seeks to deny women access to the international labor market through arguments presumedly "for their own good," nationalizing Sri Lankan women's bodies and politicizing their chastity. As illustrated in chapter 4, most Naeaegama women who told me about troublesome situations portrayed themselves as thinking and acting as rationally and forcefully as they could and, in most cases, successfully resolving their crises. The author, however, shows a "programmatic ignorance" of women's practical initiatives; in his letter, the woman as agent disappears entirely. A story line that stresses female passivity encourages legislation such as that proposed by the former chairman of the SLBFE: forbidding female migration. A story line with dynamic, creative, insightful women encourages very different government actions—perhaps on the lines of stronger labor laws, more accessible embassies, or more enforceable contracts.

A similar process of erasing female agency seems to be going on in the article "Abroad, Astray." But the man equating women's chastity with national pride in this case was Colonel Nissanka Wijeratne, the then-chairman of the SLBFE, who held a position of great power over the migration of hundreds of thousands of domestic servants. Seemingly quaint, even chivalrous images can present obstacles to individual women's migration on the village level; on the national level, such images can seriously hamper the employment opportunities for an entire country of women when internalized by policymakers. Although protest against unfair working conditions might spur reforms in labor laws, such protest might also lead to the forbidding of female migration, which would not be in the best interests of the women or the country of Sri Lanka.

Subgenre #2: Stories about Hard Work and Confinement

Many "muscular truths" (Said 1986, 219) or stereotypes of migrant women have pictured them enjoying self-indulgent, pleasurable, sensual lives in the Middle East. Given the highly charged nature of sexual infidelity (either forced or consenting) and the general ethical condemnation of migration, migrant women and their families need to negotiate the propriety of their work abroad. The second subgenre of horror stories about migration—stories about the hard work, constant supervision, and limited mobility women experienced abroad—allows story tellers, mostly returned female migrants, to defend their morality and assert their respectability in the face of widespread negative archetypes.

Unflattering stereotypes of returned migrants are prevalent. Byron, the local job agent introduced in chapter 2, half-jokingly said that one could recognize a woman who had worked abroad by her style of dress and jewelry, her knowledge of the world, and her pride. Giving an example of a woman who went to Lebanon, Byron said that before she went, she used to wear only "*haeTTiya* and cloth" [the older village woman's short blouse and ankle-length skirt]. When Byron met her upon her return three years later, she wore a short skirt, lipstick, and sunglasses (all indices of Westernization and loose morals). She had also gotten fatter (indicating luxurious, high-quality food and little work) and paler (a highly desirable trait in Sri Lankan aesthetics). Byron could hardly recognize her; he called it "a full change." Three months later, when he saw her again, she was back to her former dress, size, and complexion. Burgeoning flesh and fancy dress styles indicated well-being, new experiences, and a new identity; a return to "normal" symbolized an end to the social as well as the physical changes.

Images of decadence and sensuality have colored many people's opinions of housemaids. Byron characterized changes in returned migrants by saying, "A woman comes home with gold chains and long earrings. She finds her husband wearing a sarong, drinking *kasippu* [illicit liquor]. She doesn't want to touch him. She says, "'*mee kaeaema kanDa baeae*'" [I can't eat this food]. She wants good and expensive foods, like chicken and fish. She stays a few months at home, uses up all her savings, and has to return to the Middle East for more money and more good food." Common images about women's appetites (for food and sex) and their physical alterations while abroad do indeed mirror some on-the-ground realities, but the common tropes and embellishments clearly exceed a description of superficial changes. These images reveal a widespread fear that women's work abroad would leave them vulnerable either to abuse or to temptation (by food, money, or sex) and would irrevocably change their personalities "for the worse." Disrespect for their husbands and a new sense of independence come under the same umbrella as other disdained transformations (see also Lynch 1999; Fernandez-Kelly 1983; Ong 1987).

Although some village migrants did indeed adopt the style of dress and jewelry described above, most, in contrast, spurned such ostentation. To deflect their neighbors' jealousy over their new wealth, many women have stress how hard they had worked and how *little* food their employers had spared them. These women sought to blend back into their village setting with as little fuss as possible, presenting themselves as morally untouched by their and experiences and fully deserving of the money they had earned. Poorer neighbors enviously noted any items (such as jewelry and cassette players) obtained abroad. Whatever their material souvenirs, returnees invariably acquired a certain notoriety. Those who voiced unorthodox opinions on gender relations and family structures risked accusations of having been corrupted abroad. As "dense transfer points for relations of power" (Foucault 1978, 103), women's bodily presentations reflected and symbolized complex negotiations over the meaning of their migration.

Many returnees and some of the agents who found them jobs emphasized the restrictions that confined women's mobility overseas. Sharif, the manpower recruiting agent from Saudi Arabia introduced in chapter 2, discussed how and why employers limited housemaids' freedoms. He said that all foreigners who had sponsors surrendered their passports to the sponsors; sponsors assumed full responsibility for their employees' actions. Sharif suggested that if a sponsor let a housemaid out unsupervised, "there will be big trouble: She will fall in love with someone and run away." Men could move around freely, but religious ideals put restrictions on women's mobility. As if "in jail," housemaids went out only to the supermarket or to private houses, only with the family for whom they worked and only if covered from head to toe. Some families forbade their housemaids to speak with any men, even those in the household. Such families trained their maids to set the morning coffee outside the bedroom door, knock, and leave. Citing these restrictions, Sharif argued that Saudi Arabia, where he sent housemaids, was the best place for women to work. They could save all of their money because they had no chance "to mess around." Similarly, speaking of Filipina domestic servants working in Hong Kong, Nicole Constable argues that Hong Kong employers "consider themselves responsible for helping to assure that a domestic worker 'won't get herself into trouble'" because "even the most well-intentioned domestic workers need a bit of help resisting [sexual temptations]" (1997, 545). Images of uncontrollable sexuality seem to justify restrictions on female mobility not only in the Gulf States but also in other master-servant relations.

Naeaegama women I spoke to reported similar patterns of restricted mobility and socializing abroad. Many women started accounts of their work in the Middle East by saying that they had heard about the promiscuity of housemaids. A number independently reported that their employers had told them this sort of story and had used the image of the promiscuous housemaid to justify confining the woman in question to her sponsor's house. Some women commented on these restrictions by remarking approvingly that their employers had treated them "just like a daughter" and had protected them very well. Women then recounted the harsh working conditions they had endured: long hours, ceaseless surveillance, low pay, lack of food, and loneliness. The seemingly paradoxical juxtaposition of "good protectors" and harsh taskmasters puzzled me until I began to see the underlying logic to the argument; a housemaid locked in the house, with no time free from hard work, could not have enjoyed her job. Nor could she have possibly carried on with a boyfriend or worked as a prostitute. By relating accounts of her employers' discipline, a migrant woman effectively countered images of lazy decadence and defended her own respectability and chastity. While paying lip service to the discourse of the slothful, immoral migrant, women manipulated the "muscular truth" to validate their own diligence, credibility, and honor.

Dina, a married woman in her forties, spoke with me at length about her experiences abroad. She left for Lebanon in April 1980 and worked there for two and a half years, cleaning house and caring for children. Although she felt she had found a "good" house in comparison to some, she had knelt scrubbing the hard floor until her legs ached. On days her family had parties, she had to stay up all night to wash the dishes and set the house to rights. While her village neighbors might envy her income, having heard such stories, they would not covet her working conditions or think that she had enjoyed her life abroad.

When I asked explicitly about prostitution and sexual abuse, Dina said that she was ashamed of Sri Lankans. Early in her stay, Dina's Madam took her to the window and showed her how Sri Lankan women behaved—"They go walking in the park with Arab men, down the path and 'into a hole.'" Dina grew to recognize the women walking with Arab men, some of whom frequented the park two or three times a week. The Madam cited this spectacle as the reason why she would not let Dina go out alone or talk to Sri Lankan women living nearby. The family took Dina with them on Sunday afternoon out-ings—to the beach in the summer and to a restaurant for lunch in the winter. During her time abroad, Dina did not have a single vacation day; she said instead that she "had the evenings off." Dina's Madam explained this arrangement by suggesting that if Dina got a day off and went out, then soon she would ask for two days and start up "that pro-fession."

Dina judged her Boss and Madam as "very good"; they acted "like my parents" and were "wise." Dina said that she often cried because she was so lonely, isolated in her sponsor's house. In the next breath, she praised her employers for "protecting" her like their own daugh-ter. She seemed to accept her strict confinement as a positive aspect of her employment, one that ensured her own respectability and safety. Dina thought that whereas 10 percent of the Sri Lankan migrants might stay at home (the way she had), the remaining 90 percent "went off outside." Because they went out, they spent their money on "un-necessary things" and came back to Sri Lanka without anything to show for their work. When Dina returned to Sri Lanka, she went to a nearby town and bought a skirt and shirt for much less than she would have spent in Lebanon. Dina felt that housemaids' husbands wasted money but so did the migrants who wanted lipstick, perfume, sun-glasses, and jewelry.

Dina measured virtue in terms of frugal saving. Whereas for Elson (and for Dina's Madam) women with unlimited mobility were prone to fall into prostitution, losing their reputations but earning a great deal of money, for Dina mobile women spent their hard-earned money frivolously, returning to Sri Lanka stylish but empty-handed. Dina seemed to accept uncritically her employer's construction of the na-tionality and behavior of the women in the park, internalizing the stigma and shame of (the rumor of) Sri Lankan women's prostitution. But in her further discussion, she reversed the causality, saying that going out made one spend money unwisely instead of earning money disreputably. She prided herself on having returned with nothing but saved money, with which her husband bought a van.

Truth or fiction, the image of the stylish, full-bodied, knowledge-able, promiscuous housemaid has dogged migrant women's reputa-tions. Where the smallest infraction could lead to accusations of loose morals, the only defense is an exaggerated restriction of individual adornment and personal mobility, both in fact and in narrative self-representation. By accepting the uncomplimentary picture of the Sri

Lankan housemaid and by claiming tight, "protective" restrictions on their own movements, Dina and other women, both married and unmarried, have tried to retain their respectability through the creative manipulation of the images of the immoral housemaid and the strict, demanding Arabic employer.

Subgenre #3: Punishment

A third subgenre of horror stories emphasizes the severity of punishments meted out by Arab employers. My fieldwork did not take me to the Gulf States, so I can only speculate on the relation between stories and real situations. By stressing the constructed nature of these stories, I do not wish to deny the reality of such violent events or to minimize their importance. The images themselves, however, take on a life of their own, significantly at odds with the more mundane experiences of most housemaids with whom I spoke.

Rumors of violence, fueled by the occasional firsthand experience, can intimidate large populations by creating what Michael Taussig calls a "culture of terror" (1984). Horror stories have circulated an image of employers as strict disciplinarians who meted out sudden and terrible justice to erring maids. I asked Sharif if housemaids ever stole from their sponsors in Saudi Arabia; he said that it never happened because each housemaid knew that if she stole, her sponsors would cut off her hand. Migrant women in Naeaegama related similar horror stories of violent discipline. In a group interview, one woman said that she had heard a story of a housemaid doused with boiling water for having an affair with the Madam's son. Another woman related the story of a servant beaten and kept in a dark room without food for three days because she had stolen some jewelry and hidden it in her jar of Nivea cream. Then, with the skill of a consummate storyteller, Hera related an even more grisly narrative.

Hera, who had worked in Kuwait for four years, said that the elder brother of her Boss had hired a Sri Lankan woman to take care of the children. While the housemaid was bathing the youngest son one day, he struggled, knocked his head on the water pipe, and started to bleed. The mother heard the boy screaming in the bathroom and broke through the locked door. The mother accused the maid of deliberately injuring the child. At that same moment the Boss, an army man, came home. The boy died and the Boss shot the housemaid. Hera's family brought Hera over to see the dead bodies, and her Boss asked, "Is this what you're doing to our children?" Hera analyzed the situation by saying that the Arabs showed other housemaids the punishments meted out to those caught in error so that the rest could learn from the experience.

Stories about threats and punishments work to enforce discipline by spreading an image of the dominant group as masterful, omniscient, and omnipotent. In James Scott's terms, the powerful overdramatize their reputation in an effort to control the weak (1990, xi–xii). Scott questions the extent to which workers actually believe in such inflated reputations, suggesting "hidden transcripts" that recognize the attempted deception. In this case, I wonder how self-consciously housemaids have challenged images of employer brutality. Whatever their beliefs and personal experiences, most Naeaegama women related with passion at least one horror story during interviews.

Returned migrants described their employers as demanding loyalty without excessive familiarity and creating and maintaining boundaries using discipline and fear. Habits of interaction developed, circumscribing servants' mobility and socializing, and regulating household relations so that domestic help were simultaneously marginal insiders and intimate outsiders. Unlike unionized shop-floor workers, female domestic servants at work in the Middle East rarely have the opportunity to mingle, organize, and discuss their work situations. Instead, each works in the relative isolation of her employer's family, where issues of power, hierarchy, and workers' rights tend to seem like individual, interpersonal matters instead of topics for class solidarity and class action. Perhaps retelling stories about "the bad guys" in a common folk genre allows migrant women to create a community through fiction that they cannot easily find in fact.

Horror stories exemplify *hegemony*, which is "the lived dominance and subordination of particular classes" (R. Williams 1977, 110). While such stories can frighten workers into submission, they also create a strong group identity for migrant women. Claude Meillassoux (1981) suggests that racism, xenophobia, and discrimination keep guest workers in foreign countries afraid and disorganized. Workers think of the issues and problems facing them as questions of ethnicity and nationality instead of questions of class. In contrast, Constable (1997) suggests that Filipinas in Hong Kong do organize against oppression. While Sri Lankan housemaids have not organized either in the Middle East or in Sri Lanka, I would argue that the racist stereotype of the abusive Arab employer creates a community of "survivors" among house-maids, providing them with a badge of courage that emphasizes the importance and difficulty of their undertaking, above and beyond the menial nature of their work. Whereas domestic service isolates house-hold workers and makes class consciousness difficult to achieve, hor-ror stories bring women together in a common alliance against the im-age of the inhumane employer. Paradoxically, in this case, a racist stereotype serves both to discourage resistance and to enhance a con-sciousness and solidarity among housemaids that may eventually function as a channel for nascent class awareness.

The Life of the Image

Working within the narrative framework of the three subgenres of horror stories, individuals have colored events that "really" happened with an eye toward the messages they wished to convey to their au-diences. The *dramatis personae* for the saga of migration to the Middle East—the immoral and vulnerable housemaid, her impotent husband, and her despotic employers—have played significant roles in detailed daily negotiations over meaning and representation. Complex moti-vations underlie various rhetorical strategies in these stories.

Two main sets of power relations emerge from the horror stories. I've explored. The first set of power relations is between men and women in the local and national community. Negotiations over mean-ing, knowledge, and power center on female chastity. In the first sub-genre, sensationalized media reporting, echoed by stories told by male migrants, emphasizes the possibility of female promiscuity and sex-ual vulnerability abroad. Coupled with the sexualized female worker comes the man as impotent "donkey" (discussed in chapter 9). Images of men unable to fulfill the roles of financially secure breadwinner and of sexually gratifying husband haunt the national consciousness at many levels. A common response to the threat to female chastity and masculine pride is to argue for restricting and constraining the social-izing and mobility of women both in the Middle East and in the vil-lage.[2] The woman's body becomes a site of national identity, with only Sri Lankan men having legitimate sexual access to Sri Lankan women.

[2] The fourth subgenre of horror story, the tales of disasters at home resulting from female migration, also work to restrict women's work abroad.

In this argument, the woman as agent disappears entirely, and her freedom to work abroad comes under threat.

Women counter the images of female infidelity and defend their right to migrate with stories of the second subgenre: the supervision and hard work in their Arabic homes. The restricted mobility, (symbolic) lack of "food," and linguistic and cultural isolation that they depict help deflect jealousy over the wealth they earn abroad. By accepting and repeating tales of other housemaids' sexual immorality, village migrants paradoxically both diminish the stature of maids in general and reinforce their own individual honor and chastity. The stories these women tell of their experiences work within and strengthen the established framework of oppressive sexualized images but create space for individual respectability by emphasizing the tyrannous discipline of the employer.

The second set of power relations, between Sri Lankan women (and men) and their Arabic employers, dramatizes a racist consciousness of difference and distance. The pervasive impression, often repeated, that "Arabic people say that Sri Lankan men must be donkeys because they send their wives abroad," sets up an angry and threatened dynamic between men of the more and less affluent communities. Sri Lankans characterize Arabs as questioning the sexual and economic potency of Sri Lankan men. Considerations of poverty, the usual reply to this barb, begin to explore the international dynamics that make the Gulf States labor-importing countries and Sri Lanka a labor-exporting one. Closer to the individual, stories from the third subgenre—abuse and punishment of migrant maids—create a moral framework wherein the good but powerless housemaid braves the evils of the dominant Arabic society. Stories portraying the hard work and dangerous environment dramatize the heroism of a particular class of poor women, creating a community of "survivors" who have courageously undertaken difficult and hazardous work for the financial benefit of their families. Karen Sacks (1989) argues for a definition of "class" that focuses not on individual workers but on the communities that support their labor and profit from their wages. In this case gender and nationality heavily color an emerging sense of class identity.

By examining horror stories, this chapter has explored the layers of extra signification piled on already complicated moral, social, and economic relations surrounding migration of labor to the Middle East. The circulating stories, amplified and augmented in the telling, exaggerate the perils and predicaments housemaids face abroad. In the gray

area between fiction and fact, between word and deed, in the discrepancies between what people do and what they say they do, much of
interest awaits the researcher. The most important step in the analysis consists of doing away with artificial boundaries between word and
deed, appearance and reality. If, as anthropological common sense suggests, our cultural categories shape our behavior and pattern our interpretation of others' behavior, then clearly the horror stories analyzed in this chapter, whether "true" or not, can generate enough
power and initiative of their own to significantly, creatively affect the
lives of the original subjects.

Princess Diana was a media personality, and her brother asserted
that the media killed her. In a less literal but just as powerful move,
in the horror story of "Abroad, Astray," the media erases the individuality of the eight migrant housemaids in the photo accompanying
the text. An editor has blacked out the eyes (I's?) of the women. Disguised, masked, deprived of their individuality, these grainy images
become players in a generic story—"uprooted, isolated and defenceless," as the caption asserts. They cannot speak out to espouse their
chastity or to tell the particular, idiosyncratic, rich stories of their own
agency (Spivak 1985). They become mute pawns in a larger project of
nationality and masculinity, where the images and narrative patterns
discussed here can often sway public policy more persuasively than
sober facts, scholarly reflections, or the voices of the women themselves. Despite the very real dangers of working in the Middle East,
Naeaegama women and others like them in Sri Lanka greatly value
their work opportunities abroad. I conclude this chapter with the plea
that those in decision-making positions consider the politics of representation inherent in the horror story genre and take folk concepts of
meaning and identity with a grain of salt.

Conclusion

The proverb that inspired this book's title suggests that "A woman's understanding reaches only the length of the kitchen spoon handle."[1] The book's focus on globalization, though, demonstrates the interconnection between local and global dynamics. With the transnational migration of female domestic workers from Sri Lanka to the oil-producing states in West Asia, perhaps the spoon handle now reaches several thousand miles instead of a mere twelve inches. Village women's migration experiences have put them in contact with local, national, and international institutions and actors, including government bureaucracies, manpower recruiting agencies, and village moneylenders. Labor migration has led to the commodification of "women's work" and to shifts in local gender roles, caste hierarchies, and class relations. As individuals and families have negotiated these hierarchies, the power structures themselves have evolved and changed. Gender, class, and caste are fluid identities situated in overlapping systems of power and authority. People constantly use these systems and, through this use, re-create and change them.

A decade before I started my fieldwork in Naeaegama, Sri Lankan scholar R. B. M. Korale predicted that the migration of female labor to the Middle East would revolutionize gender roles in the family and in society, increasing women's participation in politics and community decisions: "It is also expected that the desire for greater independence

---

[1] "gaehaeniyagee nuwana haendimiTee durayi."

and participation in the social and economic process by women will be enhanced. The wealth acquired by females and the dependence of other household members on this income, will further buttress their social transformation resulting in greater social and economic rights being granted to females" (1983, 23). Korale and other social scientists ·(Dias and Weerakoon-Gunawardene 1991; Schampers and Eelens 1986) also predicted numerous adverse effects of migration on children and families. The preceding chapters, however, have shown that access to waged labor did not immediately or directly change women's roles in family or village. Nor did the absence of a large number of women throw family or village life into chaos. In both cases, preexisting social structures dampened the extremity of the predicted social transformations. The preceding chapters have explored forces that have prompted and resisted change in the village; this concluding chapter will consider the rate and direction of social change, asking how quickly social transformation has occurred and in what ways men and women have suffered and benefited.

National and International Social Structures

The term *social structure* refers to patterns of human affiliation, from the familial to the global. Research can and must focus on the connections among international, national, village, family, and individual levels of analysis. The actions of the OPEC cartel to raise the price of oil in 1973, 1979, and 1981 reached into the lives of rural Sri Lankans as families in the Middle East began to spend their wealth by hiring housemaids. Coupled with a dearth of lucrative jobs for men and women in Sri Lanka, economic opportunities abroad catapulted women into the international labor market. With one in eleven of the working-age women in Sri Lanka employed abroad, and with total out-migration growing yearly, the future of villagers in Naeaegama and elsewhere in Sri Lanka continues to grow more tightly linked with the political and economic stability of the oil-producing nations in the Persian Gulf.

From the global perspective, unpaid family labor in Naeaegama subsidizes salaries for "cheap" guest laborers in the Middle East. Families in the village provide child care, unemployment benefits, and retirement plans for migrant workers. At the same time, a housemaid's wages, while paltry in international terms, translate very generously in the national context. Fearing that regulations requiring higher minimum wages and more efficient enforcement of official contracts would decrease the demand for Sri Lankan housemaids, the Sri Lankan government has long tolerated disadvantageous labor relations for its citizens working abroad. Migration to the Middle East generates valuable foreign exchange, reduces local unemployment, and helps alleviate poverty. On the national level, though, recent government legislation regularizing agency practices and providing insurance policies benefits many migrants. Current government initiatives to improve consulate services and negotiate multi-country labor agreements may further improve women's work experiences in the future. National and international dynamics simultaneously operate to keep Sri Lankan women's labor cheap and give women the opportunity to work and to earn abroad.

Although national and international government policy initiatives could greatly streamline and support female migration, government officials remain vulnerable to the nationalist rhetoric of the horror story genre, which urges them to prohibit female migration entirely in the name of protecting Sri Lanka's women. A 1997 newspaper article reported that in 1996 172,000 Sri Lankans, most of them women, went abroad; the Minister of Labour, Mr. W. D. J. Senaviratne, was quoted as saying, "This trend must change. Married men and young bachelors should be given preference in selections" (Samarajeewa 1997). While economic forces shape and direct migration patterns, powerful gender ideologies and commonly held ideas about family, work, and travel can strongly influence national and international policy decisions.

Rethinking "The Village"

Analysis of international migration changes the concept of "the village" and its social structures. If a woman leaves Naeaegama to spend two years in West Asia, does she still count as a villager? If not, what sort of social identity and belonging does she don in her absence? If so, how should we conceptualize the village when at any one time a sixth of the adult women may live in another country?

In Sri Lanka, discussion of migration often generated nostalgia for the lost village and family of yesteryear—an idealized village community with perfect, traditional family relations that may never actually have existed in the past (Spencer 1990; Ivy 1988). This rhetoric commonly portrays women's absence from the village as a pathology bound to weaken the social and moral fabric of rural families and villages. Instead of taking these negative assumptions for granted, social scientists must carefully examine how the relationships, travels, and transactions in question actually benefit and hurt those involved, critically accounting for the power of images and horror stories to affect scholarly and general conceptions of migration.

To answer the question about migrant women's village identity or lack thereof, I draw on another example of a spatially transient but socially enduring group, Sri Lanka's large and dynamic community of commuter train passengers. Office workers from the south coast travel daily to Colombo on the *Ruhunu Kumari* [Princess of the South] and the *Samudra Devi* [Goddess of the Sea]. Regular commuters on the crowded trains form a tight-knit society where future spouses meet and court, and friends of twenty-years' standing play cards, gossip, and joke for one or two hours a trip, twice a day, five days a week. For many office workers, the journeys become as important as the destinations at either end. Although work and money draw commuters to the trains and migrants to the Middle East, new ties of affection develop that rival—even if they do not replace—identities based on occupation, family, and residence. Since all involved invariably classify both commuters and migrants as still part of the village, then to the extent that commuters commute and migrants migrate, the village shifts its elastic boundaries to encompass their multiple loyalties and identities. Thought of in terms of networks of relationships, migrant women and office train passengers weave a web of intense and meaningful personal connections that bind them strongly with more than one community.

Just as the refugee, a person without a homeland, calls into question the folk concepts of "rootedness" in "country" and "nation," so the migrant calls into question assumptions about the bounded, exclusive, and circumscribed nature of belonging in the village. Liisa Malkki suggests that we use "rhizomes" as a new base metaphor for "nomadology," a theory of identity based on travel and interpersonal relationships instead of "place" and "rooting" (1992, 37–38). Rhizomes, endlessly versatile networks of roots and shoots, spread and grow and bud into any soil they touch, much as people cultivate relationships in whatever social setting they find themselves. Recent scholarship on transnationalism focuses not on bounded spaces and exclusive loyalties but on continued ties and interactions among the different locations in which people feel at home (Clifford 1994; Gray 1996; Gupta 1992; Kearney 1995).

Although the workforce in many GCC countries consists mainly of non-nationals, these nations maintain a love-hate relationship with guest workers. Recent "Arabization" initiatives to employ local labor emphasize the dangers of growing too dependent on foreign workers (Looney 1992; *Migration News* 1996b, 1996c, 1997). Most GCC countries discourage permanent settlement by foreigners. Gulf states strictly regulate time limits on visas and work permits, restrict the number of dependents that can accompany a worker, prohibit foreigners from owning land or running businesses, and make naturalized citizenship extremely difficult to obtain. For example, Bahrain requires citizenship applicants to have a minimum residence of twenty-five years (Shadid, Spaan, and Speckmann 1992, 71), making it difficult for migrants to "take root" in the land. Despite these barriers, however, guest workers continue to flow to the Middle East.

Domestic servants working in households abroad encounter welcomes that range from hostility, racism, or indifference to love and affection. Just as governments in GCC countries distance themselves from guest workers, so housemaids' sponsors maintain a similar social distance within households. By separating the maid's living quarters from those of the family, limiting her mobility, curtailing her socializing, and imposing hard work and discipline, employers create and reinforce social separations. At the same time, many housemaids work in the same household for four, eight, or even twelve years at a stretch. Housemaids perform the most intimate of services for their employers, and some said with evident love and loyalty that their employers were like a second family. Ties of dependency, affection, and camaraderie develop despite carefully constructed boundaries and cultural differences separating sponsors and their employees. As intimate outsiders and marginal insiders, housemaids have a great deal of informal power to challenge many of the categories maintaining distance and hierarchy between employer and servant.

In his discussion of the South Asian diaspora, Peter van der Veer speaks of the dynamics of "longing and belonging," of loyalty to the place one is (either the old or the new), and nostalgia for the place one is not: "The theme of belonging opposes rootedness to uprootedness, establishment to marginality. The theme of longing harps on the desire for change and movement, but relates this to the enigma of arrival, which brings a similar desire to return to what one has left" (1995, 4).

While women asserted that their primary loyalties remained in Sri Lanka, as housemaids they also participated in the lives of their Arabic employers, speaking their language, eating their food, and preparing for their religious ceremonies. Korale speculated in 1983 that migration would cause a great deal of cross-fertilization between Arabic and Sinhala cultures. In contrast, Dias and Weerakoon-Gunawardene (1991) maintain that housemaids came home without having integrated into the foreign culture and that women easily slipped back into the role of wife and mother without having adopted Arabic ways or a foreign ethnic identity. In juxtaposition to both these predictions, my research revealed small but intriguing instances of cultural integration in Naeaegama. For example, one housemaid home for the Sinhala-Tamil New Year holidays sat in her mother's living room wearing a long Arabic-style dress and told me that despite the April heat, she felt uncomfortable with bare legs after all her years abroad. Villagers often suggested that housemaids quickly grew to miss the rich Middle Eastern diet and modern conveniences when they returned home. Neither immediately obvious nor clearly traceable, changes have gradually crept into village society, mediated through women's own preconceptions, values, ideals, and upbringing (see Gailey 1993; B. Williams 1991). Cyclically migrating between two different families and cultures, women have come to belong in, and long for, both.

Changes in the Family

Many social changes have occurred in village families as a result of migration. Dias and Weerakoon-Gunawardene (1991) predict that the extended family might break down from the effort of supporting migrant workers. In Naeaegama, I found that the extended family played a crucial role in facilitating migration by providing child care, financing agency fees, finding jobs in the Middle East for female relatives, and seeing the family through crises at home. While fragmentation and disintegration of family bonds did occur when relatives fought about the use and control of remittances, in general migration seemed to strengthen extended family relationships, not weaken or endanger them. At the same time, one could argue that family duties such as giving gifts, providing funds for ceremonies, and supporting daily consumption could weigh heavily on those trying to accumulate enough savings to buy land, build a house, or start a business. Men and women

I interviewed continually negotiated their family rights and obligations, balancing goals for more individual and nuclear family improvement against responsibilities toward larger family, caste, and village communities.

Sometimes individual interests have conflicted with family plans.
Violent confrontations over the control of money revealed the different priorities various family members held. Dramatic local examples
of betrayal prompted many migrants to counsel other women to save
their wages in private bank accounts, buy land in their own names,
and send nothing to their parents or husbands; surprisingly few, however, followed their own advice. In cases where families agreed on how
to use remittances and cooperated in reaching their goals, most family
members benefited. Prospering depended not only on the industry of
the housemaid but also on the wisdom and judgment of the person or
people controlling remittances in the village. Enmeshed in larger col-
lectives with claims on her work, time, and money, a woman has
rarely profited or suffered from her migration on a purely individual
basis.

Just as the prophets of doom predict the imminent end of "the village," so horror stories that circulated by word of mouth and through
the media emphasize how families fell apart during a housemaid's absence. Such stories often blame women for depriving their families of
their guidance and control, thus producing neglected and delinquent
children and alcohol-dependent husbands. More sober research reveals
that migrants made adequate arrangements for their offspring before
leaving the country (Samarasinghe 1989). In many cases of male alcoholism, husbands merely continued to behave as they had before their
wives went abroad. Male unemployment, domestic violence, and substance abuse often predated, and even precipitated, a woman's migration and formed part of the continuing historical context surrounding
the migration of labor. Although the media have presented the disintegration of marriages as an unwanted side effect of migration, many
village women saw this same phenomenon from a different perspective, and felt that their new financial independence offered them a way
out of untenable home situations.

Migration has affected not only the families of married women but
also the marriage prospects of unwed migrants. Young women in the
village either avoided marriage by returning abroad, agreed to marriages arranged by their parents, or eloped with young men of their
own choice. David G. Mandelbaum (1970) suggests that South Asian

families who arranged good marriages for their daughters increased their prestige. By village criteria, an eligible man should have property, education, and a job. With the money that unmarried migrants earned abroad serving as a dowry, families often found better husbands for their daughters than they could have otherwise. Older and more secure financially than the love interests of eloping peers, these men could often support their wives without further migration. In contrast, some unmarried women rebelled against their parents' authority, choosing their own husbands. Control over their own savings, and the knowledge that they could easily earn more money abroad, gave women the confidence to take this step. Migration thus increased the potential dowries for women marrying in the traditional fashion and increased the financial and social independence of those marrying "for love."

Migration has placed Naeaegama family structures and practices in flux. It has strengthened many extended families by incorporating a large set of relatives into the project of covering for an absent family member. At the same time, conflict over the control of remittances could drive wedges between husbands and wives, parents and children, nuclear families and more distant relatives. Access to lucrative jobs abroad gave unmarried women the freedom to choose their own spouses, threatening parental authority and potentially challenging older patterns of caste endogamy. Migration also gave unhappily married women the choice to leave their husbands both temporarily and permanently, challenging older patterns of gender subordination. While many local traditionalists lamented the changes occurring in family structures and values, a more anthropological approach suggests that family patterns adapt to suit the needs of the family members (Stacey 1997). We should praise, not pathologize, the innovative solutions that migrants and their relatives create.

Changes in Identity

Although the components that constitute identity may appear stable and self-evident, critical study reveals the inherent fluidity of cultural systems, such as class, caste, and gender, on which individual identity depends. Concepts of self rely on learned, internalized patterns of thought and habits of behavior. Though these taken-for-granted patterns and habits acquire a sense of permanence, legitimacy, inevitability, and authority, as the outcome of past human creativity they remain continually subject to change. People reproduce and transform norms and standards through one and the same process: living by these culturally constructed categories. Since categories shape behavior, they also reflect and channel power relations within society. Power relations are continually "renewed, recreated, defended, and modified" but are also continually "resisted, limited, altered, and challenged" (R. Williams 1977, 112). Changes in identity reflect and affect changes in economic, political, and social situations. The migration of female labor, although not the only influence on the village identities, forms a significant factor in recent social change.

Changing economic circumstances and work patterns contradict older images of ideal male and female behaviors and roles in Sri Lanka as well as around the world. Naeaegama-area women could find high-paying jobs abroad, but men were hard-pressed to find adequate employment anywhere. In a similar situation of job scarcity, Judith Stacey found a "masculinity crisis" (1990, 267) in lower-middle-class America as men came face-to-face with the impossibility of fulfilling the role of the sole breadwinner of the family. Caught between an unworkable ideal and economic reality, "young, postfeminist men ... appear uncertain whether a man who provides sole support to his family is a hero or a chump" (1990, 267). Furthermore, Stacey found that many men "express their masculinity in antisocial, self-destructive, and violent forms" (1990, 267), such as drug addiction and wife-beating. Women working for wages outside the home threw family power structures and ideal gender roles into flux, affecting the personal identities of both women and men.

Louise Lamphere provides another example of how individuals have handled changes in gender roles and household duties. Lamphere examines the division of productive and reproductive labor in several different immigrant working-class communities in Rhode Island between 1790 and 1980. She asserts that only after mothers and wives joined the workforce did substantial changes take place in authority in the home; earlier employment of unmarried daughters did not challenge power relations, as daughters gave their money to their mothers and fathers. In interviews with Colombian and Portuguese families in Central Falls, Rhode Island, in the late 1970s and early 1980s, Lamphere found that with the employment of married women, men had taken over some domestic chores. Even though women still did the bulk of the work around the house, practices were gradually changing. Because the immigrants in Lamphere's research rarely had extended family networks to call on, husbands stepped in of necessity to help with child care (1987, 288). She noted, "Males participate in some tasks now that they did not undertake before immigration, yet preserve an ideology of male authority. In general, men's behavior has changed more than have their notions about authority and respect" (1987, 41). In the communities Lamphere studied, ideology and attitudes lagged behind changes in conduct as men and women struggled to work out a new balance of power and gender roles.

Bringing domestic service into the international economy has brought about gradual and ongoing changes in Naeaegama gender roles. Domestic work—as a commodity on the global market, performed in a semi-public arena, for strangers, regulated by national laws, for foreign exchange—has became more widely recognized as "work." Migration prompted the beginnings of a local reassessment of the value of housework, made women's domestic service into a profession, and distributed a portion of women's household chores to men. These changes disrupted older patterns of power and authority, and as a result men and women struggled not only over the control of remittances but also over redefining the meaning of women's work, the nature of motherhood, and the attributes of respectable masculinity.

New money flowing into Naeaegama from migrants' work abroad has challenged older distributions of both economic and symbolic capital. Many of the newly rich constructed large cement houses, commandeering a sign of high status formerly reserved for high-caste, wealthy families. Meanwhile, poorer members of the old village elite tried to emphasize their caste status while downplaying the significance of material wealth. Despite the potential leveling power of money earned abroad, however, limited access to start-up capital perpetuated unequal class relations. Rich families paid large sums to send men abroad to earn generous salaries; poor families paid smaller sums to send women abroad to earn much more modest wages. Moneylenders provided loans and opportunities to migrants who could not otherwise have afforded to pay their agency fees but charged high rates of interest that siphoned off the bulk of a migrant's profits. Migration opened the possibility for shifts and potential shifts in economic status, but those who already had significant assets stood to benefit the most. Complex changes were occurring not only in the distribution of material wealth in Naeaegama but also in local attitudes toward caste hierarchies, class identity, and the proper use of money.

The everyday actions of ordinary men and women reproduced and transformed the overlapping structures and practices of caste, class, and gender. Always situated in multiple, cross-cutting social positions, individuals rarely acted with only one hierarchy in mind. Not only did individuals and families change their positions in existing structures; more importantly, as people jockeyed to improve their status, their actions in small but significant ways changed the structures themselves. Older ideals and horror stories influenced individual acts; in turn, as people grew used to pragmatic realities and other-than-ideal arrangements, standards and norms governing behavior gradually shifted and changed. Pierre Bourdieu refers to the time lag between material changes and ideological adjustment as "the hysteresis of habitus" or, less colorfully, "the structural lag between opportunities and the dispositions to grasp them" (1977, 83). In Naeaegama, numerous examples illustrated the slow and painful transformations in ideals and identity.

Change in Progress

Longitudinal research often reveals unexpected changes in social structures and practices. In my 1997 visit to Naeaegama, I discovered a number of developments that surprised me. First, several families that villagers in 1994 had predicted would "never come up" had clearly prospered. This brought home to me that a family who showed no "improvement" for many years might not necessarily have misused or wasted funds. Even if initial migrations had not visibly benefited the family, subsequent ones clearly might. Poor families needed a number of years to get out of debt and save enough money to buy land and build a house. Contrary to many predictions, long-term research revealed that migration brought a slow but persistent improvement to even the most "hopeless" of cases.

Second, in 1997 I found that more unmarried women were traveling to work abroad. This shift in the composition of the labor force seemed to indicate wider acceptance of more liberal gender roles, particularly those centering on ideals of female virginity and marriageability. As people grew accustomed to women's work abroad, the social stigma decreased, and more parents allowed their daughters to participate.

A third surprising change came in the shape of women's increasing reliance on "tickets" for finding jobs abroad. Cutting out the job agents and moneylenders allowed migrant women to avoid interest charges and agency fees while earning a bit on the side by providing jobs for friends and relatives. These entrepreneurial adventures increased profits for migrant women by cutting out the middlemen and middlewomen, a step that might bring more prosperity to the poorer families in the village and eventually disrupt older patterns of wealth and prestige. These rapid changes in gender ideology and entrepreneurial activities cautioned me to be careful in making estimations of the speed and extent of social change. Cultural patterns can shift quickly, with change building up under the surface before appearing in full-blown glory (R. Williams 1977).

Fourth, government efforts to professionalize migrant labor through training, legislative initiatives to regulate and systematize the migration process, and diplomatic attempts to institute international labor contracts impressed me as signs of progress. The government seemed to consider domestic work as "work" and count women's issues, such as child care and family planning, as working-class issues of national importance (Sacks 1989, Joan Scott 1988). At the same time, horror stories of female vulnerability circulated widely, and a number of men in positions of power called for a ban on migration to protect Sri Lankan women from harm. It remains to be seen whether economic pragmatism or jingoistic nationalism will carry the day.

I chose as the epigraph for this book several lines from W. B. Yeats's poem, "Among School Children."

> O chestnut-tree, great-rooted blossomer,
> Are you the leaf, the blossom or the bole?
> O body swayed to music, O brightening glance
> How can we know the dancer from the dance?
> (Yeats 1926/28, I-312)

During my stay in Sri Lanka, I grew to know and love a number of dynamic and insightful women and men in Naeaegama. Observations of the complexity of their daily dancing made me realize that I could not glorify women's resistance to gender hierarchies any more than I could argue their continual abject subjugation. Women danced with and against their embeddedness in a multitude of overlapping communities—family, caste, village, nation—and a large repertoire of identities—gender, class, ethnicity—each with a separate set of loyalties and alliances. By introducing a few of the dancers in Naeaegama village life, and describing their practices, I hope that I have preserved their ceaseless creative energy without essentializing its patterns or over-theorizing its choreography. In the case studies in this book, I have tried to show through women's own stories how they contested power relations in the village, improvising within the space of bounded innovation. In choosing stories to relate, I have called on the usual *and* the extraordinary to create a narrative impression of both the stately waltz of harmony and the discordant energies of contention and challenge.

Appendix A:
An Orthography
of Spoken Sinhala

The following orthography of spoken Sinhala is based on the works of Gordan H. Fairbanks, James W. Gair, and M. W. S. de Silva (1968) and W. S. Karunatillake (1992).

Vowels

Sinhala speakers distinguish between long and short soundings of seven vowels (see table A.1). In the text, long vowels are represented by doubling the short vowel symbols: "i" is a short vowel similar to that in the American English "bit"; "ii" is similar to the vowel in the English "deed"; "e" is halfway between the English "bet" and "bait," but without the glide found in "bait"; "ee" is similar to the vowel in "raid," again without the glide; "ae" and "aeae" are similar to the vowel in "cat"; I use the symbol "a̱" for the vowel sound similar to the last vowel in "sofa"; the corresponding long vowel, "a̱a̱," is rarely found in Sinhala, except in the occasional English loanword, where it sounds like the vowel in "bird"; "a" is like the vowel in "hot," while "aa" sounds like the first vowel in "father"; "u" is like the vowel in "shoot," but shorter and without the glide, while "uu" sounds like the

Table A.1.   Vowels in spoken Sinhala

	Front, Short	Front, Long	Center, Short	Center, Long	Back, Short	Back, Long
High	i	ii			u	uu
Mid	e	ee	<u>a</u>	<u>aa</u>	o	oo
Low	ae	aeae	a	aa		

vowel in "food," again without the glide; "o" is similar to the vowel sound in "coat," but shorter and without the glide; "oo" sounds like the vowel in "load," without the glide.

Consonants

I use "p," "c," and "k" to represent the voiced consonants similar to the first consonants in the English "pin," "chin," and "kin." I use "b," "j," and "g" to represent the corresponding unvoiced consonants similar to the first consonants in the English "bin," "jam," and "gone."

Sinhala speakers distinguish between two "t"-like and two "d"-like sounds. I use "T" to represent a sound pronounced just slightly further back in the mouth than the first consonant in the English "taxi." I use "t" to represent a dental stop consonant pronounced with the tongue positioned for the first consonant in the English "thin" but without the passage of air. Similarly, the voiced sound "D" corresponds with the first consonant in "dog," pronounced in the same place as "T," with the tongue slightly further back in the mouth, but "d" is pronounced in the same place as "t," with the tongue just behind the upper teeth.

The spirants "s," "sh," and "h" are pronounced as in the English "sip," "ship," and "hat." The sound "f" occurs mainly in English loanwords such as "phone," and many Sinhala speakers substitute "p" for it.

Sinhala speakers distinguish between what Fairbanks et al. call "full nasals" and "half nasals" (or "pre-nasals"). The full nasals "m," "n," and "ng" correspond to the first consonants in the English "mood" and "noon" and the "ng" in "sing." The half-nasals "<u>m</u>," "<u>n</u>," and "<u>ng</u>" occur only before the voiced stop consonants "b," "d," "D," and "g" and are kept short and released quickly.

Whereas "l" corresponds to the first consonant in the English "let," "r," a trill formed with the tip of the tongue against the upper tooth

Table A.2. Consonants in spoken Sinhala

	Labial	Dental	Alveolar	Retroflex	Palatal	Velar	Glotal
Voiced stops	b	d		D		g	
Voiceless stops	p	t		T		k	
Voiced affricates					j		
Voiceless affricates					c		
Pre-nasal stops	mb	nd		nD		ng	
Nasals	m		n	n		ng	
Trill			r				
Laterals			l				
Spirants	(f)	s			(sh)		h
Semi-vowel	v				y		

ridge, has no close correlate in English. I have transcribed as "v" the Sinhala sound between the English "v" and "w." The "y" corresponds to the first consonant in the English "yes." Departing from Fairbanks et al., I transcribe the Sinhala emphatic marker as "yi," similar to the "ye" in the English phrase, "Now hear ye this." Finally, Sinhala speakers note a difference between single and double consonants; "kk" is pronounced as in the English "bookkeeper."

Personal and place names have been transliterated according to the most common traditional conventions, which do not always correspond to the orthography I have set out here.

Appendix B:
Calculating Inflation
in Sri Lanka

Rampant inflation in Sri Lanka makes comparing prices from different years difficult. Throughout most of the book, unless otherwise noted, monetary figures have been adjusted for inflation and are stated in 1994 rupees. In these calculations, I have used the Colombo Consumer Price Index (CCPI) (see table B.1). This index measures the prices of consumer items and suggests the changing purchasing power of wages.

To calculate what Rs. 1000/ in 1984 would be worth in 1994, divide the CCPI number for 1994 by the CCPI number for 1984, and multiply the result (2.762) by Rs. 1000/, to obtain the figure of Rs. 2762/. This means that a consumer would spend Rs. 2762/ in 1994 to buy what he or she could have purchased with Rs. 1000/ in 1984.

Occasionally, as noted in the text, I give both nominal values (rupee values informants report) and real values (equivalents in 1994 rupees, adjusted for inflation). In these special cases this was done to show how dramatically inflation has affected the value of the rupee over the years. To avoid encumbering the text, U.S.$ equivalents are only noted for particularly salient figures. In 1994, U.S.$1 was roughly equivalent to Rs. 50/, and all dollar equivalents are calculated at that rate, except where noted.

Table B.1. Colombo consumer price index, 1975–97

Year	Colombo consumer price index
1952	100 (base year)
1975	198.3
1976	200.7
1977	203.2
1978	227.8
1979	252.3
1980	318.2
1981	375.4
1982	416.1
1983	474.2
1984	553.1
1985	561.2
1986	606.0
1987	652.8
1988	744.1
1989	830.2
1990	1,008.6
1991	1,131.5
1992	1,260.4
1993	1,408.4
1994	1,527.4
1995	1,644.6
1996	1,906.7
1997	2,089.1

Source: Central bank of Sri Lanka 1998.

Bibliography

Abu-Lughod, Lila. 1986. *Veiled Sentiments: Honor and Poetry in a Bedouin Society,* Berkeley: University of California Press.

Addleton, Jonathan S. 1991. "The Impact of the Gulf War on Migration and Remittances in Asia and the Middle East." *International Migration* 29, no. 4: 509–26.

Ahearn, Laura M. 2000. "Agency." *Journal of Linguistic Anthropology* 9, no. 1: 9–12.

Al-Chalabi, Fadhil J. 1991. "The World Oil Price Collapse of 1986: Causes and Implications for the Future of OPEC." In *After the Oil Price Collapse: OPEC, the United States, and the World Oil Market,* edited by Wilfrid L. Kohl, 1–27. Baltimore: Johns Hopkins University Press.

Ambah, Faiza S. 1995. "Death Sentence for Teenage Maid in Arab Court Raises Cry of Protest." *The Christian Science Monitor,* 20 September.

Anderson, Benedict. 1991. *Imagined Communities: Reflections on the Origin and Spread of Nationalism.* London: Verso.

———. 1994. "Exodus." *Critical Inquiry* 20, no. 2: 314–27.

Appadurai, Arjun. 1978. "Kings, Sects, and Temples in South India, 1350–1700 A.D." In *South Indian Temples,* edited by Burton Stein, 47–73. Delhi: Vikas.

———. 1981. *Worship and Conflict under Colonial Rule.* Cambridge: Cambridge University Press.

———. 1986. "Is Homo Hierarchicus?" *American Ethnologist* 13, no. 4: 745–61.

Appadurai, Arjun, and Carol A. Breckenridge. 1976. "The South Indian Temple: Authority, Honor, and Redistribution." *Contributions to Indian Sociology,* n.s., 10, no. 2: 187–211.

———. 1988. "Why Public Culture?" *Public Culture* 1, no. 1: 5–9.

Ariyawansa, D. M. 1988. "Report of the Survey on Changes in Economic and Social Status of Expatriate Labour for Unskilled Occupations." Economics Department, University of Kelaniya, Sri Lanka. Photocopy.

Athukorala, Prema-Chandra, and Piyasiri Wickramasekara. 1996. "International Labour Migration Statistics in Asia: An Appraisal." *International Migration* 34, no. 4: 539–67.

Bakhtin, Mikhail. 1981 [1935]. *The Dialogic Imagination.* Translated by Caryl Emerson and Michael Holquist and edited by Michael Holquist. Austin: University of Texas Press.

Bayly, Susan L. 1999. *Caste, Society and Politics in India from the Eighteenth Century to the Modern Age.* Cambridge: Cambridge University Press.

Becker, Uwe. 1989. "Class Theory: Still the Axis of Critical Social Scientific Analysis?" In *The Debate on Classes,* edited by Erik Olin Wright, Uwe Becker, Johanna Brenner, Michael Burawoy, Val Burris, Guglielmo Carchedi, Gordon Marshall, Peter Meiksins, David Rose, Arthur Stinchcombe, and Philippe Van Parijs, 127–56. London: Verso.

Bernstein, Basil. 1981. "Classes, Modalities, and the Process of Cultural Reproduction: A Model." *Language in Society* 10:327–63.

Berreman, G. D. 1981. *Social Inequality,* New York: Academic Press.

Beteille, André. 1969. *Caste, Class, and Power: Changing Patterns of Stratification in a Tanjore Village.* Berkeley: University of California Press.

———. 1974. *Studies in Agrarian Social Structure.* Delhi: Oxford University Press.

Bourdieu, Pierre. 1977. *Outline of a Theory of Practice.* Translated by Richard Nice. Cambridge: Cambridge University Press.

———. 1984. *Distinction: A Social Critique of the Judgement of Taste.* Translated by Richard Nice. Cambridge: Harvard University Press.

———. 1991. *Language and Symbolic Power.* Cambridge: Harvard University Press.

Brochmann, Grete. 1987. *Escape Route to Dependency? Female Migration from Sri Lanka to the Middle East.* Oslo: International Peace Research Institute.

———. 1990. *The Middle East Avenue: Female Migration from Sri Lanka— Causes and Consequences.* Oslo: Institute for Social Research.

———. 1992. "Sri Lankan Housemaids in the Middle East: An Avenue for Social and Economic Improvement?" In *Labor Migration to the Middle East: From Sri Lanka to the Gulf,* edited by F. Eelens, T. Schampers, and J. D. Speckmann, 215–37. London: Kegan Paul International.

Brow, James, and Joe Weeramunda, eds. 1992. *Agrarian Change in Sri Lanka.* New Delhi: Sage.

Carby, Hazel. 1982. "White Women Listen! Black Feminists and the Boundaries of Sisterhood." In *The Empire Strikes Back: Race and Racism in the Seventies in Britain.* London: Hutchinson in association with the Centre for Contemporary Cultural Studies, University of Birmingham.

———. 1985. "'On the Threshold of Woman's Era': Lynching, Empire, and Sexuality in Black Feminist Theory." *Critical Inquiry* 12:262–77.

Central Bank of Sri Lanka. 1998. Annual Report. <http://www.lanka.net/centralbank/economy.html>, 7 September 1999.

Central Intelligence Agency. 1998. *World Factbook 1998.* <http://www.odci.gov/cia/publications/factbook/index.html>, 16 August 1999.

Clifford, James. 1994. "Diasporas." *Cultural Anthropology* 9, no. 3: 302–38.

Cole, Douglas, and Ira Chaikin. 1990. *An Iron Hand upon the People: The Law against the Potlatch on the Northwest Coast.* Seattle: University of Washington Press.

Colen, Shellee. 1990. "'Housekeeping' for the Green Card: West Indian Household Workers, the State, and Stratified Reproduction in New York." In *At Work in Homes: Household Workers in World Perspective,* edited by Roger Sanjek and Shellee Colen, 89–118. American Ethnological Society Monograph Series, no. 3. Washington: American Anthropological Association.

Collier, Jane, and Sylvia Yanagisako. 1987. *Gender and Kinship: Essays Toward a Unified Analysis.* Stanford, Calif.: Stanford University Press.

———. 1987b. "Theory in Anthropology Since Feminist Practice." *Critique of Anthropology* 9, no. 2: 27–37.

Comaroff, Jean. 1985. *Body of Power, Spirit of Resistance: The Culture and History of a South African People.* Chicago: University of Chicago Press.

Constable, Nicole. 1997. *Maid to Order in Hong Kong: Stories of Filipina Workers.* Ithaca, N.Y.: Cornell University Press.

———. 1999. "At Home, but not at Home: Filipina Narratives of Ambivalent Returns." *Cultural Anthropology* 14, no. 2: 203–288.

Cronk, Lee. 1997. "Reciprocity and the Power of Giving." In *Conformity and Conflict: Readings in Cultural Anthropology,* 9th ed., edited by James Spradley and David W. McCurdy, 157–63. New York: Addison Wesley Longman.

Crosby, Alfred W. 1972. *The Columbian Exchange: Biological and Cultural Consequences of 1492.* Westport, Conn.: Greenwood Press.

Daily News. 1993a. "Newborn Found in Garbage Cart." 2 April.

———. 1993b. "Lankan Housemaid Dies in Abu Dhabi." 30 April.

Daniel, E. Valentine. 1984. *Fluid Signs.* Berkeley: University of California Press.

Daniel, E. Valentine, and John Chr. Knudsen, eds. 1995. Introduction to *Mistrusting Refugees.* Berkeley: University of California Press.

Danielsen, Albert L. 1982. *The Evolution of OPEC.* New York: Harcourt Brace Jovanovich.

Dean, Mitchell. 1994. *Critical and Effective Histories: Foucault's Methods and Historical Sociology.* London: Routledge.

Derrida, Jacques. 1977. "Signature, Event, Context." *Glyph* 1: 172–97.

Diamond, Irene, and Lee Quinby. 1988. *Feminism and Foucault: Reflections on Resistance.* Boston: Northeastern University Press.

Dias, Malsiri, and Nedra Weerakoon-Gunawardene. 1991. "Female Labour
    Migration to Singapore and Hong Kong: A Profile of the Sri Lankan House-
    maids." Colombo: Centre for Women's Research. Photocopy.
Dimzon, Carmelita. 1997. "Overseas Employment: Directions Toward
    Philippines 2000." In Proceedings of the Regional Meeting of Officials of
    Labour Exporting Countries March 1997, 83–92. Colombo: Sri Lanka Bu-
    reau of Foreign Employment (SLBFE).
Dirks, Nicholas B. 1989. "The Invention of Caste: Civil Society in Colonial
    India." In Identity, Consciousness, and the Past, edited by H. L. Senevi-
    ratne, 42–52. Special Issues Series of Social Analysis, Journal of Culture
    and Social Practice, no. 25, Bedford Park, South Australia: University Re-
    lations Unit, Flinders University of South Australia.
———. 1990. "The Original Caste: Power, History, and Hierarchy in South
    India." In India through Hindu Categories, edited by McKim Marriott,
    59–77. New York: Sage.
———. 1992. "Castes of Mind." Representations 37: 56–78.
Dirks, Nicholas B., Geoff Eley, and Sherry B. Ortner, eds. 1994. Introduction
    to Culture / Power / History: A Reader in Contemporary Social Theory.
    Princeton, N.J.: Princeton University Press.
Douglas, Mary. 1966. Purity and Danger: An Analysis of the Concepts of
    Pollution and Taboo. London: Ark Paperbacks.
Dumont, Louis. [1970] 1980. Homo Hierarchicus: The Caste System and Its
    Implications. Chicago: University of Chicago Press.
Eelens, Frank, T. Mook, and Toon Schampers. 1992. "Introduction." In La-
    bor Migration to the Middle East: From Sri Lanka to the Gulf, edited by F.
    Eelens, T. Schampers, and J. D. Speckmann, 1–25. London: Kegan Paul In-
    ternational.
Eelens, Frank, and Toon Schampers. 1992. "Survival Migration: The Sri
    Lankan Case." In Labor Migration to the Middle East: From Sri Lanka to
    the Gulf, edited by Frank Eelens, Toon Schampers, and Johann Dirk
    Speckmann, 27–38. London: Kegan Paul International.
Energy Information Administration. 1997. "The World Oil Market." [May
    1997.] <http://www.eia.doe.gov/oiaf/ieo97/oil.html>, 26 July 1999.
———. 1998a. "Kuwait." [October 1998.] <http://www.eia.doe.gov/emeu
    /cabs/kuwait.html>, 26 July 1999.
———. 1998b. "United Arab Emirates." [December 1998.] <http://www.eia
    .doe.gov/emeu/cabs/uae.html>, 26 July 1999.
———. 1999a. "Saudi Arabia." [January 1999.] <http://www.eia.doe.gov
    /emeu/cabs/saudi.html>, 26 July 1999.
———. 1999b. "OPEC Revenue Fact Sheet." [May 1999.] <http://www.eia
    .doe.gov/emeu/cabs/opecrev.html>, 26 July 1999.
———. 1999c. "Persian Gulf Oil Export Fact Sheet." [June 1999.] <http://
    www.eia.doe.gov/emeu/cabs/pgulf.html>, 26 July 1999.
———. 1999d. "OPEC Fact Sheet." [July 1999.] <http://www.eia.doe.gov
    /emeu/cabs/opec.html>, 26 July 1999.

Escobar, Arturo. 1988. "Power and Visibility: Development and the Invention and Management of the Third World." *Cultural Anthropology* 3, no. 4: 428–43.

Etherington, Norman. 1988. "Natal's Black Rape Scare of the 1870s." *Journal of Southern African Studies* 15, no. 1: 36–53.

Fairbanks, Gordon H., James W. Gair, and M. W. S. de Silva. 1968. *Colloquial Sinhalese*. 2 Vols. Ithaca, N.Y.: South Asia Program, Cornell University.

Fekjaer, Hans Olav. 1993. *Alcohol and Illicit Drugs: Myths and Realities*. Colombo: IOGT Alcohol and Drug Information Centre.

Fernandez-Kelly, Maria Patricia. 1983. *For We Are Sold, I and My People: Women and Industry in Mexico's Frontier*. Albany: State University of New York Press.

Foucault, Michel. 1978. The History of Sexuality. Vol. 1. New York: Vintage.

———. 1979. *Discipline and Punish*, translated by Alan Sheridan. New York: Vintage.

———. 1991. "Governmentality." In *The Foucault Effect: Studies in Governmentality*, edited by Graham Burchell, Colin Gordor, and Peter Miller, 87–104. Chicago: University of Chicago Press.

———. 1994. "Two Lectures." In *Culture / Power / History: A Reader in Contemporary Social Theory*, edited by Nicholas B. Dirks, Geoff Eley, and Sherry B. Ortner, 200–221. Princeton, N.J.: Princeton University Press.

Friedrich, Paul. 1989. "Language, Ideology, and Political Economy." *American Anthropologist* 91: 295–312.

Gailey, Christine Ward. 1993. "Mediated Messages: Gender, Class and Cosmos in Home Video Games." *Journal of Popular Culture* 27, no. 1: 81–97.

Gamburd, Geraldine E. 1972. "The Seven Grandparents: Locality and Lineality in Sinhalese Kinship and Caste." Ph.D. diss., Columbia University.

Gamburd, Michele R. 1995a. "Housemaids at Home and Abroad: Labor Migration and Gender Transformations in a Sri Lankan Village." Ph.D. diss., University of Michigan.

———. 1995b. "Sri Lanka's 'Army of Housemaids': Control of Remittances and Gender Transformations." *Anthropologica* 37:49–88.

———. 1998. "Absent Women and Their Extended Families: Sri Lanka's Migrant Housemaids." In *Negotiation and Social Space: A Gendered Analysis of Changing Kin and Security Networks in South Asia and Sub-Saharan Africa*, edited by Carla Risseeuw and Kamala Ganesh, 276–91. New Delhi: Sage.

———. 1999. "Class Identity and the International Division of Labor: Sri Lanka's Migrant Housemaids." *Anthropology of Work Review* 19, no. 3: 4–8.

———. 2000. "Nurture for Sale: Sri Lankan Housemaids and the Work of Mothering." In *Home and Hegemony*, edited by Kathleen M. Adams and Sara Dickey, 179–205. Ann Arbor: University of Michigan Press.

Gill, Lesley. 1994. *Precarious Dependencies: Gender, Class and Domestic Service in Bolivia.* New York: Columbia University Press.

Gordon, Colin. 1991. "Governmental Rationality: An Introduction." In *The Foucault Effect: Studies in Governmentality,* edited by Graham Burchell, Colin Gordon, and Peter Miller, 1–52. Chicago: University of Chicago Press.

Gough, Kathleen. 1969. "Caste in a Tanjore Village." In *Aspects of Caste in South India, Ceylon, and North-west Pakistan,* edited by E. R. Leach, 11–60. Cambridge: Cambridge University Press.

Graber, Marjorie. 1992. "The Occidental Tourist: *M. Butterfly* and the Scandal of Transvestism." In *Nationalisms and Sexualities,* edited by Andrew Parker, Mary Russo, Doris Sommer, and Patricia Yaeger, 121–46. New York: Routledge.

Gramsci, Antonio. 1971. *Selections from the Prison Notebooks of Antonio Gramsci.* Edited and translated by Q. Hoare and G. Nowell Smith. New York: International Publishers.

———. 1988. *An Antonio Gramsci Reader: Selected Writings, 1916–1935.* Edited by D. Forgacs. New York: Schocken Books.

Gray, Breda. 1996. "Irish Women in London: National or Hybrid Diasporic Identities?" *National Women's Studies Association Journal* 8, no. 1: 85–109.

Gumperz, John J. 1977. "Sociocultural Knowledge in Conversational Inference." In *Linquistics and Anthropology,* edited by M. Saville-Troike, 191–212. Washington: Georgetown University Press.

Gunatilleke, Godfrey. 1995. "The Economic, Demographic, Sociocultural, and Political Setting for Emigration from Sri Lanka." *International Migration* 33, nos. 3/4: 667–98.

———, ed. 1992. "Sri Lanka." In *The Impact of Labour Migration on Households: A Comparative Study in Seven Asian Countries.* 227–63. Tokyo: United Nations University Press.

Gunatilleke, Godfrey, and P. D. A. Perera. 1987. "The Asian Migration to Arab Countries." Colombo: Marga Institute (Sri Lanka Centre for Development Studies) document M933. Manuscript.

Gupta, Akhil. 1992. "The Song of the Nonaligned World: Transnational Identities and the Reinscription of Space in Late Capitalism." *Cultural Anthropology* 7, no. 1: 63–79.

Gupta, Akhil, and James Ferguson. 1992. "Beyond 'Culture': Space, Identity, and the Politics of Difference." *Cultural Anthropology* 7, no. 1: 6–23.

Hall, Jacquelyn Dowd. 1983. "The Mind That Burns in Each Body: Women, Rape, and Racial Violence." In *Powers of Desire: The Politics of Sexuality,* edited by A. Snitow, C. Stansell, and S. Thompson, 328–49. New York: Monthly Review Press.

Hall, Stuart. 1996. "Gramsci's Relevance for the Study of Race and Ethnicity." In *Stuart Hall: Critical Dialogues in Cultural Studies,* edited by David Morley and Kuan-Hsing Chen, 411–40. London: Routledge.

Halle, David. 1984. *America's Working Man*. Chicago: University of Chicago Press.

Hansen, Karen. 1989. *Distant Companions: Servants and Employers in Zambia, 1900–1985*. Ithaca, N.Y.: Cornell University Press.

———. 1990. "Body Politics: Sexuality, Gender, and Domestic Service in Zambia." *Journal of Women's History* 2, no. 1: 120–42.

Harrison, Faye V. 1997. "The Gendered Politics and Violence of Structural Adjustment." In *Situated Lives: Gender and Culture in Everyday Life*, edited by Louise Lamphere, Helena Ragoné, and Patricia Zavella, 451–68. New York: Routledge.

Hedges, Chris. 1992. "Foreign Women Lured into Bondage in Kuwait." *New York Times*, 3 January.

Heng, Geraldine, and Janadas Devan. 1992. "State Fatherhood: The Politics of Nationalism, Sexuality, and Race in Singapore." In *Nationalisms and Sexualities*, edited by Andrew Parker, Mary Russo, Doris Sommer, and Patricia Yaeger, 343–64. New York: Routledge.

Herath, K. M. K. P. 1993. "Monthly Statistics on Labour Migration: October 1993." Colombo: Sri Lanka Bureau of Foreign Employment. Manuscript.

Herring, Ronald J. 1983. *Land to the Tiller: The Political Economy of Agrarian Reform in South Asia*. New Haven, Conn.: Yale University Press.

Hettige, S. T. 1992. "Migration to the Middle East, Social Stratification, and Social Mobility: Three Case Studies." In *Labor Migration to the Middle East: From Sri Lanka to the Gulf*, edited by F. Eelens, T. Schampers, and J. D. Speckmann, 137–58. London: Kegan Paul International.

Inglis, Amirah. 1975. *The White Woman's Protection Ordinance: Sexual Anxiety and Politics in Papua*. London: Chatto and Windus for Sussex University Press.

International Labor Organization (ILO). 1996. "Female Asian Migrants: A Growing but Increasingly Vulnerable Workforce." [5 February 1996.] <http://www.ilo.org/public/english/235press/pr/96–1.htm>, 6 May 1999.

The Island. 1992. "Safe-House Set up for Housemaids in UAE." 1 December.

———. 1993. "Woman Dies of Hemorrhage," 19 May.

Ivy, Marilyn. 1988. "Tradition and Difference in the Japanese Mass Media." *Public Culture* 1, no. 1: 21–29.

Jacobs, E. J. J., and A. Papma. 1992. "The Socio-Economic Position and Religious Status of Sri Lankan Muslim Women Migrating to the Gulf." In *Labor Migration to the Middle East: From Sri Lanka to the Gulf*, edited by F. Eelens, T. Schampers, and J. D. Speckmann, 199–214. London: Kegan Paul International.

Jacobson, Doranne. 1995. "The Women of North and Central India: Goddesses and Wives." In *Women in India: Two Perspectives*, edited by Doranne Jacobson and Susan S. Wadley, 15–109. Columbia, Mo.: South Asia Publications.

Jacobson, Doranne, and Susan S. Wadley. 1995. *Women in India: Two Perspectives*. Columbia, Mo.: South Asia Publications.

Jordanova, L. J. 1980. "Natural Facts: A Historical Perspective on Science and Sexuality." In *Nature, Culture, and Gender,* edited by Carol MacCormack and Marilyn Strathern, 42–69. Cambridge: Cambridge University Press.

Kapferer, Bruce. 1983. *A Celebration of Demons: Exorcism and the Aesthetics of Healing in Sri Lanka.* Bloomington: Indiana University Press.

———. 1997. *The Feast of the Sorcerer: Practices of Consciousness and Power.* Chicago: University of Chicago Press.

Karunatillake, W. S. 1992. *An Introduction to Spoken Sinhala.* Colombo: Gunasena.

Kearney, Michael. 1995. "The Local and the Global: The Anthropology of Globalization and Transnationalism." *Annual Review of Anthropology* 24:547–65.

Kendrick, Andrew J. 1992. "Landholding and Service in a Temple Village in the Kandyan Highlands." In *Agrarian Change in Sri Lanka,* edited by James Brow and Joe Weeramunda, 191–228. New Delhi: Sage.

Kiribamune, Sirima, ed. 1992. Introduction to *Reconciliation of Roles: Women, Work, and Family in Sri Lanka.* International Centre for Ethnic Studies Series, no. 3. New Delhi: Navrang.

Kirk, Colin. 1992. "Perceiving Agrarian Change: Past and Present in Ratmale, a Sinhalese Potter Village." In *Agrarian Change in Sri Lanka,* edited by James Brow and Joe Weeramunda, 389–422. New Delhi: Sage.

Knapman, Claudia. 1986. *White Women in Fiji.* Boston: Allen and Unwin.

Kohl, Wilfrid L. 1991. *After the Oil Price Collapse: OPEC, the United States, and the World Oil Market.* Baltimore: Johns Hopkins University Press.

Korale, R. B. M. 1983. *Migration for Employment to the Middle East: Its Demographic and Socio-Economic Effects in Sri Lanka.* Colombo: Ministry of Plan Implementation.

———. 1989. "Reintegration of the Sri Lankan Returned Migrant." Paper presented at the National Seminar on Sri Lankan Migrant Labour. Colombo: Marga Institute. Photocopy.

Lamphere, Louise. 1987. *From Working Daughters to Working Mothers: Immigrant Women in a New England Industrial Community.* Ithaca, N.Y.: Cornell University Press.

———. 1997. "The Domestic Sphere of Women and the Public World of Men: The Strengths and Limitations of an Anthropological Dichotomy." In *Gender in Cross-Cultural Perspective,* 2d ed., edited by Caroline B. Brettell and Carolyn F. Sargent, 82–92. Upper Saddle River, N. J.: Prentice Hall.

Lancaster, John. 1995. "Maid Jailed for Killing after Rape." *The Washington Post.* 11 July.

Lappé, Frances Moore, Joseph Collins, and Peter Rosset, with Luis Esparza. 1998. *World Hunger: Twelve Myths.* New York: Grove.

Leach, Edmund R. 1961. *Pul Eliya, A Village in Ceylon: A Study of Land Tenure and Kinship.* Cambridge: Cambridge University Press.

————, ed. 1969. *Aspects of Caste in South India, Ceylon, and North-west Pakistan.* Cambridge: Cambridge University Press.

Lee, Richard B. 1997. "Eating Christmas in the Kalahari." In *Conformity and Conflict: Readings in Cultural Anthropology.* 9th ed., edited by James Spradley and David W. McCurdy, 26–33. New York: Addison Wesley Longman.

Limón, José. 1989. "Carne, Carnales, and the Carnivalesque: Bakhtinian Batos, Disorder, and Narrative Discourses." *American Ethnologist* 16, no. 3: 471–86.

Looney, R. E. 1992. "Manpower Options in a Small Labour-Importing State: The Influence of Ethnic Composition on Kuwait's Development." *International Migration* 30, no. 2: 175–200.

Lynch, Caitrin. 1999. "The 'good girls' of Sri Lankan Modernity: Moral Orders of Nationalism and Capitalism." *Identities: Global Studies in Culture and Power* 6, no. 1: 55–89.

Mahawewa, W. A. S. 1993. "The Process of International Female Migration: The Case Study of Sri Lanka." Master's thesis, Population and Human Resources Programme, School of Social Sciences, Flinders University of South Australia.

Malkki, Liisa. 1992. "National Geographic: The Rooting of Peoples and the Territorialization of National Identity among Scholars and Refugees." *Cultural Anthropology* 7, no. 1: 24–44.

Mananwatte, Sarath. 1993. Interviews by author. 10 December and 17 December.

Mandelbaum, David G. 1970. *Society in India.* Vol. 1, *Continuity and Change.* Berkeley: University of California Press.

Marecek, J. 1992. "Through American Eyes. Women, Work, and Family Life: Old Myths, New Realities." In *Reconciliation of Roles: Women, Work, and Family in Sri Lanka,* edited by Sirima Kiribamune, 264–91. International Centre for Ethnic Studies Series, no. 3. New Delhi: Navrang.

————. 1998. "Culture, Gender, and Suicidal Behavior in Sri Lanka." *Suicide and Life Threatening Behavior* 28, no. 1: 69–81.

Marriott, McKim, ed. 1990. *India Through Hindu Categories.* New York: Sage.

Marx, Karl. 1971. "Manifesto of the Communist Party." In *On Revolution,* edited by Saul K. Padover, 79–107. New York: McGraw-Hill.

————. 1978. *The Marx-Engels Reader,* 2d ed., edited by Robert C. Tucker. New York: W. W. Norton.

Mascia-Lees, Frances E., Patricia Sharpe, and Colleen Ballerino Cohen. 1989. "The Postmodern Turn in Anthropology: Cautions from a Feminist Perspective." *Signs* 15, no. 1: 7–33.

Mauss, Marcel. 1990 [1925]. *The Gift: The Form and Reason for Exchange in Archaic Societies.* Translated by W. D. Halls, with a foreword by Mary Douglas. New York: W. W. Norton.

McGilvray, Dennis B., ed. 1982. *Caste Ideology and Interaction.* Cambridge: Cambridge University Press.

————. 1998. "Arabs, Moors and Muslims: Sri Lankan Muslim Ethnicity in Regional Perspective." *Contributions to Indian Sociology*, n.s., 32, no. 2: 433–83.

Meillassoux, Claude. 1981. *Maidens, Meal, and Money: Capitalism and the Domestic Economy*. Cambridge: Cambridge University Press.

Migration News. 1996a. "Foreigners in the Middle East." 3, no. 1, January. <http://migration.ucdavis.edu/Archive/jan_1996–22.html>, 10 August 1999.

————. 1996b. "Foreigners in the Gulf." 3, no. 5, May. <http://migration .ucdavis.edu/Archive/may_1996–23.html>, 10 August 1999.

————1996c. "Foreign Workers in the Middle East." 3, no. 12, December. <http://migration.ucdavis.edu/Archive/dec_1996–27.html>, 10 August 1999.

————. 1996d. "Philippines Maid Returns Home." 3, no. 9, September. <http://migration.ucdavis.edu/Archive/sep_1996–16.html>, 10 August 1999.

————. 1997. "Middle East: Crackdown." 4, no. 11, November. <http:// migration.ucdavis.edu/Archive/nov_1997–24.html>, 10 August 1999.

————. 1999. "Sri Lanka, Pakistan." 6, no. 10, January. <http://migration .ucdavis.edu/Archive/jan_1999–27.html>, 6 May 1999.

Ministry of Manpower, Directorate General of Development for Manpower Placement, Republic of Indonesia. 1997. "Recent Development of Indonesian Migrant Workers." In *Supporting and Organization Documents from the International Conference on Migrant Women Workers, October 1997*. Colombo: American Center for International Labor Solidarity in Collaboration with the All Ceylon Federation of Free Trade Unions.

Mitchell, Timothy. 1990. "Everyday Metaphors of Power." *Theory and Society* 19, no. 5: 545–77.

Miyoshi, Masao. 1993. "A Borderless World? From Colonialism to Transnationalism and the Decline of the Nation-State." *Critical Inquiry* 19, no. 4: 726–51.

Mohanty, Chandra. 1988. "Under Western Eyes: Feminist Scholarship and Colonial Discourses." *Feminist Review* 30: 61–88.

Mook, T. 1992. "Middle East Migration at the Micro-Level: A Village Case Study." In *Labor Migration to the Middle East: From Sri Lanka to the Gulf*, edited by F. Eelens, T. Schampers, and J. D. Speckmann, 107–35. London: Kegan Paul International.

Nair, P. R. Gopinathan. 1999. "Return of Overseas Contract Workers and Their Rehabilitation and Development in Kerala (India): A Critical Account of Policies, Performance, and Prospects." *International Migration* 37, no. 1: 209–42.

Nelson, Cynthia. 1997. "Public and Private Politics: Women in the Middle Eastern World." In *Gender in Cross-Cultural Perspective*, 2d ed., edited by Caroline B. Brettell and Carolyn F. Sargent, 111–23. Upper Saddle River, N. J.: Prentice Hall.

O'Hanlon, Rosalind. 1988. "Recovering the Subject: Subaltern Studies and Histories of Resistance in Colonial South Asia." *Modern Asian Studies* 22, no. 1: 189–224.

Ong, Aihwa. 1987. *Spirits of Resistance and Capitalist Discipline: Factory Women in Malaysia.* Albany: State University of New York Press.

———. 1988. "The Production of Possession: Spirits and the Multinational Corporation in Malaysia." *American Ethnologist* 15, no. 1: 29–42.

———. 1999. *Flexible Citizenship: The Cultural Logics of Transnationality.* Durham, N. C.: Duke University Press.

OPEC Press Release. 1999. "One-Hundred-and-Seventh (107th) Meeting of the OPEC Conference." 23 March 1999. <http://www.opec.org/pr299.htm>, 26 July 1999.

Ortner, Sherry. 1974. "Is Female to Male as Nature Is to Culture?" In *Women, Culture, and Society,* edited by Michelle Z. Rosaldo and Louise Lamphere, 67–88. Stanford, Calif.: Stanford University Press.

———. 1984. "Theory in Anthropology Since the Sixties." *Comparative Studies in Society and History* 26, no. 1: 126–66.

———. 1989. *High Religion: A Cultural and Political History of Sherpa Buddhism.* Princeton, N. J.: Princeton University Press.

Parliament of the Democratic Socialist Republic of Sri Lanka. 1985. Sri Lanka Bureau of Foreign Employment Act no. 21 of 1985. Supplement to Part II of the *Gazette of the Democratic Socialist Republic of Sri Lanka.* 7 June.

Pedersen, Susan. 1991. "National Bodies, Unspeakable Acts: The Sexual Politics of Colonial Policy Making." *Journal of Modern History* 63, no. 4: 647–80.

Perera, P. D. A. 1992. "Needs of Kuwait Returnees of Sri Lanka: An Assessment." Marga Institute Study, commissioned by the Sri Lanka Bureau of Foreign Employment (SLBFE). Manuscript.

Poopalan, T. 1993. Letter to the editor. *The Island,* 5 May.

Quigley, Declan. 1993. *The Interpretation of Caste.* Oxford: Clarendon Press.

Raheja, Gloria Goodwin. 1988. *The Poison in the Gift: Ritual, Prestation, and the Dominant Caste in a North Indian Village.* Chicago: University of Chicago Press.

———. 1990. "Centrality, Mutuality and Hierarchy: Shifting Aspects of Inter-caste Relationships in North India." In *India through Hindu Categories,* edited by McKim Marriott, 79–101. New York: Sage.

Rand McNally. 1987. *Universal World Atlas.* Chicago: Rand McNally and Co.

Ratnapala, Nandasena. 1985. *Alcohol and People.* Ratmalana, Sri Lanka: Sarvodaya Research.

Razik, Z. M. 1997. "Painter Remanded in Wife Stabbing." *Daily News,* 8 September.

Risseeuw, Carla. 1991. *Gender Transformation, Power, and Resistance Among Women in Sri Lanka: The Fish Don't Talk about the Water.* New Delhi: Manohar.

Rodrigo, Chandra. 1998. *Country Study: Sri Lanka—The Impact of Employment Agencies on the Functioning of Labor Markets.* International Labor Organization. <http://www.ilo.org/public/english/80relpro/admitra/papers/1998/lanka/index.html, 6 May 1999.

Rollins, Judith. 1985. *Between Women: Domestics and Their Employers.* Philadelphia: Temple University Press.

———. 1990. "Ideology and Servitude." In *At Work in Homes: Household Workers in World Perspective,* edited by Roger Sanjek and Shellee Colen, 74–88. American Ethnological Society Monograph Series, no. 3. Washington: American Anthropological Association.

Rosaldo, Michelle Z. 1974. "Women, Culture, and Society: A Theoretical Overview." In *Women, Culture, and Society,* edited by Michelle Z. Rosaldo and Louise Lamphere, 17–42. Stanford Calif. Standford University Press.

Rose, Nikolas. 1999. *Powers of Freedom: Reframing Political Thought.* Cambridge: Cambridge University Press.

Roseberry, William. 1989. *Anthropologies and Histories: Essays in Culture, History, and Political Economy.* New Brunswick, N. J.: Rutgers University Press.

Rudner, David W. 1994. *Caste and Capitalism in Colonial India: The Nattukottai Chettiars.* Berkeley: University of California Press.

Ruhunage, L. K. 1993. Interview by author. 13 December.

Ryan, Bryce. 1953. *Caste in Modern Ceylon: The Sinhala System in Transition.* New Brunswick, N. J.: Rutgers University Press.

Sacks, Karen. 1989. "Towards a Unified Theory of Class, Race and Gender." *American Ethnologist* 16, no. 3: 534–49.

Sahlins, Marshall. 1981. *Historical Metaphors and Mythical Realities.* Ann Arbor: University of Michigan Press.

Said, Edward. 1979. *Orientalism.* New York: Vintage.

———. 1986. "Orientalism Reconsidered." In *Literature, Politics, and Theory,* edited by Francis Barker, 210–29. London: Methuen.

Samarajeewa, Neminda. 1997. "Big Demand for Employment Abroad." *The Island,* 9 September.

Samarasinghe, Gameela. 1989. "The Psycho-Social Implications of Middle East Migration on the Family Left Behind." Colombo: Centre for Women's Research (CENWOR). Photocopy.

Sanday, Peggy. 1974. "Female Status in the Public Domain." In *Women, Culture and Society,* edited by Michelle Z. Rosaldo and Louise Lamphere, 189–206. Stanford Calif.: Stanford University Press.

Sanjek, Roger, and Shellee Colen, eds. 1990. *At Work in Homes: Household Workers in World Perspective.* American Ethnological Society Monograph Series, no. 3. Washington: American Anthropological Association.

Sapir, Edward. 1949. *Edward Sapir: Selected Writings in Language, Culture, and Personality.* Edited by David G. Mandelbaum. Berkeley: University of California Press.

Schaeffer, Robert K. 1997. *Understanding Globalization: The Social Consequences of Political, Economic and Environmental Change.* New York: Rowman and Littlefield.

Schampers, Toon, and Frank Eelens. 1986. "The Effect of Migration on the Well-Being of Sri Lankan Children Left Behind." Colombo: Marga Institute Document M899. Photocopy.

Scheper-Hughes, Nancy. 1992. *Death without Weeping: The Violence of Everyday Life in Brazil.* Berkeley: University of California Press.

Schiller, Nina Glick, Linda Basch, and Cristina Szanton Blanc. 1995. "From Immigrant to Transmigrant: Theorizing Transnational Migration." *Anthropological Quarterly* 68, no. 1: 48–63.

Schneider, Jane. 1978. "Peacocks and Penguins: The Political Economy of European Cloth and Colors." *American Ethnologist* 5, no. 3: 413–47.

Schrijvers, Joke. 1985. *Mothers for Life: Motherhood and Marginalization in the North Central Provinces of Sri Lanka.* Delft: Eburon.

Scott, David. 1994. *Formations of Ritual: Colonial and Anthropological Discourses on the Sinhala Yaktovil.* Minneapolis: University of Minnesota Press.

Scott, James C. 1990. *Domination and the Arts of Resistance: Hidden Transcripts.* New Haven, Conn.: Yale University Press.

Scott, Joan. 1988. *Gender and the Politics of History.* New York: Columbia University Press.

Seneviratene, Dharshini. 1996. "Abroad, Astray." *Sunday Times Plus,* 4 August.

Shadid, W. A., E. J. A. M. Spaan, and J. D. Speckmann. 1992. "Labour Migration and the Policy of the Gulf States." In *Labor Migration to the Middle East: From Sri Lanka to the Gulf,* edited by F. Eelens, T. Schampers, and J. D. Speckmann, 63–86. London: Kegan Paul International.

Shah, Nasra M. 1994. "Arab Labour Migration: A Review of Trends and Issues." *International Migration* 32, no. 1: 3–28.

———. 1995. "Emigration Dynamics from and within South Asia." *International Migration* 33, nos. 3/4: 559–626.

Shah, Nasra M., and Indu Menon. 1999. "Chain Migration Through the Social Network: Experience of Labour Migrants in Kuwait." *International Migration* 37, no. 2: 361–82.

Spencer, Jonathan. 1990. *A Sinhala Village in a Time of Trouble.* Delhi: Oxford University Press.

Spivak, Gayatri C. 1985. "Can the Subaltern Speak? Speculations on Widow Sacrifice." *Wedge* 7–8:120–30.

Sri Lanka Bureau of Foreign Employment (SLBFE). 1997. *Statistical Handbook on Foreign Employment.* Colombo: Sri Lanka Bureau of Foreign Employment.

Sri Lanka National Department of Census and Statistics. 1996. *Census Statistics.* <http://www.lk/national/census/sl_figures95.html#population>, 3 September 1998.

Srinivas, M. N. 1955. "The Social System of a Mysore Village." In *Village India*, edited by McKim Marriott, 1–35. Chicago: University of Chicago Press.
———. 1962. *Caste in Modern India and Other Essays*. Bombay: Asia Publishing House.
———. 1987. *The Dominant Caste and Other Essays*. Delhi: Oxford University Press.
Stacey, Judith. 1990. *Brave New Families*. London: Basic Books.
———. 1997. "The Neo-Family-Values Campaign." In *The Gender/Sexuality Reader: Culture, History, Political Economy*, edited by Roger N. Lancaster and Michaela di Leonardo, 453–70. New York: Routledge.
Stahl, C. W. 1991. "South-North Migration in the Asia-Pacific Region." *International Migration* 29, no. 2: 163–94.
Steedly, Mary Margaret. 1993. *Hanging without a Rope: Narrative Experience in Colonial and Postcolonial Karoland*. Princeton, N. J.: Princeton University Press.
Stoler, Ann. 1989. "Making Empire Respectable: The Politics of Race and Sexual Morality in 20th Century Colonial Culture." *American Ethnologist* 16, no. 4: 634–60.
———. 1991. "Carnal Knowledge and Imperial Power." In *Gender at the Crossroads of Knowledge*, edited by Micaela di Leonardo, 51–101. Berkeley: University of California Press.
———. 1992. "Sexual Affronts and Racial Frontiers: European Identities and the Cultural Politics of Exclusion in Colonial Southeast Asia." *Comparative Studies in Society and History* 34:514–51.
Taussig, Michael. 1984. "Culture of Terror—Space of Death." *Comparative Studies in Society and History* 26, no. 3: 467–97.
Tsing, Anna Lowenhaupt. 1994. "From the Margins." *Cultural Anthropology* 9, no. 3: 279–97.
van der Veer, Peter. 1995. *Nation and Migration: The Politics of Space in the South Asian Diaspora*. Philadelphia: University of Pennsylvania Press.
Washbrook, David. 1976. *The Emergence of Provincial Politics: The Madras Presidency, 1870–1920*. Cambridge: Cambridge University Press.
Waters, Anne B. 1999. "Domestic Dangers: Approaches to Women's Suicide in Contemporary Maharashtra, India." *Violence Against Women* 5, no. 5: 525–47.
Whitaker, Mark P. 1999. *Amiable Incoherence: Multiple Histories and Modernities in a Batticaloa Hindu Temple*. Amsterdam: Vu University Press.
Williams, Brett. 1991. "Good Guys and Bad Toys." In *The Politics of Culture*, 109–31. Washington: Smithsonian Institution Press.
Williams, Raymond. 1977. *Marxism and Literature*. Oxford: Oxford University Press.
Wolf, Eric R. [1982] 1997. *Europe and the People Without History*. Berkeley: University of California Press.

Wright, Erik Olin. 1997. *Class Counts: Comparative Studies in Class Analysis.* Cambridge: Cambridge University Press.

Yalman, Nur. 1967. *Under the Bo Tree.* Berkeley: University of California Press.

———. 1969. "The Flexibility of Caste Principles in a Kandyan Community." In *Aspects of Caste in South India, Ceylon, and North-West Pakistan,* edited by Edmund R. Leach, 78–112. Cambridge: Cambridge University Press.

Yeats, W. B. 1926/1928. "Among School Children." In *Chief Modern Poets of Britain and America,* edited by Sanders et al., 1:131–32. New York: Macmillan.

Zimmer-Tamakoshi, Laura. 1997. " 'Wild Pigs and 'Dog Men': Rape and Domestic Violence as 'Women's Issues.' " In *Gender in Cross-Cultural Perspective,* 2d ed., edited by Caroline B. Brettell and Carolyn F. Sargent, 538–53. Upper Saddle River, N. J.: Prentice Hall.

Index